Growth Management Principles and Practices

Growth Management Principles and Practices

by

Arthur C. Nelson, AICP
James B. Duncan, AICP

with

Clancy J. Mullen, AICP
Kirk R. Bishop

Planners Press
AMERICAN PLANNING ASSOCIATION
Chicago, Illinois   Washington, D.C.

Copyright 1995 by the American Planning Association
122 S. Michigan Ave.
Suite 1600
Chicago, IL 60603
Paperback edition ISBN 0-918286-92-1
Hardbound edition ISBN 0-918286-93-X
Library of Congress Catalog Card Number 94-70284

To John M. DeGrove, indefatigable growth management
champion, and Thomas G. Pelham and David J. Russ,
growth management litigators extraordinaire

To Margaret, Katy, and Bryant
Mother, wife, and son

Contents

Acknowledgments

A book of this sort requires the special effort of many individuals. We were fortunate to have the professional services of Kirk Bishop and Clancy Mullin in gathering background information. Without their tireless effort and insights, this book would not be possible. It is for this reason that we extend coauthorship to them.

We want to acknowledge four other people. Frank So and Jim Hecimovich were most enthusiastic about our concept and gave us the encouragement needed to see this book through. We consider Sylvia Lewis and Richard Wright saints for their extraordinary patience, timely recommendations, and willingness to track down bits and pieces we could not.

The greater share of our acknowledgment is given to you who create the real solutions—the planner, the developer, the conscientious citizen, and the public official committed to doing the right thing.

Arthur Christian ("Chris") Nelson
James ("Jim") Bryant Duncan
January 1995

Preface

There is a mood in America. Increasingly citizens are asking what urban growth will add to the quality of their lives. They are questioning the way relatively unconstrained, piecemeal urbanization is changing their communities and are rebelling against the traditional processes of government and the marketplace which, they believe, have inadequately guided development in the past. They are measuring new development proposals by the extent to which environmental criteria are satisfied—by what new housing and business will generate in terms of additional traffic, pollution of air and water, erosion and scenic disturbance. WILLIAM K. REILLY

Written two decades ago, these words continue to provide a succinct description of citizens' feelings about growth in America's rapidly expanding communities. In the 1970s, the mood was characterized by the terms *slow growth* and *no growth*. Gradually, the term *growth management* came to encompass a whole range of policies designed to control, guide, or mitigate the effects of growth. Today, we still talk in terms of growth management, although increasingly the emphasis is on sustainable growth on a local, regional, and global scale.

At the theoretical level at least, growth management has legions of supporters. Scratch beyond the surface, however, and you're likely to come away with the impression that this advocacy is due to the fact that the term means both everything and nothing. Depending on one's perspective, growth management is either a panacea or a hollow promise. Those communities that have successfully employed growth management techniques view it as everything they always wanted, but never got, from traditional comprehensive planning programs. Those who have initiated growth management strategies after much of

the damage has been done may view it as a remedial measure at best. The term *growth management* is defined in the *Encyclopedia of Community Planning and Development* (Schultz and Kassen 1984: 175) as the

> [i]mplementation of government regulations that control the type, location, quality, scale, rate, sequence or timing of development. The prohibitions contained in a traditional zoning ordinance are a form of growth management, but the term implies a much greater involvement of local government in development decisions. Sophisticated growth management systems are closely tied to comprehensive land use plans and specific development policies.

By attempting to guide growth rather than react to its effects, communities engaged in growth management are assuming a proactive stance in ensuring that the very qualities that attract growth are not destroyed for existing residents and future generations. Sound growth management entails more than simply conserving existing community assets. Implicit in the notion of growth management is an awareness of the double-edged nature of growth and local government's use of various planning tools to shape the future of the community in a way that goes beyond merely responding to market trends. It is part of a larger effort to shape the desired community of tomorrow, based on a vision of the future that recognizes global resource limits and our responsibilities to future generations. To be politically and morally sound, it must also insist that the economically disadvantaged aren't forced to shoulder the heaviest burden of growth management policies.

This book provides an overview of various local, regional, and state approaches to growth management and an analysis of the applicability of selected growth management techniques. Chapter 1 begins with a review of the theoretical underpinnings of growth management, including the need for public intervention into the land market, the economic purposes of growth management, and issues of efficient urban form.

Chapter 2 presents a discussion of what many believe to be a prerequisite for successful growth management at the local level—a state or regional planning framework. It highlights a number of policies designed to ensure that communities tackle growth issues in a comprehensive manner and coordinate their activities with surrounding communities and regional agencies.

The next six chapters focus on growth management techniques. Chapter 3 reviews the role of resource land preservation as the backbone of urban growth management. Chapter 4 presents techniques for protecting special areas of public concern, another pillar of urban growth management. Chapter 5 discusses rural growth management as integral to both urban growth management policies and resource land preservation. Chapter 6 reviews techniques that are used to contain urban development in an effort to prevent urban sprawl and encourage more compact development, stressing the roles of infill, redevelopment, and new communities. Chapters 7 and 8 detail the role of public facilities planning and finance in achieving desired development patterns.

The final two chapters pull the material together. Chapter 9 presents the administration of growth management programs, which we believe is the key to effective growth management. Chapter 10 summarizes the key ingredients of successful growth management, culled from reviews of state and regional growth management initiatives. This chapter also develops an effectiveness continuum, wherein each growth management technique reviewed in preceding chapters is assessed for its effectiveness, both in isolation from and in combination with other techniques. While an attempt has been made to organize various growth management techniques according to their purpose and effect, we must clarify at the outset that any given technique may have consequences and effects that make precise categorization difficult. Little attempt has been made here to dismiss or promote growth management approaches on the basis of past success or failure.

1

The Purposes of Growth Management

Many growth management techniques have been developed as a direct response to the problems and processes associated with urban sprawl. In recent times, growth management has also come to be viewed as a way to protect taxpayers from certain financial exposure, and of providing for equity among taxpayers. At its heart, however, growth management aims to offset certain imperfections in the otherwise unregulated land market.

Figure 1–1. Aerial view of one of many subdivisions in southwestern Florida. The state has millions of lots platted far in excess of market demands and often removing land from important resource uses such as farming, forestry, and wetlands. *Source:* Photo by Arthur C. Nelson.

This leads to the pursuit of efficient urban form through growth management policies. Ultimately, growth management policies aim to improve the quality of life through good planning.

PREVENTION OF URBAN SPRAWL

The term *urban sprawl* refers to several distinct urban development patterns. In its broadest application, it refers to the pattern of low-density suburban development that has spread out around most cities in this country during the postwar era. More narrowly applied, it refers to premature leapfrog or "highway ribbon" development or low-density scattered development that occurs beyond the current perimeter of contiguous development. A synthesized definition of urban sprawl drawn from the planning literature is:

> unplanned, uncontrolled, and uncoordinated single-use development that does not provide for an attractive and functional mix of uses and/or is not functionally related to surrounding land uses and which variously appears as low density, ribbon or strip, scattered, leapfrog, or isolated development.

Because urban sprawl is viewed as wasteful of land and resources, costly to serve, damaging to the environment, and among other things, unsightly, much public policy aims to discourage it. To some extent, these concerns are shared by the development community. For example, the Urban Land Institute was referring to the narrow meaning of *urban sprawl* when it observed that:

> Isolated or scattered projects for small acreage tracts or a series of lots developed with houses strung out along existing highways in rural areas and bearing little or no relation to any neighborhood idea, are a thing of the past. Apart from its wastage of land, this type of scattering is expensive to service and is unsuitable as an urban environment (Urban Land Institute 1968: 94).

In recent years, several state legislatures have adopted policies to contain urban sprawl (Bollens 1992; DeGrove 1984, 1992; Gail 1992; Innes 1992; Leonard 1983). Either directly or indirectly, the statewide land-use planning statutes adopted by California, Florida, Georgia, Hawaii, Maine, Maryland, New Jersey, Oregon, Rhode Island, Vermont, and Washington aim to prevent or contain urban sprawl. All Florida counties and cities are specifically required to discourage the proliferation of urban sprawl.

Causes of Sprawl

We now review some of the causes of sprawl, some of which are actually induced by planning policy. Urban sprawl, when broadly conceived as the predominance of low-density, single-family suburban development, is primarily a product of American affluence. Rising standards of living in the postwar period enabled the majority of families to afford an automobile and a house located a considerable distance from work. The suburban boom leading to sprawl was fueled by national investment policies, generous subsidies, and outright discrimination against high-density development. Local policies have also contributed to sprawl. Thus, ironically, one of the primary aims of growth management is to offset the sprawl-inducing effects of many public policies.

Investment Policies. National transportation and housing policies have been major contributors to urban sprawl. The construction of the interstate highway system provided access to large areas outside of central cities, making them available for suburban development. Furthermore, state and federal transportation investment policies tend to support the construction of new roads over maintenance of existing roads or development of alternative transport modes. Federally guar-

Figure 1–2. Generous tax laws and local zoning for low-density development result in many people buying pieces of former farms for hobby farms or ranchettes only to find, in this case, that two acres is really more than can be managed and is not suitably sized for farming. Notice that only about one-quarter acre of land is mowed and landscaped; the balance is merely a thistle farm. *Source:* Photo by Arthur C. Nelson.

anteed and insured home mortgage programs tend to favor investment in new housing (National Commission on Urban Problems 1968). Federal and state allowance of first-home mortgage and property tax deductions on taxable income allow more families to own single-family dwellings. While on the whole this is desirable, one of the additional features is that families can use the deductibility of interest payments to afford larger homes on larger sites farther away from urban areas. That such policies result in more home owners is desirable, but that those home owners consume more housing resources as a consequence may not be. Moreover, since these programs stimulate the production of new single-family housing over multiple-family or attached housing options and are not readily extended to infill, rehabilitation, or redevelopment of urban areas, they stimulate urban sprawl (Bourne 1980). Finally, these programs do not discourage single-family developments in rural areas that require long-distance, wasteful commuting, so long as basic construction standards are met and buyers meet minimum financial criteria.

Speculation. Speculation is a natural feature of the development process. It results in certain land being withheld from development while nearby or surrounding properties are developed. Eventually, the withheld parcel becomes more valuable as a higher intensity use—for example, a shopping center or higher density housing—than other surrounding development. Early development of such parcels in more intensive land uses would be financially imprudent. Later development rewards speculators for waiting until the optimal moment of development when returns to a more intensive use justify the risk of waiting.

But speculation can be inefficient and actually induce sprawl if it is subsidized by public policies. For example, tax policies, preferential assessment policies such as greenbelt taxation, and undervaluation of land for property tax assessment purposes will actually stimulate speculation (Harvey and Clark 1965; Brown and Roberts 1978; Brown, Phillips, and Roberts 1981; Gurko 1972). While tax laws have changed in recent years, notably the elimination of preferential capital gains taxation and the introduction of active/passive investor rules, the general premises remain. The result is more land being withheld from development than is efficient. Development that is needed is forced to bypass parcels on which it would otherwise have located. A certain amount of sprawl development is thus caused by too much urban land speculation in the market.

Speculation also invades open spaces near urban areas (Nelson 1990a, 1992a). In growing urban areas, speculators will naturally acquire and hold larger rural parcels in the path of development. When policies stimulate speculation, more rural land and rural land farther away from urban development will be acquired for speculation. Land held for speculation will gradually lose productivity as speculators or farmers acting as speculators are unwilling to make or maintain agricultural investments in production for long periods of time (Berry 1978).

Land Use Regulation. Public regulation of land use can also lead to sprawl (Clawson 1972; White 1975). Land-use controls that are more restrictive inside urban areas than outside can make rural areas more attractive (Nelson 1990b, 1992b). This will cause some urban development to seek out rural areas (Lafferty and Frech 1978). Indeed, bad land-use planning is the result (Hirsch 1977). Development of rural areas to serve urban land-use needs will occur as long as the returns to rural development exceed those of urban development. One of the aims of growth management is therefore to make development of rural areas less attractive, while making development of urban areas more attractive (Whitelaw 1980).

Facility Pricing. Most public facilities are priced based on average costs and not on marginal costs (Blewett and Nelson 1988). It is usually less costly to serve higher density development closer in than lower density development farther away. Marginal cost pricing strategies would assess lower density development farther away more than higher density development closer in. Average cost pricing assesses all development the same amount. As a result, lower density development farther away is subsidized by higher density development closer in. The perverse effect is that low- and moderate-income households, which dominate closer-in development, subsidize affluent households farther out.

Effects of Urban Sprawl

What are the effects of urban sprawl, and why is it important to discourage it? First, sprawl is an inefficient development pattern to serve with public facilities. Second, it leads to the loss of valuable agricultural land. Third, it results in lower land values and amenities due to conflicting land uses.

Capital Facility Costs. The costs of sprawl literature has focused chiefly on its impact on capital facilities (Frank 1989a, 1989b). In general, higher density development is less costly to serve than lower density development (Windsor 1979; Peiser 1984; National Association of Home Builders 1986), with most of the

Figure 1–3. Rapidly growing Taft's Corner, Vermont, shows how the scattered, single-use, auto-dependent pattern of development wastes land, increases traffic congestion, and violates the strong historical distinction between town and countryside. *Source:* Photo by Peter Owens.

cost savings from less expensive on-site facilities (e.g., less street and utility frontage per unit). In addition, the cost of major system facilities, such as arterial roads and water and wastewater transmission lines, can vary greatly by location and intensity of development.

Figure 1–4. This single-family, low-density, single-use residential subdivision, planted amid farms in rural southern New Jersey, has no services and is miles removed from any. *Source:* New Jersey Department of Agriculture.

The costs of extending facilities can greatly increase if an area develops initially in a low-density, leapfrog, or at times radial pattern and then later needs facilities (Harvey and Clark 1965). Development of one-, two-, or five-acre lots on septic systems and private wells in a few places may not require the full array of public facilities and services. However, the long-term effect of continued development will result in the need for capital facilities such as water and sewer, drainage, and roads (Nelson and Dueker 1989). Such facilities may be required to serve low density or scattered areas for reasons of health hazard, pollution, and congestion (Gaffney 1964). Extension of such facilities over large areas developed at low density can be very costly. Moreover, such facilities may be financed at the expense of facilities needed for infill, redevelopment, and planned expansion of urban areas. Thus, urban sprawl can and often does require extension of facilities and services in an economically inefficient manner (Sullivan 1985; Peiser 1984; Frank 1989a, 1989b; Lee 1981).

An opposing view holds that facility capacity expansion costs to accommodate urban development could be more expensive on an infill basis than building new facilities to serve lower density development outside built-up areas. According to this argument, it may be prudent to facilitate development outside built-up areas rather than to inhibit it. In response to such a view there are three considerations. First, many urban systems actually will have excess capacity. As household size is shrinking over time, many systems now at or near capacity may actually realize increasing capacity (Nelson 1989). For example, replacing eight large but old single-family residences in an inner-city neighbor-

hood with twenty row houses may absorb no more sewer and water facility capacity than the original eight homes did thirty years ago because of declining household size. Second, many urban facilities are in need of replacement anyway; they easily may be replaced with higher capacity facilities. For example, replacing an old six-inch line with an eight-inch line will nearly double the carrying capacity of the system for a relatively small increase in cost (Gaffney 1964). Third, urban sprawl can result in more expensive design of infrastructure. Gaffney (1964:118–19) analyzes the impacts of sprawl on the cost of water distribution systems:

> Consider water distribution. If demand doubles within a fixed service area by doubling density, we need simply expand all pipe diameters—not by double, but by the square root of two, since cross-sections increase with the square of the radius. But if demand doubles by doubling service area, at constant density, we must (a) double our pipe mileage; (b) double the cross-section of our old pipe system at its base, and more than double it elsewhere, to transmit the extra load through to the new extension; (c) increase pressure at system load center to maintain it at the fringes (especially if new lands are higher); and (d) upgrade our pipe-joints to hold extra pressure.
>
> Actually those four simplest considerations understate the case a good deal. We should add the factor of peaking. The fewer customers on a given line, the higher is the usual ratio of peak demand to mean daily demand because there is less pooling of offsetting demand patterns, and more lawn sprinkling. There is also the factor of planning expansion. "Containing urban sprawl" does not imply halting growth, but holding it inside compact increments, whose ultimate density is known in advance and will be reached quickly, saving utilities

from the waste of under- or oversizing their lines in the face of uncertainty. Urban sprawl as known today not only reduces density but breeds extreme uncertainty of future density.

Frank (1989a, 1989b) synthesized all major studies evaluating the public facility costs of different urban forms, including those of Wheaton and Schussheim (1955), Isard and Coughlin (1957), Urban Land Institute (1968), Kain (1967), Stone (1973), Real Estate Research Corporation (1974), Dougherty, Tapella, and Sumner (1975), Downing and Gustely (1977), and the National Association of Home Builders (1986). Frank combined the findings of these studies to establish average public facility costs per residential unit for various development patterns.

Frank's analysis includes facility costs installed by developers. Although these costs are borne by consumers, rather than by the general public, their maintenance, operation, repair, and replacement become a community liability. A development with twice the cost per unit for public facilities relative to the community average will cost, generally, twice the cost for replacement. Less densely developed areas will cost more on a per-unit basis for operations, maintenance, and repair than more dense areas, at least to a certain point. Thus, it is appropriate for Frank to consider the costs of internal as well as external public facilities.

The results of his assessment, adjusted to 1992 dollars, are shown in Table 1–1. His analysis suggests that density has a much stronger effect than urban form on public facility costs. Frank's work shows that although the greatest savings are at fifteen to thirty units per acre, density at ten units per acre is only 10 percent more costly than density at fifteen units per acre, but it is nearly a quarter less expensive than five units per acre based on contiguous development patterns. At less than three units per acre, development becomes very costly.

Development of Agricultural Land. Another cost is the loss of agricultural land for the production of food and fiber that occurs when farmland is subdivided into residential lots. But there are more insidious ways in which productive farmland is reduced.

Urban development is incompatible with farming (Sinclair 1967; Berry 1978; Nelson 1986, 1992). Urban residents object to the noise, glare, dust, smoke, hours of operation, spraying, fertilizing, and other operational

Table 1–1. Summary of Capital Costs by Urban Form and City Center Distance
(1992 Dollars Per Dwelling Unit, All Urban Facilities)

DENSITY	CONTIGUOUS		LEAPFROG	
	5 Miles	10 Miles	5 Miles	10 Miles
1 Unit/4 Acres	$94,949	$103,111	$94,949	$103,111
1 Unit/Acre	57,822	65,985	57,822	65,985
3 Units/Acre	42,586	50,748	47,390	45,408
5 Units/Acre	40,246	48,409	37,245	45,408
10 Units/Acre	33,677	41,364	35,902	40,098
12 Units/Acre	33,355	38,728	34,717	40,090
15 Units/Acre	30,185	37,872	32,410	40,098
30 Units/Acre	18,445	24,975	20,670	27,200

Notes: This table updates Frank's (1989a, 1989b) figures for 1988 using the 1992 *Engineering News & Record* construction cost index. Frank adapted this from Real Estate Research Corporation (1974).

activities of farmers (Plaut 1976). Urban residents also cause damage to crops and small livestock. Farmland is therefore less productive the closer it gets to urban development (Nelson 1986, 1992; Sinclair 1967). Nelson shows that urban development casts a shadow of negative effects on farmland that can extend three miles from the boundary of urban development (Nelson 1986, 1990a, 1992a).

Yet another way in which the farmland base is reduced is through erosion of the farming economy (Daniels 1986). Productive farms depend on a variety of support services, including farm implement dealers and repair shops, fertilizer and pesticide distributors, and certain trades. To justify serving an area, these support services depend on a certain volume of activity. At some point, as productive farmland is reduced through development or as a consequence of the shadow effect, the critical mass of productive farmland needed to sustain some support services is removed. As support services erode, the farming economy further declines (Daniels and Nelson 1986; Nelson 1990a). These concerns are not limited to farmlands: they also apply to all lands used for the production of goods and for the preservation of important natural resources (Thompson 1986).

Conflicting Development. A third kind of cost is the loss in values and amenities of urban real property from the development of conflicting, undisciplined land uses on the periphery of cities. Sites more appropriate for high-density development, perhaps high-rise or mixed-use developments, may be prematurely developed into low density. Certain development at the urban fringe, such as certain kinds of industry, may dissuade prudent expansion of urban areas. Sprawl can thus prematurely restrict efficient development patterns. One solution offered by the National Commission on Urban Problems (1968: 245) is "that . . . local governments establish holding zones in order to postpone urban development in areas that are inappropriate for development."

Other Consequences of Urban Development Patterns. Popenoe (1972, 1974) observes that low-density development has led to an intensification of residential segregation by race and social class. Feagin (1985) observes the several social costs imposed on citizens of Houston because of the lack of planning and other land-use regulations. The National Research Council (1974) notes that:

1. The benefits of urban sprawl are distributed regressively with respect to wealth.
2. Of all the alternative forms of urban expansion, urban sprawl is the one that is most destructive of the center city.
3. Urban sprawl has led to the proliferation of fragmented and overlapping governmental units.

Gaffney (1964) argues that containment of sprawl is necessary to provide urban facilities and public service in an efficient manner, to maximize the ease of contact between people, and to stimulate the revitalization of underutilized sites. Freilich (1978: 29) summarizes the benefits of growth management in discouraging or preventing urban sprawl:

> Controlling sprawl by redirecting growth would benefit central city dwellers through rehabilitation and revitalization of the central city, would be environmentally beneficial by preserving agricultural land and open space, would aid in reducing energy consumption and would, by limiting the area over which services must be extended, reduce the cost of services to suburbanites and aid in the fiscal solvency of local governments.

In response to urban sprawl, planners have evolved a system of approaches that is now broadly termed urban growth management.

TAXPAYER PROTECTION

Growth management policies should be viewed as an important way in which to protect taxpayers from imprudent private investment decisions resulting in overbuilding. A prime example is the failure of hundreds of savings and loans in the 1980s and 1990s. By the beginning of 1993, U.S. taxpayers had paid out more than $80 billion in federal revenues to bail out failed savings-and-loan institutions (Resolution Trust Corporation 1993). The Congressional Budget Office (CBO) estimates that the present value of taxpayer costs to bail out failed S&Ls will be as high as $215 billion in 1990 dollars. Federal debt service payments will increase by about $15 billion annually (CBO 1992: 13). Total cost to the gross national product is estimated to run as much as $0.5 *trillion* in 1990 dollars (CBO: 35). Indeed, the CBO notes that it will not be the current but rather the future generation of taxpayers that will bear the economic burden of the bailout (CBO: 20).

As the CBO points out, overbuilding in the real estate industry was a significant contributor to the bailout crisis. Overbuilding robs the private sector of economic development investment capital and prevents local governments from making economically efficient infrastructure decisions. Overbuilding induces development of new, suburbanizing areas while diverting development opportunities from central cities. For example, data suggest that the aggregate supply of vacant suburban office space is greater than the aggregate supply of vacant downtown office space (Urban Land Institute 1992).

What caused the overbuilding of the 1980s? The CBO points out that the one-two tax punch of the 1981 Economic Recovery Act that induced real estate development coupled with the Tax Reform Act of 1986 that undid many of the 1981 policies caused many S&Ls to fail. But this begs the question: Was real estate development tax-driven or market-driven? If development occurred commensurate with demand, the bailout may not ever have happened. Overbuilding was probably driven by tax policies and unrealistic assessments of markets by speculators and their financiers. It was also linked to the absence of growth management, as will be shown here.

For our purposes, ten states are defined as growth management states: California, Florida, Hawaii, Maine, Maryland, New Jersey, Oregon, Rhode Island, Vermont, and Washington (Bollens 1992; DeGrove 1984, 1992; Gail 1992; Glickfeld and Levine 1992; Knaap and Nelson 1992). Table 1–2 shows that bailout costs totalled $80 billion for all states that grew between 1980 and 1990 (all states except Iowa, North Dakota, West Virginia, and Wyoming, and excluding the District of Columbia). The ten growth management states collectively grew by more than 11.5 million people while the remaining thirty-six states grew by slightly more than 11 million. Despite more growth, the growth management states account for only $19 billion in bailout costs while the remaining thirty-six states account for $61 billion. The bailout costs average $1,642 per new resident among the growth management states but $5,582 per new resident among nongrowth management states.

Here are a few interesting comparisons between selected states:

• Arizona (a nongrowth management state) and Florida (a growth management

Table 1–2. Savings-and-Loan Bailout Costs Compared between Growth Management and Nongrowth Management States

Indicator	Growth Management States	Nongrowth Management States
Growth during 1980s	11,511,000	11,201,000
Total bailout costs ($billions)	$18.90	$61.44
Bailout costs per new resident	$1,642	$5,485

state) grew by comparable rates (25.8 percent and 24.7 percent, respectively) and each incurred comparable bailout costs. Yet, the per-new-resident bailout costs in Arizona exceed $6,500 while the costs in Florida are slightly more than $2,000.

• Texas (a nongrowth management state) and California (a growth management state) are the two largest states in terms of land area within the contiguous forty-eight states and had reasonably comparable growth rates (16.2 percent and 20.5 percent, respectively). The per-new-resident bailout costs in Texas exceed $9,300 while the costs in California are slightly less than $2,000.

• New Mexico (a nongrowth management state) and Oregon (a growth management state) have comparable land area and added nearly identical population amounts. The per-new-resident bailout costs in New Mexico are nearly $10,000 while the costs in Oregon are slightly less than $1,000.

Growth management states clearly performed better than nongrowth management states in protecting taxpayers from bailout costs. Some will argue that such comparisons are not realistic on two grounds. First, high growth projections in some nongrowth management states may have induced overbuilding. This would be true if, for example, projected growth in Texas was considerably less than actual growth. Yet Texas' 1990 population was less than three percent lower than projected, a situation similar to the growth

management states of Florida and Washington. New Mexico nearly matched its projected growth, yet Oregon, because of its timber economy shakeout, was nearly 15 percent lower than projected. The logical conclusion of blaming underachieved population projections as an excuse for the magnitude of the bailout costs would mean that Florida and should have had the same magnitude of losses per capita as Texas; New Mexico should have had the same magnitude of losses per capita as Oregon; and Oregon should have shown gargantuan per-capita bailout costs.

Some may also argue that certain states are heavily dependent upon oil and that oil price variations will have wild effects on state economies, especially on the demand for and value of development. Much of the bailout is attributable to S&Ls securing loans with overvalued real estate during high oil price years, only to see that security erode as oil prices fell. Crude oil production data indicate that Texas produces one-quarter of the nation's oil and California produces about half as much as Texas. Although Texas is the most costly bailout state, Arkansas, New Mexico, and Arizona are the second, third, and fourth most costly bailout states on a per-new-resident basis, and none of those states produce significant volumes of oil. While a contributing factor, oil dependency alone cannot account for the magnitude of the taxpayer bailout cost.

In a prophetic 1986 article, Prof. David Dowall warned of overbuilding and the role

Overbuilding

of planners in preventing it (Dowall 1986). His original prose is the basis for elaboration on the role of planners in protecting society against overbuilding:

• Empty buildings blight surrounding areas, undercut viable markets, and can create economically devastating overcorrections in the local construction industry. Given historical patterns of overbuilding (whether office overbuilding in the 1980s or condominium overbuilding in the 1970s), planners must no longer believe that the developer knows the market best. Planners should confront those developers who claim it is their right to invest their own money even if it means overbuilding by replying that *any* risk that may be borne by taxpayers gives planners the right to just say no. For their part, planners must gauge the market feasibility of projects or require that developers provide convincing evidence of market demand and perhaps engage a third party to evaluate the veracity of the developer's claims.

• Overbuilding exaggerates the demand for scarce, and increasingly expensive, public facilities. Local governments may build infrastructure prematurely to serve development, thereby robbing it of resources that may be better spent on other more pressing problems. Even if a developer is willing to pay for infrastructure improvements, the cost of maintaining facilities still falls on all taxpayers and ratepayers. If a building lies vacant, its phantom tenants will not pay their share of debt service or operating costs. Moreover, local government is obliged to reserve infrastructure capacity to serve vacant buildings, though this may rob the local government of the capacity to accommodate other development that may be more timely or appropriate.

• In overbuilt markets, planners have a more difficult time levying exactions or im-

posing impact fees since developers will argue that they cannot compete with overhung supplies in other communities if they have to pay those exactions. This ultimately robs the local government of the resources it needs to expand future infrastructure capacity commensurate with needs. It also ultimately results in local taxpayers footing the bill for future infrastructure.

• Empty buildings may bankrupt developers and force them to breach contracts with local suppliers, subcontractors, and even the local government itself in terms of paying downstream fees, exactions, or financial support for ongoing programs such as transportation management associations.

• Where a development is a product of a public-private partnership, overbuilding may cause the private developer to fold, leaving the local government footing the entire bill.

Professor Dowall observes that developers and lenders have demonstrated their inability to exercise responsible stewardship over real estate markets (Dowall 1986). In a few (but growing) number of states, planners who are given growth management tools are demonstrating their ability to protect taxpayers from unwise developments. This is but one, albeit significant, policy rationale for growth management.

THE ECONOMIC PURPOSES OF GROWTH MANAGEMENT

There are some who claim that urban sprawl does not exist, or that it is desirable. Jack Lessinger, for example, argues the case for scattered development. Only through "scatteration" can tracts of land be reserved for future development to greater intensity than is justified in the present (Lessinger 1962). Others suggest that efforts to contain sprawl may do more harm than good, and that sprawl is really an efficient form of land use (Fischel 1990). The general contention is that sprawl is part of an orderly market process and is a product of an efficient market process.

Foremost among the arguments posed by those opposing growth management aimed at discouraging urban sprawl is that the unregulated urban land market is inherently efficient. Private property owners are viewed as best able to determine the use of their own land and thus to produce more efficient development than would result from growth management policies. The problem with this view is that efficient behavior by private property owners is impossible to achieve because the conditions of efficient behavior are nonexistent.

Lee (1981) succinctly reviews the nature of market failure and the need for public policy intervention. The market economy is composed of many interrelated markets, such as markets for housing, industry, recreation, agricultural land, school sites, and baseball stadiums. Society achieves efficiency among markets when resources are allocated to each market to generate the largest net benefits. This can be achieved if the output of each market is increased until the marginal cost of the next unit of production is just equal to its marginal benefit. Too low a level of production means that some benefits are not realized despite increasing investment and declining cost per unit. Too high a level of production means that the last units cost more than the benefits received.

Lee observes that in the ideal situation these markets achieve efficiency without any government intervention. Yet, there are several, highly restrictive assumptions inherent in these claims. According to Lee, perfectly functioning markets must meet seven conditions including (1) many buyers and sellers

for any given property; (2) perfect information about any given property; (3) ease of entry and exit of developers within each market; (4) no transaction costs such as complex title searches, negotiations, legal services, and enforcement of contracts; (5) constant returns to scale in the long run so that profit is predictable; (6) buyers and sellers fully internalizing any externalities imposed on others or society because of the manner in which they use property; and (7) all consumers have the same tastes and preferences.

Of course, the problem is that (1) for many properties there are not many buyers and sellers; (2) information is always imperfect and so there will be risks and uncertainty; (3) there are considerable barriers to entry and exit; (4) there are always transaction costs; (5) it is impossible to receive predictably constant returns to scale; (6) buyers and sellers do not internalize their externalities and this results in other individuals or society as a whole paying those costs in many ways; and (7) consumers do not have the same tastes and preferences.

As a result, urban land markets fail to provide efficient development patterns because none of these conditions is ever completely present. Private property owners never fully internalize their marginal social costs, and they never know their marginal social benefits.

One purpose of government intervention in the market—in part through growth management—is to correct conditions causing inefficiencies. These interventions create a complex web that aims to balance public interest with principles of efficiency. Intervention usually takes the form of restrictions, and economic incentives and disincentives. However, unless their effects are anticipated, these policies may cause greater inefficiencies (Richardson and Gordon 1993). Indeed, while some analysts bemoan the inefficient effects of development regulation on land markets, they often fail to consider inefficiencies caused by government subsidies and investment policies. The logical solution would be to (1) eliminate all development subsidies; (2) eliminate mortgage interest deductions; (3) require full marginal cost pricing of facilities and services regardless of ability to pay; (4) eliminate all preferential property taxation programs including those on elderly, low-income, farmers, and other special groups; (5) settle all conflicting land-use problems in the courts under nuisance theories despite any potential for further clogging courts; (6) reform the entire system of land transaction to eliminate transaction costs or, through government subsidy, make free all transactions; (7) undertake a full impact assessment on every development proposal including individual building permits for homes—as well as on all public works projects regardless of size so that social costs can be identified and mitigated; and (8) tax the public to buy the development rights to open spaces it deems socially important, even in situations causing taxpayers to pay twice (once for the facilities that create value and again for the value they create). Only if these steps are taken—and only when the seven conditions of efficient markets are present—would the market achieve efficiency and growth management would be unnecessary.

In effect, planning systems are in place to: (1) offset inefficient development patterns stimulated by government subsidies and sprawl-inducing policies; (2) take improved (although imperfect) account of the nature of conflicts among different land uses; (3) inform buyers and sellers of the overriding public interest in the environment; and (4) achieve development patterns that make more efficient use of taxpayer investments.

Economic texts also point out reasons for planning that are ultimately aimed at preventing urban sprawl. Those reasons include (1) the reduction of negative externalities that result from interdependencies among land uses, as when development of one parcel has adverse effects on the use or value of another (Bish and Nourse 1975); (2) the provision of the optimal level of public goods (Ervin et al. 1977); and (3) the reduction of the costs of providing public services (Ervin et al. 1977).

Prof. Marion Clawson (1962: 109) offers a view of how to design a comprehensive planning system that aims to contain urban sprawl and counter the sprawl-inducing effects of both public policy and market imperfections, while accommodating the development needs of an urban area:

> If planning, zoning, and subdivision were firm—enforceable and enforced—then the area available at any one time for each kind of use would bear some relationship to the need for land for this use. That is, area classified for different purposes could be consciously manipulated or determined in relation to market need. Sufficient area for each purpose, including enough area to provide some competition among sellers and some choice among buyers, should be zoned or classified for development, *but no more.* By careful choice of the areas concerned sprawl would be reduced, perhaps largely eliminated.

ISSUES OF EFFICIENT URBAN FORM

Growth management is intimately associated with the achievement of more efficient urban development patterns. The more efficient urban development is, the greater the wealth of society since scarce resources are not wasted.

The goals of efficient urban form include (1) achieving jobs-housing balance; (2) integrating socioeconomic classes (since both low- and high-income workers often work in the same place); (3) reducing the need for expansion of transportation capacity; (4) enhancing redevelopment; (5) minimizing environmental pollution; (6) preventing costly or conflicting land-use patterns; and (7) minimizing public facility costs.

As to the most efficient urban development pattern, we turn to four groups of studies. The first group of studies are simulations of energy and accessibility among six archetypal urban development patterns. The second is a number of studies undertaken by several U.S. urban areas focusing on effects of alternative development patterns on accessibility. The third is an economic impact assessment of the New Jersey state plan conducted for the State of New Jersey by the Rutgers University Center for Urban Policy Research. The fourth group is a series of studies on urban growth containment in Oregon conducted by several researchers.

Alternative Settlement Pattern Simulations

Rickaby (1981, 1987; with Steadman 1981; with de la Barra 1982) evaluates the energy and accessibility implications of six settlement patterns under three different energy conservation scenarios. It is the only such evaluation in the literature. The settlement patterns include (1) status quo configuration composed of a moderately compact urban area and low-density development sprawling into the rural countryside; (2) highly compact urban development (based on Dantzig and Saaty 1973); (3) moderately compact urban core with development along major corridors, based on *Soria y Mata* (Spreiregen 1981;

March 1967); (4) moderately compact urban core with satellite towns (based on Howard 1898); (5) moderately compact urban core with scattered linear development along minor corridors (Steadman 1977); and (6) moderately compact urban core surrounded by an integrated system of urban villages, involving infill of existing settlements (Department of the Environment 1974).

Total population for all scenarios is 124,129, and total land area is 175,685 acres. In all but the highly compact urban core scenario, 72,000 people or about 60 percent of the population live in the urban area. Nearly 80 percent of the population is allocated to the urban area in the highly compact urban core development scenario. About 20 percent of the population is allocated to the rural area in all scenarios other than the status quo, where about 33 percent are allocated. In all but the status quo and highly compact development scenarios, about 20 percent of the population is allocated to different planned development patterns and some unplanned development around the compact urban area.

Three energy consumption scenarios were considered: (1) high consumption wherein there is no change over twenty-five years in energy consumption or lifestyle; (2) middle consumption wherein technological improvements are made to reduce energy consumption without any change in lifestyle; and (3) low consumption wherein both technological improvements and changes in lifestyle are effected. Table 1–3 summarizes results for the middle energy consumption scenario.

The highly compact urban core development pattern is the most energy efficient and provides the greatest degree of access relative to all other patterns. Although highly compact development requires more roads to dis-

Table 1–3. Evaluation Results for Different Development Patterns

Comparison	Compact with Urban Sprawl	Highly Compact	Compact with Linear	Compact with Satellite Towns	Compact with Scattered Linear	Compact with Urban Villages
LAND-USE FEATURES						
Land Area Planned (acres)	175,685	175,685	175,685	175,685	175,685	175,685
Urban Area (acres)	5,244	5,244	5,244	5,244	5,244	5,244
Rural Area (acres)	98,147	98,147	98,147	98,147	98,147	98,147
Urb Fringe Unplanned Dev (acres)	67,050	67,050	63,319	65,135	64,662	64,897
Linear/Satellite Dev (acres)			3,731	1,915	2,388	2,153
Developed Urb/Lin/Sat (acres)	5,244	5,244	8,975	7,159	7,632	7,397
Employment	49,418	49,418	49,418	49,418	49,418	49,418
Population	124,129	124,129	124,129	124,129	124,129	124,129
Urban Population	72,000	96,652	72,000	72,000	72,000	72,000
Rural Population	8,815	8,815	8,815	8,815	8,815	8,815
Urb Fringe Pop in Unplanned Dev	43,314	18,662	17,604	18,246	17,141	18,114
Linear/Satellite Population			25,630	25,068	26,173	25,200
Urban Population/Sq Mi	8,787	11,794	8,787	8,787	8,787	8,787
Rural Population/Sq Mi	57	57	57	57	57	57
Urb Fringe Pop/Sq Mi in Unpl Dev	383	178	178	179	170	177
Linear/Satellite Pop/Sq Mi			4,396	8,388	7,015	7,491
Urban+Lin/Sat Pop/Sq Mi	8,787	11,794	6,962	8,678	8,233	8,410
Households	49,318	49,318	49,318	49,318	49,318	49,318
Energy Consumed (gigajoules)	5,232	3,798	4,309	3,781	4,200	4,111
TRANSPORTATION						
Roads (miles)	413	455	451	508	440	430
Modal Split-Public (percent)	24.54	25.67	24.78	24.96	24.10	24.41
Public Passenger Miles	137,586	113,325	179,016	158,631	136,391	132,756
Private Passenger Miles	533,356	435,924	650,403	581,343	538,423	516,499
Total Passenger Miles	670,942	549,249	829,419	739,974	674,814	649,255
Energy Consumed (gigajoules)	908	803	1,073	958	1,028	888
TOTAL ENERGY (gigajoules)	6,140	4,601	5,382	4,739	5,228	4,999

Source: Adapted from Tables 7–9 in Rickaby (1987).

tribute trips more efficiently throughout the urban area relative to most other patterns including the status quo, total passenger miles is at least 20 percent less than all alternative development patterns including the status quo. Energy consumption is reduced about 25 percent over the status quo.

What of the other patterns? The second most efficient pattern is satellite towns with a compact urban area. However, this pattern has most of its energy savings attributed to households while its transportation related energy consumption is greater than the status quo. The urban village (infill) with compact urban area emerges as the better second choice since it involves energy savings in both households and transportation relative to the status quo.

Energy savings implies increased disposable income. Transportation savings include both energy and time. Both kinds of savings are capitalized by land. The result of these efficiencies is higher housing costs, which is to be expected in any program that creates efficiencies. Among all the alternative schemes, urban village (infill) with a compact urban area involves the greatest energy savings with the least increase in housing costs.

To some extent, the analysis prepared by Rickaby, based as it was on data and development patterns in England, is not directly applicable to much of the United States. Nonetheless, certain implications are offered. The pattern of distributed nodes of concentrated development (Rickaby's "villages") around a compact urban area, wherein the nodes are connected to the urban area by public transit and major highways, is not only the pattern Rickaby generally advances (1987: 219–20), but the one most commonly advanced by planners and architects to reshape American urban areas (Duany and Plater-Zyberk 1991; Ewing 1991; Kelbaugh 1989; Moudon 1990; Stern 1981; Van der Ryn and Calthorpe 1986).

American Urban Region Simulations

Since 1990, at least six urban areas have studied effects of alternative development patterns on vehicle-miles of travel (VMT): Baltimore, Dallas-Fort Worth, Middlesex, San Diego, Seattle, and Washington. All involved comparing existing development patterns to patterns along various combinations of employment and housing concentration and dispersal. Table 1–4 summarizes the findings of each study.

Table 1–4. Summary of Urban Form Analysis of Selected Metropolitan Regions

City	Development Pattern	Change in VMT
Baltimore, Maryland	Centralized Residential with Concentrated Job Centers	−1%
	Decentralized Residential with Concentrated Job Centers	+2%
	Transit-Accessible Res. with Concentrated Job Centers	−1%
Dallas-Fort Worth, Texas	Rail Corridors with Concentrated Job Centers	−1%
	Activity Centers with Concentrated Job Centers	−1%
	Development of Presently Uncontested Areas	−4%
Middlesex, New Jersey	Concentrate Jobs and Housing in Existing Centers	−12%
	Concentrate Jobs and Housing in Dispersed Centers	−9%
San Diego, California	Move Jobs to Housing	−6%
	Move Housing to Jobs	−8%
	Move Jobs to Housing Along Transit Corridors	−5%
	Move Housing to Jobs Along Transit Corridors	−9%
	Concentrate Jobs into Regional Centers	+11%
Seattle, Washington	Concentrate Jobs into Regional Centers	−4%
	Achieve Jobs-Housing Balance with Smaller Centers	−1%
	Continued Dispersal of Jobs and Housing	+3%
	Concentrate Jobs and Housing to Achieve Balance	−3%
Washington, D.C.	Achieve Jobs-Housing Balance with Smaller Centers	−9%
	Concentrate Jobs and Housing to Achieve Balance	−9%

Sources: Baltimore Regional Council of Governments (1992), North Central Texas Council of Governments (1990), Middlesex–Somerset–Mercer Regional Council (1991), San Diego Association of Governments (1991), Puget Sound Council of Governments (1990), Metropolitan Washington Council of Governments (1991), and Fehr and Peer Associates (1992).

In all cases, failure to achieve some improvement in the accessibility of housing to jobs results in increased VMT over the projection periods. In contrast, all scenarios resulting in locating housing where jobs are and vice versa decreases VMT. The greatest magnitudes of VMT reduction are associated with locating new housing *closer* to existing job centers. In most situations, the greatest reductions in VMT are associated with locating housing along transit corridors that improve access to major employment centers.

New Jersey Simulation

Between 1990 and 2010, New Jersey expects to add 520,000 residents and 654,000 jobs. New Jersey recently adopted a statewide development plan after nearly a decade of preparation. Prior to adoption, the State of New Jersey contracted with the Center for Urban Policy Research at Rutgers (CUPR 1992) to review the draft plan to determine whether the state would be better off with or without it. The plan at that time was called the Interim State Development and Redevelopment Plan, or simply the State Plan. It has since been adopted and is now being implemented. The state plan calls for concentrating new development in existing urbanized areas, creating commercial centers in existing suburban areas, and preventing the further development of most remaining farmland and other fragile land. In general, the state plan would

 • concentrate employment in specially targeted employment centers.

 • concentrate development where excess facility capacity exists or where new facilities are extended contiguous to existing development.

 • increase redevelopment and infill activity.

 • shift development away from farmlands and other important open spaces.

 • reduce air pollution principally by reducing VMT and increasing public transit use.

 • improve housing affordability principally by increasing housing supply and density at selected urban centers.

 • improve intergovernmental coordination in growth management and delivery of public services.

The general conclusion drawn from CUPR's analysis is that by establishing employment centers and either putting housing in those centers or connecting housing to centers by transit, several improvements are effected. Table 1–5 summarizes CUPR's findings.

Oregon Growth Management Studies

Oregon's statewide growth management system forces urban development to concentrate inside urban growth boundaries (UGBs) and prohibits development of resource lands unless such development is needed to improve resource productivity (Knaap and Nelson 1992). Generally speaking, the kind of development pattern pursued in Oregon is similar to Rickaby's urban villages with a moderately compact urban core. Generally speaking, Oregon's growth management approach has led to

 • preservation of resource land for resource purposes with associated improvements in productivity (Nelson 1992).

 • efficient provision of public facilities with associated taxpayer savings (Nelson and Knaap 1987; Nelson 1987).

 • efficient allocation of land for various kinds of development (Knaap and Nelson 1992).

 • VMT reductions (Moore and Nelson).

 • improved housing opportunities (Knaap 1991; Knaap and Nelson 1992).

Suburbs in metropolitan Portland, for example, are being converted into centers of

Table 1–5. Evaluating Impacts of New Jersey Development Plan

Issue	Outcome
Employment Location	The State Plan would shift 300,000 jobs away from dispersed suburban and rural areas into suburban and rural centers, and add 62,000 jobs to urban centers.
Housing Location	The State Plan results in up to 300,000 more households gaining access to various modes of public transit chiefly by locating new housing in and near employment centers.
Land Consumption	The State Plan will consume 130,000 fewer acres of land. Without it, development will consume 30,000 more acres of environmentally sensitive land. Development will also consume 30,000 more acres of prime farmland.
Pollution	Nitrogen oxide emissions will be 21 percent less, carbon monoxide emissions will be 12 percent less, and nonmethane hydrocarbons will be 17 percent less under the State Plan. Water pollutants in stormwater runoff from new development will be 4,560 tons tons less under the State Plan.
Public Facilities	The State Plan will save $440 million in new water and sewer facility investments.
Roads	The State Plan will save $740 million in new road costs.
Transit	The State Plan will provide transit access to up to 300,000 more homes.
Housing Costs	By increasing densities slightly and improving access of housing to employment centers, housing costs will be slightly lower under the State Plan.
Governmental Efficiency	State and local agencies will improve their coordination and delivery of services under the State Plan.

Source: Center for Urban Policy Research 1992).

employment, commerce, and housing. Many are being linked by light rail transit to each other and to moderately compact downtown Portland.

RELATION TO QUALITY OF LIFE

Anthony Downs (1989) dismantles the prevailing ethos favoring urban sprawl and then offers a program aimed at achieving compact development patterns. Downs observes that the prevailing vision of the ideal form of urban development (urban sprawl) is centered on the auto-dependent, low-density suburban housing model. That ideal is based on four pillars: (1) ownership of single-family homes on large lots; (2) ownership of a private automobile, with a highway system that accommodates traffic without congestion; (3) low-rise workplaces on land-extensive arrangements with plenty of free parking; and (4) highly decentralized governance of public facilities and services.

Downs observes that large U.S. metropolitan areas have generally achieved that ideal but are beginning to find it unacceptable. This is because there are three fatal flaws rooted in the ideal, including (1) excessive travel that results from the urban form resulting from the first and second pillars; (2) no provision of housing for the low-wage earner, including the very education, public safety, and public works personnel whose services are demanded by suburban communities; and (3) no consensus on how to best pay for urban infrastructure, with the result that many urban residents in higher density areas actually subsidize residents in lower density areas, and existing residents effectively subsidize the costs of providing expensive infrastructure to new residents. Downs (1989: 7) parenthetically observes the central problem inherent in changing the present arrangement of how benefits are distributed:

> Once a majority of citizens has begun receiving . . . short-run benefits, its members do not want to give them up. But they often fail to agree about how to distribute long-run costs necessary to sustain those short-run benefits. Each subgroup among the beneficiaries tries to shift as much of its share of the costs as possible onto other subgroups. No consensus arises about how to pay for these costs. In some cases, the costs are not paid at all.

Downs also observes that the planning profession has been in the forefront of critics claiming that the prevailing vision of the ideal urban form will not work in the long run.

Downs notes that most suburbanites in fast-growing metropolitan areas are now discovering this fact, to their dismay.

Downs offers a vision that is composed of five parts. In his view, a new vision of urban form must (1) contain sizable areas of at least moderately high-density development, especially of housing and workplaces; (2) encourage people to live nearer to where they work; (3) have governance structures that preserve substantial local authority but within a framework that compels local governments to act responsibly to meet regional needs; (4) have incentive arrangements that encourage individuals and households to take a more realistic account of the collective costs of their individual actions, such as marginal cost pricing of public facilities and services (one example being peak-hour traffic charges through metering of automobiles); and (5) incorporate stable and predictable strategies to adequately finance infrastructure to accommodate growth. With these and other strategies, the quality of urban life can be improved. But these strategies require substantial growth management efforts.

2

State and Regional Growth Management Approaches

The kinds of problems that growth management systems attempt to address—urban sprawl, costly development patterns, traffic congestion, environmental degradation, and farmland conversion—have causes and effects that typically extend beyond local government boundaries. Yet, growth management programs historically have been developed and administered at the local level, due to local governments' role in the areas of land-use regulation and infrastructure provision.

Beginning in the early 1970s, state governments began to assert more control over environmental problems and growth management issues. Since that time many states have prepared statewide land-use and infrastructure plans, mandated planning at the local level, and adopted requirements that local plans be consistent with state and regional planning goals. This shift, often referred to as planning's quiet revolution, was due partly to strong popular initiatives and partly to federal programs that provided funding and guidelines for state efforts.

Regional approaches to planning and growth management issues have long been championed as a necessary alternative to the problems associated with fragmented, unco-

ordinated, and competitive local government policies. As with state programs, regional growth management approaches were spurred by federal funding opportunities. State mandates for regional planning provided the impetus to some regional programs.

State and regional involvement in planning and growth management requires a large degree of intergovernmental cooperation and support. These intergovernmental arrangements, though necessary, often produce considerable tension among state, regional, and local interests. Questions that continue to be worked out in state and regional growth management programs include (1) how much authority should reside at each level, (2) how the authority should be carried out, and (3) how much monitoring by state or regional agencies should take place. This chapter presents several examples of state and regional growth management frameworks.

STATE APPROACHES

Since the 1970s, state governments, recognizing the inability of local governments to effectively manage their growth, have taken a stronger role in mandating and coordinating planning and growth management activities by state, regional, and local governments. The most basic state mandate is that local governments prepare and adopt a comprehensive plan to guide their land-use regulations and decisions. While the U.S. Department of Commerce's Standard State Enabling Act of 1926, upon which most states patterned their original enabling legislation, seem to require local comprehensive plans, the courts in most states have interpreted the act's rather vague language as requiring no more than a comprehensive zoning map. About half of all states now explicitly require their local governments to adopt a comprehensive plan with at least some minimum content specifications.

Several states have gone beyond planning mandates and adopted comprehensive approaches to growth management. In general, state strategies involve the establishment of statewide goals and policies, the creation of regional agencies charged with reviewing and coordinating local plans, and requirements that local governments prepare plans that implement state goals. State planning and growth management strategies exhibit key differences of approach. Vermont and Hawaii, small states with relatively weak local governments, have emphasized state land-use planning and a direct permitting role for state government. Others, like Oregon and Florida, have pursued integrated strategies that rely on local plans and regulations to implement state and regional goals. In some cases, state-initiated growth management programs are limited to substate areas, such as the coastal zone management programs of California and North Carolina. Many states now require that planning be done, but relatively few mandate planning coordination among local, regional, and state agencies. Table 2–1 summarizes growth management

statutes among states considered leaders in growth management.

State-Imposed Planning

As the name implies, state-imposed planning is planning imposed on local governments by a state agency. Hawaii is the only state that imposes top-down planning upon its local governments.

Hawaii. Almost since statehood, Hawaii has had the nation's most centralized planning structure. Original planning laws in Hawaii were aimed principally at preventing the 1950s practice of buying large tracts of land and dividing them into smaller tracts for low-density development, a practice that accelerates the process of urban land conversion and reduces farmland inventory. Act 187, the original statewide land-use law adopted in 1961, resulted in classifying all island lands into four categories: urban, agriculture, low-density rural, and conservation. Only the first three permit any kind of development (De-Grove 1984).

The use and development of urban, agricultural, and low-density rural land is managed by a seven-member, gubernatorially appointed state land use commission and its staff, the department of planning and economic development. Before 1975, changes in land use had to be approved on an incremental basis. Conservation lands, which may not be developed, are managed by the board of land and natural resources and its staff. Although there were land-use studies, there was no formal overall land-use plan. Nor were there clear administrative procedures or decision-making criteria to guide review of land-use changes. Interim guidelines for development were not implemented until 1975. The official state plan itself was not adopted

Table 2–1. State Comprehensive Growth Legislation

State	Legislation
California	Coastal Act of 1976 (Cal Pub Res Code (30000-30900) Coastal Zone Conservation Act, 1972 (Cal Pub Res Code 27000-650) Tahoe (Lake) Regional Planning Compact, 1969 (Cal Government Code 66801)

Florida	Omnibus Growth Management Act
	    Local Government Comprehensive Planning and Land Development Regulation Act, 1985
	    (Fla Stat 163.3161-.3215)
	    State Comprehensive Plan, 1985 (Fla Stat 187.201)
	    State and Regional Planning Act, 1984 (Fla Stat 186.001-.911)
	    Environmental Land and Water Management Act, 1972 (Fla Stat 380 et seq.)

Georgia	Coordinated Planning Legislation, 1989 (O.C.G.A. 50-8-1 et seq.)
Hawaii	Hawaii State Plan, 1978. Hawaii Department of Planning and Economic Development. Adopted by legislature as Act 100. Hawaiian Land Use Law, 1961 (Haw Rev Stats Chapter 205)
Maine	Comprehensive Planning and Land Use Regulation Act, 1988 (30 M.R.S.A. Sec O4960)
Maryland	Economic Growth, Resource Protection, and Planning Act, 1992 (House Bill 1195. Chapter 437 of the Laws of Maryland) Chesapeake Bay Critical Area Law, 1984 (NRA 8-1801-1816)
Massachusetts	Cape Cod Commission Act, 1989 (Chapter 716 of Acts and Resolves) Martha's Vineyard Commission Act, 1974 (Chapter 637 of Acts and Resolves)
New Jersey	State Planning Act, 1985 (NJSA 52:18A-196 et seq.) State Pinelands Protection Act, 1979 (NJ Rev State 13-18A)
New York	Adirondack Park Agency Act, 1971 (Article 27, NYS Executive Law, NY Consolidated Laws Service, NY Statutes, vol 14A)
Oregon	Land Conservation and Development Act, 1973 (SB 100; Oregon Statutes 197)
Rhode Island	Comprehensive Planning and Land Use Regulation Act, 1988 (Chapter 45-22.1 of the Rhode Island General Laws)
Vermont	Amendments to Chapter 117 (Act 280), 1990 Growth Management Act (Act 200), 1988 (24 Vermont Statutes Ch. 117) Environmental Control Act (Act 250), 1970 (10 Vermont Statutes Ch. 151)
Washington	Amendments to the 1990 Growth Management Act, 1991 (ReSHB 1025) Growth Management Act, 1990 (Sub House Bill 2929)

Note: Programs above met two selection criteria: (1) they are comprehensive and multifunctional, and (2) they were initiated through and in response to state actions. Thus, not included here are numerous state acts focused on single land use–related functions, and the many state coastal management acts created in response to federal legislation. The California coastal program is included because it was initially adopted prior to and independent of federal action. *Source:* Scott A. Bollens (1992)

until 1978. Since 1978, requests for changes in land use designation have required commission approval. Counties that are composed of individual islands cannot make their own plans and are obligated to administer the state plan.

By the thirtieth anniversary of Hawaii's program in 1991, 95 percent of the land originally classified as rural in the 1960s remained rural (Callies 1992). There has recently emerged, however, some dissatisfaction with the lack of local government influence in plan-making and with the perceived lack of responsiveness of state agencies to development pressures. Low vacancy rates (among the nation's lowest) combined with high housing prices, has led to a call for local flexibility in allowing more land to be developed. On the other hand, vacancy rates are high by other nations' standards and high housing prices may be mostly attributable to inefficient building codes and contracting practices peculiar to Hawaii. Hawaii may eventually move toward an Oregon-style process in which plans are prepared locally and reviewed by state agencies for consistency with state planning policies but not implemented locally until they are approved.

Mandatory Planning with Strong State Role

The second approach is mandatory planning with a strong state role. This applies mainly to Oregon and Florida, but nominally as well to Maine, New Jersey, Rhode Island, and Washington. In these interventionist, bottom-up planning states, local plans are prepared and reviewed for consistency with state planning policies. Plans found to be noncompliant are either not approved or prevented from being implemented. In essence, states practicing this approach have redelegated planning authority to the state, only to delegate back to local government when plans are in compliance.

Oregon. Oregon's pioneering state planning program was initiated in 1973, with the passage of the Land Conservation and Development Act. The act established the land conservation and development commission (LCDC), a state agency charged with developing a set of statewide planning goals and guidelines and overseeing implementation of the state planning program. Under the act,

cities, counties, and state agencies are required to adopt comprehensive plans that are coordinated with each other and that are in compliance with adopted state goals. The LCDC has formulated nineteen state goals dealing with major issues such as

• preservation of agricultural and forest land.

• preservation of sensitive lands and areas of scientific, historical, and cultural significance.

• encouragement of compact development patterns and urban growth boundaries.

• housing affordability.

• economic development.

• transportation and public facilities to facilitate urbanization.

The Oregon program has two primary and complementary objectives: containing urban sprawl and preserving forests and farmland. To limit urban sprawl, the urbanization goal requires cities to delineate urban growth boundaries, beyond which municipal water and wastewater services will not be extended. To preserve forests and farmland, the agriculture and forestry goals mandate the designation of exclusive farm use and/or resource zones that exclude incompatible uses and afford sharply reduced property taxes. In Oregon's original legislative proposal, coordination of local plans was to be accomplished by regional agencies. Political opposition to this arrangement resulted in a compromise that requires counties to review the plans of cities, special districts, and state agencies within their boundaries for consistency with state goals. Portland's regional growth boundary is administered by Metro, a regional agency charged with coordinating the planning activities of area counties, cities, and service districts. Final authority for ensuring compliance, however, remains with the LCDC.

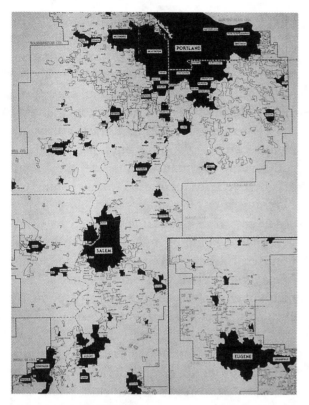

Figure 2–1. Oregon's statewide growth management program results in the separation of urban and exurban land uses from agriculture, forestry, and other resource land uses. This map, prepared by 1,000 Friends of Oregon, shows how this is accomplished in the Willamette Valley, the state's most populous region and the state's most productive in agricultural income; the valley rivals several European countries in overall density. In this map, urban areas—denoted in black—are contained within urban growth boundaries; exurban areas, which are suitable for neither urban nor resource uses, are contained within "exception" areas—denoted as white area bounded by black borders—and resource lands, principally agriculture, compose the balance. *Source:* 1,000 Friends of Oregon.

Local plans were required to be acknowledged by LCDC as being in compliance with state goals by January 1976. The LCDC was appropriated state funds to distribute to local governments to assist them in preparing their plans and was also authorized to issue extensions. The LCDC itself, however, has historically been inadequately funded and understaffed (DeGrove 1984: 264). This fact, coupled with the enormous technical and political difficulties of defining urban growth boundaries and complying with the other state goals, resulted, at least initially, in slow progress on local plan approvals. The LCDC rejected most local plans on first submittal, due in part to their inconsistency with state goals. The final local plan was not approved by LCDC until 1986, ten years after the original deadline for local plan submittal (Bollens 1992). Despite the lengthy period required for adoption of local plans, and the problems of administering and enforcing state goals, Oregon's planning program is widely considered one of the most comprehensive and effective in the nation.

Florida. Florida's original planning legislation, the Local Government Comprehensive Planning Act, was adopted in 1975. It required all local governments to prepare and adopt comprehensive plans. Although the act did not require state approval of plans, by mid-1982, 419 of 461 Florida cities and counties had adopted plans that had been reviewed and commented on at the local and regional levels (DeGrove 1984: 162). With the enactment of the State and Regional Planning Act (1984), the Growth Management Act (1985), and the Local Government Comprehensive Planning and Land Development Regulation Act (1987), Florida established a much more rigorous and detailed state planning framework. In 1985, the legislature adopted a state comprehensive plan that spelled out goals and policies on twenty-five major planning issues. By 1987, all of the state's regional councils had adopted policy plans consistent with the state plan. State agencies also adopted "functional plans" to implement the state plan.

Florida's second-generation system requires cities and counties to adopt a future-land-use map denoting the density and intensity of residential and nonresidential uses permitted. Land-use maps must also depict the location of major natural systems and existing and proposed transportation networks. Major amendments to adopted plans may be made only twice per year. Measurable goals, objectives, and policies must be spelled out for nine mandated plan elements: land use, conservation, housing, capital improvements, infrastructure, coastal management, traffic circulation, recreation, and intergovernmental coordination.

The Florida Department of Community Affairs (DCA) has the authority to approve or disapprove local plans based on their consistency with state and regional goals. Local governments are under pressure to comply because of the threat of losing state funds. DCA initially rejected one-half of the local plans submitted. Recognizing that many local governments would likely submit unacceptable plans a second time, the agency began negotiating compliance agreements with local governments (Innes 1992). All of Florida's local governments submitted plans by the July 1991 deadline imposed by the 1985 Growth Management Act. Local governments are not only required to plan, they must also adopt local land development regulations that implement and are consistent with the

adopted comprehensive plan. If the implementing regulations are not adopted, the DCA can take the case to the state administrative hearing board and ultimately to the state court system to force compliance (Gale 1992). Florida's second-generation planning mandate may be resulting in more consistent comprehensive planning, but it is not without controversy, as many plans are challenged and there are frequent calls for abolishing the planning laws altogether.

Maine. In 1988, Maine adopted its Comprehensive Planning and Land Use Regulation Act. The act sets out ten statewide growth management goals and requires that all municipalities develop comprehensive plans by 1996 that are consistent with those goals. The act also provides a strong role for newly created regional councils that are authorized under the act to determine if local plans are consistent with regional and state plans. The Maine act does not require state approval of local plans. It does, however, require review by the state office of comprehensive land use planning. It also provides a voluntary certification process. Local plans must be consistent with statewide goals in order to be certified. Only those communities with certified plans are able to impose impact fees or receive certain state funds. The real impetus for compliance, however, is that failure to adopt a new plan by the deadline will invalidate the community's zoning ordinance and render it susceptible to legal challenge. Maine's act requires that two general land-use categories be included in local comprehensive plan maps: growth areas suitable for orderly residential and economic development, and rural areas that should be protected for agricultural, forest, open-space, and scenic values.

New Jersey. New Jersey's alternative to top-down planning and growth management is unique among state planning programs. Instead of requiring the preparation and adoption of local comprehensive plans, the State Planning Act of 1985 created the state planning commission and charged it with preparing a state development and redevelopment plan. Despite the focus on state planning, local governments have been actively involved in preparing the plan through an innovative process called cross-acceptance. Under the act, the state's twenty-one counties acted as coordinating bodies between municipalities and the state planning commission. The draft plan was released in early 1989 and underwent an extended negotiation process aimed at reconciling state planning goals and policies with the interests of city and county governments. In June, 1992, the state planning commission adopted the final state development plan. All local governments chose to participate in the process.

The central tenet of the New Jersey state plan is to accommodate projected growth by directing it to existing urban areas and to defined, compact locations in rural and environmentally sensitive areas. The real strength of New Jersey's approach lies in its use of the plan to guide public investment and finance decisions. Under the plan, state spending for infrastructure improvements will be concentrated in areas where growth or redevelopment is most cost-effective. An economic impact report prepared by the Rutgers University Center for Urban Policy Studies in February 1992 estimated that, by channeling growth to established population centers, the plan could save the state and local governments $1.18 billion in road and infrastructure costs and $0.40 billion in road maintenance and school operating costs (Lawlor 1992).

Rhode Island. Rhode Island enacted its Comprehensive Planning and Land Use Regulation Act in 1988. It organizes all 247 communities into fourteen regional commissions and requires them to prepare plans consistent with state planning policies. Those policies are found in the state plan. The program is administered by the division of planning within the department of administration, which is the governor's principal administrative agency. Plan amendments must be reviewed by the state agency. Individual community plans must be compatible with plans of adjacent communities (Gale 1992). Substantive goals of the plan include

• making growth compatible with the natural characteristics of land.

• assuring jobs and overall economic well-being.

• providing affordable housing.

• protecting natural resources, open space, recreational, cultural, and historic resources. Should a local plan not be approved by the state, the community loses eligibility for state planning grants. The state may prepare plans on behalf of recalcitrant communities. Plans that are not approved by the state agency can be appealed to the state comprehensive plan appeals board. Plans must be revised every five years, or sooner, and whenever the state plan is changed. Unfortunately, regional plans are not part of the state planning system, and state agency plans do not need to be consistent with local plans if local plans are not approved by the state.

Washington. Washington's Growth Management Act was originally adopted in 1990, then substantially amended in 1991. The law applies to counties with more than 50,000 residents where the rate of growth during the 1980s was 10 percent or more and in counties with fewer than 50,000 residents where the growth rate was 20 percent or more. Counties that do not meet these criteria can opt to participate in growth management planning, but once involved they cannot opt out. As of January 1992, sixteen counties were required to undertake growth management planning and another eight opted into the program, for a total of twenty-four counties out of thirty-nine (Gale 1992: 426). Substantive goals of the Washington act include

- protecting the environment.
- connecting greenways and separating cities.
- conserving agricultural and forest lands.
- preserving lands and resources of state-wide significance.
- sharing economic growth.
- making cities more livable.
- designating urban growth areas and providing services.
- providing affordable housing.
- linking land use and public facilities.
- resolving not-in-my-backyard problems (DeGrove 1992).

The Growth Management Act is administered by the Washington Department of Community Development. City and county plans are submitted to the DCD for review and comment, but the department has no authority to declare a plan inconsistent with state planning policy. Counties must coordinate by plans of their constituent cities. The governor can direct the office of financial management to withhold motor vehicle fuel tax, liquor profit and excise taxes, and sales and use tax revenues to noncomplying cities and counties. Borrowing from Georgia and Vermont,

the Washington act created three multicounty regional growth planning hearings boards to review petitions from cities, counties, and state agencies on questions of compliance with the act. In effect, these boards have the authority to determine whether city and county plans are consistent with state planning policies. At the state level, the DCD mediates disputes involving the implementation of urban growth boundaries.

Mandatory Planning with Weak State Role

The third state planning style is referred to as mandatory planning with a weak state role. Under this approach, local (and sometimes regional) governments prepare plans and have them reviewed for general consistency with state planning criteria. The state, however, has very little authority to prevent implementation of local plans even if they are inconsistent with state planning policies. Such an approach might be called noninterventionist bottom-up planning (DeGrove 1984). States utilizing this approach include California, Vermont, and Georgia.

California. California has a long history of state-mandated local planning. As early as 1955, it required local governments to adopt general plans that contained land-use and transportation elements. In 1971, the California legislature passed AB 1301, the state's landmark planning legislation. Among other things, the law requires that county or city zoning and subdivision ordinances, as well as specific development approvals be consistent with an adopted general plan. A local general plan may be amended no more than four times per year. California's general plan law requires local governments to engage in planning, but imposes procedural and organizational requirements, rather than policy requirements. In most cases, the state does not require local general plans to achieve specific state policy goals other than the act of planning itself. The only exception is the housing element of the general plan, which must advance the state's goal of providing housing opportunities to all segments of the community and all income groups. Housing elements must contain both a needs assessment and action strategies to achieve state goals.

California general plans must contain seven elements: land use, housing, circulation, conservation, open space, safety, and noise. Local governments often add other elements, such as human resources, historic preservation, and community design. The state also requires certain types of information to be included in each element. The land-use element, for example, must contain a diagram as well as text laying out the proposed distribution of housing, business, and industry. Certain other uses (schools, landfills) must be more specifically located. Similarly, the noise element must include noise contour studies, and land uses in high-noise areas must reflect the results of these studies. The California planning program does not include a state administrative enforcement mechanism; instead it relies on citizens or the attorney general to file civil suits to enforce compliance. The governor's office of planning and research does, however, perform supporting functions, including drafting of guidelines. The department of housing and community development also has review and comment power on housing elements, although local governments are not bound to follow department suggestions.

Vermont. Very few states have gone as far as Vermont in attempting to impose substantial control over land development and

growth management at the state and regional level. The fact that the state's growth management efforts have largely bypassed local governments reflects the weakness of Vermont's local governments. In 1970, the Vermont legislature passed the Environmental Control Act (Act 250), which established a state permitting process for large-scale developments. Act 250 created nine regional commissions with responsibility for issuing development permits, and established criteria for its approval, including that a proposed project must be in conformance with statewide plans adopted pursuant to Act 250, as well as local and regional plans or capital programs. While the permitting process has been relatively well accepted, Act 250's mandate for a state land-use plan generated a storm of controversy, especially after a copy of the draft plan map was mailed to every household in the state. The state environmental board, consisting of citizens appointed by the governor, favored broad policy statements, while the administrative agency charged with preparing the plan favored map-specific detail. Conflict over this issue resulted in the failure to adopt a statewide land-use plan (APA, November 1989).

In the wake of Act 250's failure to produce a state plan, the Vermont legislature passed the Growth Management Act (Act 200) in 1988. Act 200 specified thirty-two statewide goals to be followed by state agencies, regional commissions, and municipalities in all planning decisions. Participating municipalities had until 1991 to submit local plans for confirmation. Regional planning commissions and state agencies had until 1992 to submit their plans to the council of regional commissions, which has responsibility and authority for reviewing state agency and regional plans for consistency and compatibility with the state's planning goals. Act 200 provides a much stronger role for local governments in the growth management process than Act 250. Local participation is optional, but towns that participate are eligible for financial assistance. They may impose impact fees and insist that state agencies heed their plans. Local opposition to the act, starting in the economically depressed rural areas of northeastern Vermont, mushroomed and, on town meeting day in 1989, nearly half the towns voted not to participate in Act 200 (Innes 1992). In response to this expression of local dissatisfaction, the legislature amended the state planning law in 1990 (Act 280). Act 280 reduced the number of state planning goals from thirty-two to twelve, and the new goals are more general and less enforceable. It also lifted the requirement that local governments submit their plans to the regional commissions, and moved the deadline for voluntary compliance to 1996.

Georgia. Georgia is one of the most recent additions to the list of states with growth management programs, a fact explained largely by growth pressures in its booming Atlanta metropolitan area. In 1989, departing from a long tradition of strong local home rule and laissez-faire state government, the state enacted legislation outlining a comprehensive planning program involving local, regional, and state action. Georgia's Coordinated Planning Act of 1989 requires all cities and counties to adopt and implement a comprehensive plan if they wish to remain eligible for state economic development funds or to enact impact fees. The legislation also creates regional development centers, which prepare regional plans, mediate disputes among local governments, and provide technical assistance for local planning efforts. A state development council, chaired by the governor and composed of officials from all key state agencies, is charged with developing a state plan that integrates local and regional plans.

The Georgia Department of Community Affairs (DCA) is designated as the lead implementation agency. The agency has established minimum content requirements for local plans, but, with the exception of certain environmental criteria, local communities are free to establish their own planning goals. The regional development centers (RDCs) are the primary coordinating body for planning in Georgia. The RDCs review local plans for compliance with state standards and for compatibility with the plans of neighboring localities and regions. However, the DCA retains final authority for determining if a local plan is in compliance. Georgia's regional plans will be essentially an aggregation of local plans, although state and regional policies on regionally important resources may supersede local plans. The state plan is likely to be a policies plan that incorporates major features of the local and regional plans (Gale 1992).

Consistency Doctrine

While many communities have adopted plans that provide a framework for land-use policies and decision-making, adherence to adopted plan goals and policies is often the exception rather than the rule. Local government officials, citing the need for flexibility and fairness, have instead relied upon zoning and subdivision regulations and ad hoc decision-making to control the amount, type, and location of land development. State laws mandating consistency are intended to address the historic schism between land-use planning and land-use regulation. Consistency requirements traditionally take the form of state laws that mandate a strong link between adopted plans, land development regulations, and land-use decision-making. Increasingly, such mandates also require internal consistency among plan elements and intergovernmental consistency among local, county, and regional planning policies. The most common interpretation of consistency requirements is that zoning or development may be approved at or below the densities specified in the general plan. While this definition of consistency has promoted the preservation of agricultural land, it has worked against the promotion of infill development and more compact development patterns (Johnston, Schwartz, and Tracy 1984).

Oregon. Oregon has established a multi-tiered system of consistency. Implementing ordinances for zoning, subdivision, site plan review, and special permits must be consistent with local comprehensive plans. In questions of inconsistency, the local plan prevails. In the metropolitan Portland area, local plans must themselves be consistent with the regional plan. All local plans and the metropolitan Portland regional plan must be consistent with state planning goals and policies. Where a local or regional plan is found inconsistent with state planning goals and policies, state goals and policies prevail. Inconsistency even after state approval can be determined through periodic review (which occurs every three to five years, depending on the nature of the local or regional government), or through local plan amendments (Knaap and Nelson 1992).

Florida. The Florida approach mandates that local plans shall promote and be consistent with state and regional comprehensive plan policies. State planning statutes also re-

quire that land development regulations that implement and are consistent with adopted comprehensive plans be prepared and adopted within one year of a community's required comprehensive plan submittal date. Until a local government amends its regulations to conform to the adopted comprehensive plan, the provisions of the plan prevail over the regulations with respect to any actions taken by the local government on a development application. Internal consistency between plan elements is also mandated, including adopted capital improvement elements.

California. California's consistency requirements are considerably less rigorous than Florida's. Local general plans are not required to be consistent with regional plans, and general plans of neighboring communities need not take much account of each other. With the exception of open space plans, there is no express statutory requirement that capital improvement programs or public works projects be consistent with general plans. The end result is that local general plans often work at cross-purposes, dealing with growth issues effectively in one jurisdiction while ignoring problems created in a neighboring jurisdiction.

Consistency requirements, however, have brought about consistency between general plans and zoning ordinances—a major change from the past. While the state's zoning consistency requirements apply only to general-law cities and the city of Los Angeles, most of the eighty or so charter cities in the state have adopted similar requirements in their city charters. The consistency legislation has led courts in California to call the general plan "the constitution for all future development" in a community, which has given much greater legal weight to the planning process in each jurisdiction. One appellate court even went as far as to throw a ballot-box zoning initiative off the ballot because it would have resulted in a zoning ordinance inconsistent with the general plan. The consistency requirement in California has greatly enhanced the power of the local general plan vis-à-vis the traditional source of land-use regulatory power, the zoning ordinance (Fulton 1990).

California state law also authorizes cities and counties to adopt specific plans for implementing their more policy-oriented general plans. Specific plans may apply to all or part of the area and to all or part of the elements included in the general plan. Specific plans must be consistent with the local government's adopted general plan and include implementation measures, such as zoning regulations, capital improvement programs, and financing mechanisms necessary to carry out the plan. All implementation measures must also be consistent with the specific plan. Fees to cover the cost of preparing, adopting, and administering specific plans may be imposed upon applicants seeking development approvals, which are required to be consistent with the specific plan. Such fees must be prorated in accordance with the relative benefit that the applicant derives from the specific plan (Curtin 1984).

REGIONAL GROWTH MANAGEMENT APPROACHES

Growth management issues are often best addressed at a regional level, particularly in the case of large metropolitan areas containing multiple local governments. Regional growth management approaches include metropolitan planning, regional tax-base sharing, city-county consolidation, interlocal planning agreements, and a state or regional role in approving developments with regional impacts. This section provides an overview of several regional growth management approaches.

Metropolitan Planning

Minneapolis-St. Paul, Minnesota. The Twin Cities Metropolitan Council in Minneapolis-St. Paul is widely considered the nation's most innovative and successful experiment in regional government. The Twin Cities area covers seven counties and includes over 100 municipalities. The council was created by the Minnesota legislature in 1967, replacing a largely ineffective COG-type metropolitan planning commission. Instead of representing local governments and special districts, as the previous body did, the council's seventeen members are appointed by the governor to ensure that the council will not be the captive of local governments. Sixteen members represent districts of equal population and one, the chair, is selected on an at-large regionwide basis.

The council is not a level of general government. Its taxing power is set by the legislature and its responsibilities are generally limited to functions that cannot be performed by city and county governments. Actual regional services are provided by other metropolitan agencies under council coordination, including a transit commission, waste control commission, and airport commission. The council has the authority to review major public and private projects for consistency with its regional plan. The council can suspend action on these projects for one year if there are major conflicts to be resolved. It also has the power to suspend the long-range plans of wastewater and other special districts if they conflict with the comprehensive regional plan. Finally, the council has the right to issue bonds for regional transit, regional sewer facilities, and regional park acquisition and development. The 1976 Metropolitan Land Planning Act requires local governments to prepare comprehensive plans consistent with the council's metropolitan systems plans for wastewater, parks, transit, and airports. The council reviews all amendments to local comprehensive plans and must approve the amendments as being consistent with adopted regional plans before a community can proceed with development.

Portland, Oregon. The Metropolitan Service District (Metro) of Metropolitan Portland was the nation's first regional agency with a directly elected governing board. It was authorized by the state legislature in 1977 and subsequently approved by the voters, replacing the Columbia Region Association of Governments (CRAG). Metro is responsible for coordinating the planning activities of three counties, twenty-seven cities, and many water and wastewater districts. Metro is responsible for a number of regional planning functions and for maintaining and enforcing the area's urban growth boundary, which currently includes 223,000 acres, most of which is unincorporated.

Silicon Valley, California. In the 1980s, six jurisdictions in the Silicon Valley area near San Jose joined together to create the Golden Triangle Task Force in an attempt to resolve regional growth issues through interagency cooperation. The chief growth-related problem was an imbalance of jobs (which were located north of San Jose along Route 101) and housing (which was centered south of San Jose). After months of negotiation, all jurisdictions agreed to rezone nonresidential property within their boundaries to an average floor area ratio of 0.35 (0.40 near rail stops).

The task force also agreed on several other joint strategies, including transportation demand management and capital improvement goals. Some jurisdictions actually rezoned industrial property for residential use in order to achieve the stated goal. One city dropped out of the rezoning effort and left its zoning unchanged. All of the remaining task force members, however, proceeded with the growth management effort (Fulton 1990).

Cape Cod, Massachusetts. The Cape Cod Commission was created by the Massachusetts legislature in 1990. It is responsible for preparing and implementing a regional plan to guide development and preserve important environmentally sensitive features (Connors and Jackowitz 1992). The commission is composed of nineteen members with one from each of the cape's fifteen municipalities, a county commissioner, and three minority representatives. The commission was formed in response to four concerns raised by residents, businesses, and people otherwise interested in the future of the cape. First, Cape Cod needed more effective land-use planning to properly guide development and preserve the cape's environmentally sensitive resources. Second, greater authority for regulating land uses was needed. Third, a better way to manage urban development patterns was needed. And fourth, new tools were needed to protect or manage natural resources that are shared by all interests on the cape. The commission is required to

• prepare and implement a regional land-use policy plan for the cape.

• oversee the regulation of districts of planning concern.

• review and regulate developments of regional impact.

• assist local government planning efforts.

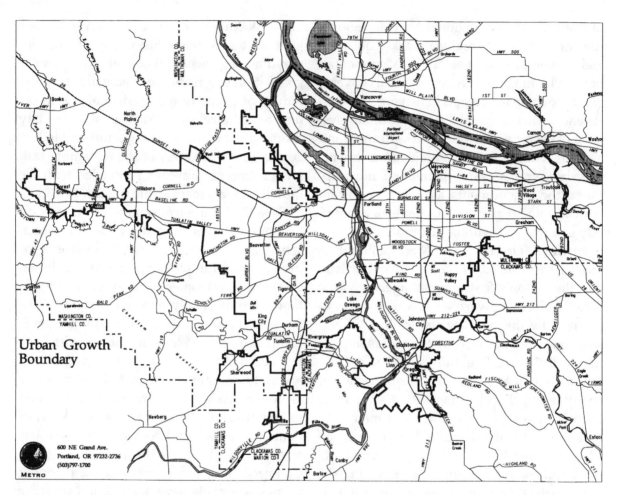

Figure 2–2. Urban growth boundary, January 5, 1995. *Source:* Map courtesy Metro Regional Services.

By 1992, a regional planning policy plan had been prepared and submitted to Barnstable County, the principal local governing body on the cape (Carbonell and Hamilton 1992).

Regional Planning Mandate

Florida. Florida's 1972 Environmental Land and Water Management Act established state review authority over local approval of major development proposals. The law designated areas of critical state concern and defined thresholds for developments of regional impact (DRI). The program requires in-depth review of DRI projects by one of the state's eleven regional planning councils before the local government with jurisdiction over the development is allowed to take action on the application. Chapter 380 of the state code defines a DRI as a development that will have "a substantial impact on the citizens of more than one county." Those projects that meet threshold DRI criteria are reviewed in terms of their anticipated impacts upon land-use patterns, public services, and the environment. While the authority of state and regional agencies over major development approvals is limited to review and comment, they can appeal local decisions to the state land and water adjudicatory commission, which does have the authority to override local decisions. The system is designed to ensure that local governments take into account both positive and negative externalities of major projects. It can be used to override local approval of an environmentally damaging project, or denial of a project with significant regional benefits, such as economic development or affordable housing. However, many projects subject to local resistance fall outside the definition of a DRI or below its threshold (Bollens 1992).

Georgia. Georgia's brand of state planning is unique for its extensive reliance on eighteen regional development centers (RDCs), which have four principal planning functions. First, RDCs coordinate planning by cities and counties within and between regions. The aim is to ensure that local plans are compatible with each other, and that regional plans are consistent along their edges. Second, RDCs are required to identify, map, and manage the use of regionally important resources (RIRs). For example, the Atlanta Regional Commission has identified the Chattahoochee River as one of its RIRs, and imposed development controls 5,000 feet on either side of it. Third, RDCs review and comment on the economic, infrastructure, fiscal, and environmental effects of developments of regional impact (DRIs). Although approval of DRIs remains a local prerogative, the RDCs' determination of negative impacts may be used by affected local governments to challenge approval through mediation or in court. The fourth role of the RDCs is mediation of planning disputes involving local governments.

Tax-Base Sharing

Competition for tax revenue from new development among neighboring cities and counties often tends to undermine regional growth management efforts. Although the negative effects of a major employment center, such as additional traffic, may affect an entire region, the benefits of the increased tax base are often confined to a single local jurisdiction. Since expenditures for the provision of services to nonresidential development are generally lower than for residential uses, municipalities tend to compete fiercely to include such development in their local tax base. Cities may overzone for commercial and industrial development and approve developments without regard for regional impacts. This problem may be particularly severe where there are multiple local jurisdictions. In Washington's Puget Sound region, for example, coordinated planning is hampered by the existence of seventy-two separate taxing districts in Pierce County alone, each of which covets tax-base-improving developments (Gerbers 1989: 564).

Regional tax-base sharing involves redistributing the tax base without necessarily changing jurisdictional boundaries or government organization. A portion of the growth in the property tax base is pooled and redistributed back to the taxing districts via a formula that favors those districts with below-average per-capita-assessed property values. All jurisdictions thus share in the economic development of the region, regardless of where development occurs. Advantages of tax-base sharing include some equalization of tax base among jurisdictions, a reduction in competition among jurisdictions for commercial and industrial development, and a reduction of the incentive for exclusionary zoning practices. Tax-base sharing preserves local autonomy and does not interfere with a community's right to establish its own level of taxation, while facilitating regional cooperation in growth management planning. Critics argue, however, that "winner" jurisdictions may be forced to shoulder most of the infrastructure costs imposed by new development without sufficient new tax revenues, and that some communities will be less inclined to accept new commercial and industrial development under a tax-base-sharing arrangement (Olson 1988). Few regions across the nation have actually adopted tax-base-sharing programs, although several have considered it. In addition to the Twin Cities and Hackensack Meadowlands programs discussed next, a program in Virginia's Charlottesville-Albemarle County area was implemented in the mid-1980s (APA, December 1987).

Hackensack Meadowlands, New Jersey. In New Jersey's Hackensack Meadowlands, a regional commission controls development and apportions property tax revenue among fourteen municipalities. The tax-base-sharing program is aimed at ensuring that those communities that contain valuable tidal wetlands do not suffer financially because wetlands cannot be developed for business or industrial development. According to a former chair of the Hackensack Meadowlands Development Commission, the tax-base-sharing program has made regional zoning possible (APA, December 1987). The 1972 Hackensack Meadowlands Development Commission and Redevelopment Act provides the legal basis for the tax-base-sharing arrangement. The New Jersey Supreme Court upheld the constitutionality of the tax-base-sharing section of the act and its formula in May 1972. Each town's tax base as of 1970 is unaffected by the arrangement, and all the revenues from that tax base continue to go to the individual towns. Forty percent of the increase in the tax base over the 1970 valuation is subject to the tax-sharing arrangement. Redistribution is based on the number of schoolchildren and the proportion of property the town has in the Meadowlands district. Each town continues to be the sole administrator of its own budgeting, property value assessment, rate setting, and tax billing. All new tax revenues are distributed among the fourteen towns, with no diversion of tax revenues to the regional commission (York 1989).

Minneapolis-St. Paul, Minnesota. Regional property tax-base sharing in the seven-county Minneapolis-St. Paul metropolitan area was established by the Fiscal Disparities Act of 1971, although the state legislation was not implemented until 1975 due to legal challenges. Under the act's requirements, a local jurisdiction compares its commercial and industrial property values with its 1971 assessment for those properties. As in the case of the Hackensack Meadowlands, 40 percent of the increase over the 1971 assessment is put in a metropolitan pool, which is then redistributed according to each community's population and overall tax base. When the program began, Minneapolis and St. Paul were the major beneficiaries. Minneapolis is now a net contributor due to the successful redevelopment of its downtown, and St. Paul's redevelopment efforts have reduced its dominance of the recipient pool (York 1989: 201). Small communities are now the major beneficiaries of the program.

The tax-base-sharing program has reduced the per capita disparity between the area's richest and poorest communities from what would otherwise be a 21-to-1 ratio to 4-to-1 (York 1989: 201–2). The effects of the tax-base-sharing program may be misleading, however, because the state's two major aid programs—School Aids and Local Governments Aids—automatically adjust for the size of each taxing jurisdiction's tax base, thereby partially offsetting both the gains and losses of tax-base sharing. One unanticipated spin-off from the program has been the equalization of tax rates within the region.

The tax-base-sharing program allows local governments with low property values to remain competitive by not having to institute a higher tax rate. In theory, tax-base sharing will help local jurisdictions make prudent land-use decisions without the panic and political pressure that can accompany economic development recruiting. The fact that a community can keep 60 percent of its increase in assessed commercial/industrial property value preserves the incentive to continue competing for development. Whether tax-base sharing has resulted in better land-use planning in the Twin Cities region is difficult to determine. However, without it, according to the metropolitan council's first chairman, there would be "no way in which land-use controls or any sensible development controls could be imposed at the regional level" (Whiting 1989). In addition, it is clear that the tax-base-sharing arrangement has reduced fiscal disparities between local governments.

Contra Costa County, California. Under California law, counties are permitted to impose local sales taxes for transportation purposes. Most large counties in California have received voter approval for at least one-half cent in local taxes. However, Contra Costa County, a large suburban county east of San Francisco, has tied the sales tax funds to growth management efforts. Eighteen percent of the roughly $5 million annually raised under the tax will be returned to local governments to improve streets and roads. Local governments do not get the money unless they have adopted a growth management plan that meets the approval of the county transportation commission, which administers the funds. To receive the funds, each jurisdiction must meet several requirements, including adding a growth management element to its general plan, establishing traffic level-of-service standards, adopting a development fee program, adopting a five-year capital improvement program, and participating in a cooperative, multijurisdictional planning process "to reduce cumulative regional traffic impacts of development."

CONCLUDING COMMENTS

Most growth management efforts will fail if done in isolation from regional or state interests. Local governments are usually incapable of influencing regional development patterns in ways consistent with local growth management objectives. On the other hand, any change in regional development patterns associated with a local government's growth management policies may distort development patterns in ways that leave many other local governments worse off. As this chapter attempts to show, growth management is most effective when done within a statewide context, so that all governmental units are fully informed about and coordinate their plans with all other governmental units. While regional growth management efforts can also be effective, there will be problems if the region per se grows beyond the original regional boundary, which has already happened in the Twin Cities region, or if some members of the region can opt out, as in the case of Contra Costa County. In the absence of coordinated statewide growth management efforts, regions should be empowered to un-

dertake coordinated regional growth management, local governments within regions should not be able to opt out, and regional boundaries should be expanded as the region grows.

3

Resource Land Preservation

While resource land preservation programs are adopted for the primary purpose of protecting resource land from urban development pressures, they are often components of a more comprehensive urban containment program. In fact, many programs now included under the "urban containment" banner owe their origins to state and local agricultural programs adopted in the 1960s and 1970s.

Within the context of growth management, the protection and preservation of resource land can be viewed in two ways. First, resource land preservation measures often are implemented as a means of managing the *effects* of regional urban growth and development. Second, regulations adopted for the primary purpose of resource land protection may work to control the *location* of urban development.

This chapter begins with an overview of the theoretical and policy considerations in the use of resource land preservation as a significant growth management technique. It then provides an overview of selected growth management techniques that are employed around the country for diminishing the negative impacts of urban development upon various natural and man-made land resources that are considered worthy of preservation.

OVERVIEW

There are some who argue that there is no compelling need to preserve resource land since there is so much of it. There are about 540 million acres of arable farmland, according to the U.S. Department of Agriculture, of which about 400 million acres are in cropland use. There are more than 700 million acres of forested land, or nearly twice as much as cropland. Estimates of additional cropland needed for food production by the year 2000 range from 22 million acres (Batie and Healy 1983) to 113 million acres (Sampson 1981). A doubling of land used for urban purposes would not significantly affect the supply of arable land. Moreover, land developed for urban uses can be converted back to resource uses if economics justify it, and technology may soon do away with the need for soil in which to raise crops anyway (Fischel 1982). Given those considerations, why is resource land preservation necessary?

First of all, not all arable cropland is of high productivity or in the best location. There are about 384 million acres of prime farmland (Soil Capability Class I and II) in the contiguous forty-eight states of which about 250 million acres are cultivated. About 50 million acres of such prime farmland are within fifty miles of the 100 largest urbanized areas (Furuseth and Pierce 1982). Most prime farmland is located within the suburban and exurban counties of metropolitan areas (Nelson 1990b). In effect, the very land that is most important for its location and productive qualities is also the most vulnerable for development (Solomon 1984). Between 500,000 and 1 million acres of prime agricultural land is lost each year to urban or scattered suburban development (National Agricultural Lands Study ["NALS"] 1981; Dideriksen and Sampson 1976; Berry and Plaut 1978).

As prime farmland is lost, marginally productive land is brought into use through brute force means such as heavy applications of fertilizers and chemicals, but this is costly and has adverse environmental effects (Platt 1985). While the Urban Land Institute (1982) has argued that new farmland can come from land presently in swamps or forest, or other land that may be intensively irrigated and heavily fertilized. But conversion of swamps and forests to agriculture has come under criticism in recent years. In semiarid areas, increased reliance on irrigation runs contrary to present concerns about wise use of water. As the U.S. Department of Agriculture (1975) notes, preservation of resource land for food, fiber, and other forms of production at least guards against future uncertainties since such land requires fewer economic and environmental inputs relative to marginal lands.

Yet, the problem of resource land reductions stems more from inefficient market interactions with urban development than from land conversion per se. There are four ways in which resource land is at a disadvantage relative to urban development: (1) overvaluation of land for urban development; (2) urban spillovers; (3) failure of the land market to reflect the value of resource land to society; and (4) the impermanence syndrome that induces resource land operators to withdraw from resource activities prematurely.

Overvaluation of Land for Urban Development

One of the problems with resource land preservation is that such land is sometimes made more valuable in the market for urban uses through subsidies such as (1) inefficient inducements to industrial development through tax concessions and subsidized utility extensions; (2) inefficient home construction caused partly by tax concessions given to home owners through the federal income tax system; (3) inefficient urban land allocation caused by local government planning policies oversupplying land for lower densities while undersupplying land for higher densities, thereby forcing more lower residential development than is efficient; and (4) inefficient average public facility pricing resulting in higher density development in urban areas—where facility costs are relatively low per unit—subsidizing suburban lower density development—where facility costs are relatively high per unit (Sullivan 1985; Frank 1989a, 1989b; Harvey and Clark 1965; Clawson 1971; Gurko 1972). The urban land market internalizes these economic subsidies into higher valued land at the urban-rural fringe. The effect is more land used for low-density urban development than would occur without those subsidies.

Another effect is inefficient speculation of farmland for potential conversion to urban development. While speculation, per se, is an important element of an efficiently operating urban land market, it has adverse effects on land markets when speculative behavior is induced through policy. Urban development subsidies signal speculators to expect more lower density development than would occur without such policies (Clawson 1962, 1971; Harvey and Clark 1965).

Of course, resource land also receives subsidies in the form of preferential taxation and federal commodity price supports. To some extent, resource land subsidies offset urban land subsidies. However, urban land subsidies are many times higher than resource land subsidies along the urban-rural fringe. Moreover, resource land subsidies tend to go where urban development pressures are minimal.

The overall effect of public policies is to make land artificially more valuable for urban uses than for resource uses along the urban fringe. (See Figure 3–2.)

Spillovers and the Undervaluation of Land for Farming

Another factor giving urban development disproportionate advantages over resource land is spillovers. As urban development

Figure 3–1. Newly built homes advertised for sale next to farmland. Haphazard land-use patterns and higher valued nonfarm uses put pressure on farmers to sell out prematurely. *Source:* Photo by Thomas L. Daniels.

invades rural areas, it imposes spillovers on farmland. These spillovers reduce the productivity of resource land, thereby making such land less valuable for resource uses and more attractive for speculation. The following are five common spillover effects:

• Regulation of resource activities deemed nuisances by nonfarm residents in rural areas. These include restrictions on fertilizers, manure disposal, smells, and slow-moving farm vehicles on commuter roads; limitations on use of pesticides and herbicides; restrictions on farm noises and hours of operation; restrictions on dust and glare; limitations on irrigation; and restrictions on other activities that may upset the lifestyle of urban households located in rural areas (Berry 1978).

• Increased property taxation to pay for new schools, roads, services, and facilities intended to serve needs of urban households. Resource land operators pay for those new facilities and services on the basis of the amount and value of land they own and not necessarily on how much they use such facilities and services (Keene et al. 1976).

• Air pollution damage to crops and trees caused by automobiles, industrial activity, and even residential space heating (Prestbo 1975).

• Destruction of crops or equipment or harassment of farm animals by urban households living in rural areas. Theft of tree crops, berries, and vegetables is common (Berry, Leonardo, and Bieri 1976).

• Use of eminent domain to acquire at relatively low cost resource land for public uses serving primarily new residential development (Berry and Plaut 1978). Eminent domain for roads and reservoirs is common.

For timber land, an additional spillover occurs when urban households living in rural areas oppose timber harvesting sometimes ostensibly on environmental grounds but often for the real reason that the loss of trees removes an amenity urban households enjoy without cost.

The effect of these and related spillovers is that resource land is made artificially less valuable for resource uses the closer it is to urban development in the manner illustrated in Figure 3–2. Indeed, as urban development becomes scattered throughout rural areas, spillovers are imposed everywhere and the value of land for resource uses falls. This is illustrated in Figure 3–3. Eventually, spillovers can reduce the supply of resource land to a level below the critical mass needed to sustain the regional resource economy base, as shown in Figure 3–4.

Unpriced Benefits

Resource lands offer value to society in ways that are not reflected in the land market. Common societal benefits include groundwater recharge and water purification, flood and erosion control, air cleansing, and scenery. Moreover, the value of such lands to future generations may be greater than it is to the current generation. In sum, farmland has important features making it inherently worthy of preservation (Lee 1979).

The Impermanence Syndrome

The combination of overvaluation of resource land for urban development and undervaluation of resource land because of urban spillovers is the impermanence syndrome (Keene et al. 1975; Currier 1978; Nelson 1992). The impermanence syndrome is characterized by resource landowners who believe that resource activities in their area has limited or no future and that urbanization will absorb their holdings sooner than later. It is manifested

through disinvestment in inputs; sale of tracts for hobby farms, ranchettes, or small woodlots; and shifting of crop selection away from high to low investment options. The impermanence syndrome causes many resource landowners to become speculators in their own land. The result is vast areas of underutilized and idle land near and between urban areas (Gottmann 1961; Berry 1976; Vining, Bieri, and Strauss 1977). There is some evidence to suggest that for every acre of resource land that is urbanized, another half-acre to one acre becomes idle due to the impermanence syndrome (Plaut 1976.) Ultimately, the critical mass of farming production needed to sustain key components of the local farming economy collapses (Berry 1976; Daniels and Nelson 1986; Daniels 1986; Lapping and FitzSimmons 1982). Thus, a fundamental purpose of a resource land preservation scheme is to remove the impermanence syndrome (Plaut 1976; Berry, Leonardo, and Bieri 1976; Berry 1978; NALS 1981; Nelson 1984, 1986).

RESOURCE LAND PRESERVATION TECHNIQUES

Nearly two-thirds of the nation's total farmland is within or near the fringes of a metropolitan area. Not surprisingly, state and local governments have taken a variety of steps to protect farmland from encroaching urban development. All fifty states have some type of right-to-farm law protecting farmers from legal actions by residential neighbors. In at least twenty-two states, local governments can apply special protective zoning to agricultural land (Walmer 1990). Resource land preservation policies are used to protect resource operations from incompatible urban sprawl development and to slow or prevent the premature conversion of productive resource

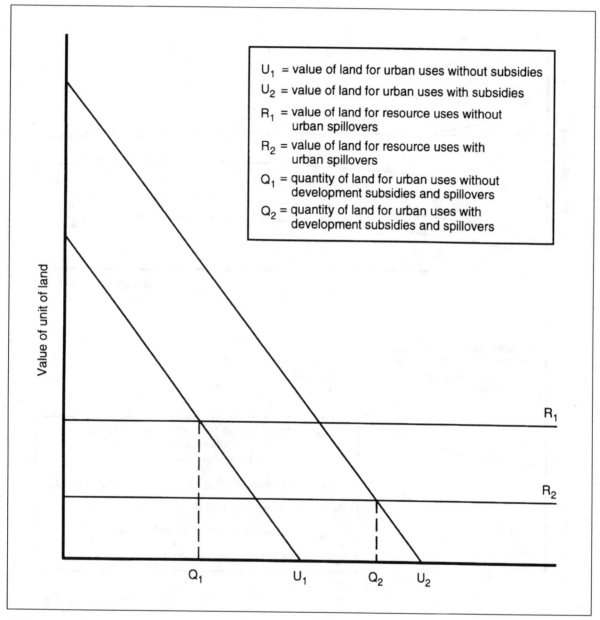

Figure 3–2. Effect of urban subsidies and spillovers on land uses at the urban fringe. In the absence of urban subsidies and spillover effects of urban development on farmland, equilibrium in land used for urban and farming activities is at Q_1. One effect of subsidies given to urban development—such as mortgage interest deductions, inefficient pricing of public facilities, and inefficient pricing of highways—is that the value of land for urban uses rises above its value for farming, shown here as the difference between U_2 and U_1. However, the effect of urban spillovers on farmland is to lower the value of land for farming shown here as the difference between R_2 and R_1. The overall effect is inefficient urban development, also called urban sprawl.

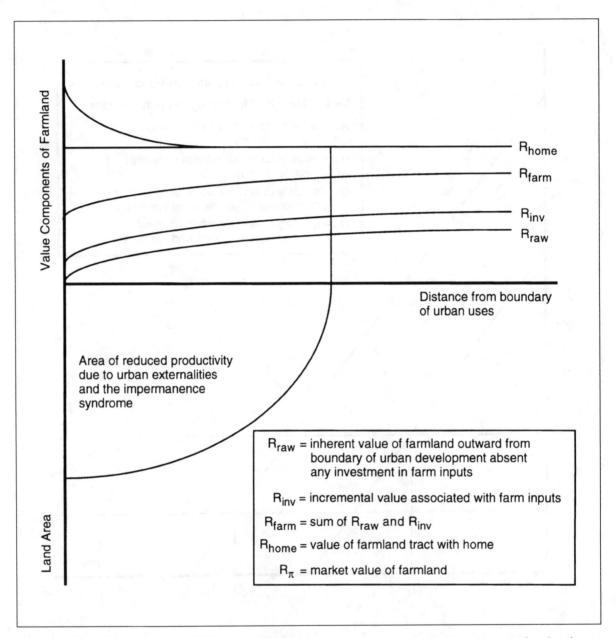

Figure 3–3. Effect of urban spillovers and the impermanence syndrome on resource-land value and productivity. This figure shows the effect of urban spillovers on the value of farmland beyond the boundary of urban development; value rises with distance from urban development. The impermanence syndrome affects the area shown emanating from the boundary of urban development outward to the location where urban spillovers are not felt. In the area affected by the impermanence syndrome, farmland owners (or speculators acquiring farmland for future conversion) disinvest in farming.

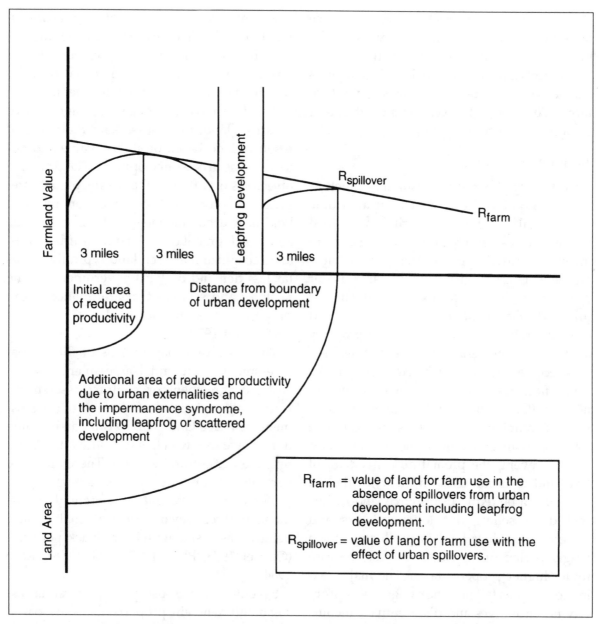

Figure 3–4. Effect of scattered urban development on resource-land value and productivity. This figure shows the effect of leapfrog urban sprawl on a region's farmland. Studies have suggested that urban spillovers and the impermanence syndrome can be felt by farmland owners three or more miles beyond the boundary of urban development. The effect of leapfrog development is to riddle the regional landscape with pockets of urban development, thereby greatly expanding the area affected by the impermanence syndrome. Such development patterns can, and do, eliminate the critical mass of farmland needed to sustain a region's agricultural and timber economic base.

areas to urban land uses. A variety of resource land preservation techniques are available, but few are really effective by themselves. These techniques fall into broad categories characterized as taxation policies, right-to-farm, acquisition of development rights, and resource land-use districting.

Taxation Policies

Real property taxes can consume as much as 20 percent of a farmer's net farm income (Keene et al. 1975). In urban fringe areas, real property taxes can equal or exceed net farm income (Leutwiler 1986). This occurs when farmland is assessed not for its farm use or productive value but for its potential value as urban development. Farmers owning land close to urban development incur a property tax burden considerably in excess of the benefits received because such taxes help pay for urban facilities and services that farmers do not use (Gloudemans 1974). To respond to this apparent inequity, all fifty states use some form of tax incentive or disincentive to slow, if not prevent, the premature conversion of farmland to urban uses. In theory, if the tax burden can be reduced, resource landowners will defer selling out to speculators and thereby keep their land in production for a longer period of time than may be the case under higher property taxes. The major taxing techniques fall into the categories of property tax incentives and disincentives, income taxes, and capital gains penalties.

Property Tax Incentives and Disincentives. By far the most common taxation techniques are property tax incentives and disincentives. Such tax policies include *differential assessments* and *deferred assessments.*

Differential Tax Assessments. Forty-eight states employ some form of differential assessment of resource land. Differential assessment usually involves (1) reducing the tax rate that is applied to the assessed value of farmland so that taxes are assessed only for certain services; (2) reducing the assessed value of resource land to a percentage relative to urban land; or (3) assessing the value of resource land based on its use value and not its value as urban development. The principal objectives of differential assessment are to reduce the property tax burden on resource land near urban development, delay the sale and development of such land for urban uses, and recognize that such land typically places far less demand on local government for the facilities and services that are financed from property taxes (Keene et al. 1975; Currier 1978; Plaut 1977).

There are two major forms of differential assessment: preferential assessment and restrictive agreement or contract assessment. Under all variations of preferential assessment, resource land is taxed only on its value in resource use, which is typically established by state agricultural experts. There are three variants of preferential assessments: pure preferential assessments, preferential assessments with conveyance or use penalties, and deferred assessments with rollback penalties (Currier 1978; Plaut 1977; NALS 1981; Rose 1984).

Seventeen states use pure preferential assessments wherein property taxes are based on the productive value of resource land as established by state agencies. There is no penalty for converting resource land to urban development. There is also no penalty for idling land once it has been designated for preferential treatment. In Indiana, for example, all resource landowners receive pure preferential assessment, whether they use the land or not. In other states, the local assessor may revoke pure preferential assessment for land that is removed from production over a number of years. Since there is no direct penalty for developing land, enrollment in pure preferential assessment programs is popular among speculators. Not surprisingly, preferential assessment policies do not slow the conversion of resource land to urban uses; indeed, such programs may facilitate conversion (Forkenbrock and Fisher 1983). Near urban areas, pure preferential assessment policies increase speculative value and do not increase productive value. Such programs may actually push some urban development farther away from urban areas when speculators owning land near urban areas use low property taxes to subsidize their holding costs, thereby affording them the luxury of withholding their land from development.

To counteract the potentially perverse effects of pure preferential assessment, seven states penalize conversion with conveyance or use-change taxes. The penalty is triggered when preferential status is revoked. The penalty may be assessed if the use changes simultaneously with sale of the property, as when an option on a property is exercised by a developer who then proceeds with development. More typically, it is assessed when the owner voluntarily withdraws from preferential assessment status, usually in anticipation of use change. Least typically, it is assessed when the local tax assessor determines the property has not been used as farmland in recent years. In some states, the tax is a percentage (10 percent to 30 percent) of the difference between agricultural-use value and market value.

Restrictive agreements or contract assessments require resource landowners to enter into long-term contracts with counties in exchange for receiving preferential assessment. If land subject to such agreements is developed while the contract is in force, property tax penalties are assessed. In California, for example, the principal technique for preserving farmland is the Williamson Act, a state law that provides tax breaks to rural landowners who keep their property in agricultural uses. Under the act, a landowner and a county enter into a contract in which landowner agrees not to develop the land for ten years in exchange for county commitments to assess the property on the basis of its value as agricultural land, rather than its market value to developers. Contracts exclude nonagricultural uses and are binding on succeeding owners. Contracts are automatically extended by one year on the anniversary date of the contract unless nonrenewal notice is given by either the local government or the landowner. Contracts are canceled if development occurs. The owner is assessed a cancellation fee equal to 12.5 percent of the then full market value of the land. A landowner wishing to remove the land from a contract may usually do so only through nonrenewal of the contract. Under nonrenewal, property assessments will rise gradually over a ten-year period, after which the property is available for development.

The Williamson Act is credited with limiting sprawl in the vast Central Valley region of California, where 90 percent or more of all land remains in agricultural production. Its usefulness around metropolitan areas, however, is questionable. Recent state statistics show that most of the state's nonrenewal land is located in the rapidly urbanizing areas of southern California, especially Riverside, Ventura, and San Diego counties. Furthermore, the Williamson Act has contributed to the financial problems of rural counties. To compensate the counties for lost tax revenue, the state provides subventions of between $0.40 and $8.00 per acre per year. The fact that this amount has not been increased since 1976 has led to political unrest among some rural counties (Fulton, 1990).

State Income Tax Credits. Michigan and Wisconsin use "circuit breaker" programs in which property tax relief for resource landowners takes the form of a state income tax rebate. In Michigan, an income tax rebate is triggered when local property taxes assessed on a farmer exceed 7 percent of her or his net farm income. The state refunds income taxes equal to the property taxes paid in excess of that threshold. The program applies only to those landowners who contract with the state for at least a ten-year period. Michigan landowners who do not renew their contracts must repay the state the last seven years' rebates. Landowners allowed to withdraw from the program before contract expiration must repay the state all property taxes rebated plus 6 percent interest.

Such programs have little effect on preserving farmland and actually encourage reduced productivity to reduce net farm income to a level that would qualify for property tax rebates. Participants in the programs are typically retired, other low-income nonfarm households, farmers earning a few thousand dollars annually, and farmers who lost money (Barrows and Bonderud 1988). Speculators can purchase existing farms and maintain them at minimal levels until conversion—all the while enjoying subsidized holding costs in the form of rebates by placing title for tax purposes in low-earning corporate entities or individuals. The penalty at conversion is minimal compared to the costs of development.

The policy thus reduces farmland productivity but increases speculative value. Less than 5 percent of Michigan's land base is enrolled in this program (Barrows and Bonderud 1988) and such land is located within or near metropolitan areas.

Capital Gains Penalties. Two states, Connecticut and Vermont, attempt to discourage land speculation by assessing a special capital gains tax on it. Vermont's land sales tax applies a sliding scale to all land sold or exchanged within six years of purchase. For land sold within one year of purchase, the tax ranges from 30 percent on any gain of less than double the purchase price, up to 60 percent on gains of more than triple the purchase price. Parcels of less than ten to fifteen acres in size (depending on location) are exempt. The practical effect of the capital gains tax is to withhold land from the market until the tax is too small to matter (or until the capital gains no longer applies). This has the perverse effect of driving land values up by restricting urban land supply everywhere. The policy does initially slow the pace of conversion, though once a full six-year cycle has run its course, farmland may actually be traded at a faster rate for higher prices to accommodate pent-up demand.

Effectiveness of Tax Programs. By themselves, these various tax programs do little to preserve resource land and actually stimulate speculation while also displacing urban development from areas near cities to areas farther away. One simple correction to all such programs would be to impose a tax penalty equal to the present value of all property taxes not assessed between initial enrollment and development. Another solution would be to assess a lump-sum tax equal to the difference between the market value of land at the time of development and the value of such land for resource uses. No states have such corrective policies. The result is inefficient land-use behavior near urban areas that must be corrected with land-use planning schemes.

Right-to-Farm Laws

Right-to-farm laws protect farmers from land-use actions or restrictions over which they have little or no control (Leutwyler 1986). The central feature of such laws is to make it difficult for nearby nonfarm residents to restrict operations through nuisance suits. Without right-to-farm, neighbors are free to allege nuisance due to chemical spray drift, smells, noises, hours of operation, and so forth. Right-to-farm laws attempt to tip the balance in favor of farmers through statutory declarations that standard farming practices are reasonable land uses, despite their possible adverse impacts on neighboring property. Such laws often go further by stating that the social utility of farming outweighs, to some degree, incidental harm to nearby properties. Moreover, such laws put new residents on notice that they may be "coming to the nuisance" if they choose to live near a farm.

Right-to-farm laws have several shortcomings. First, they do not prevent farmers from converting land to urban uses or selling it to speculators. Second, right-to-farm laws may not apply to the operations of a succeeding owner; the practices of one owner may become ineligible for right-to-farm protection if they are continued by a new owner. Third, right-to-farm laws may not protect nuisance suits brought against operators who change agricultural practices, no matter how insignificant the change may appear (Lapping and Leutwiler 1987). Fourth, farmland that is fallow during the year in which new development occurs nearby may not be protected from conversion to more intensive use in the future. Fifth, local governments often retain statutory power to regulate (and ban) the use of fertilizers, pesticides, and herbicides as an expression of their police power rights to protect the health, safety, and general welfare of residents (Rose 1984).

An even more insidious problem is that right-to-farm laws address nuisance, not trespass. Traditionally, courts have required plaintiffs to demonstrate physical invasion of property in order to show trespass. The trespass test has evolved in recent years, however, to the point where a plaintiff may need only demonstrate that the actions of another deprived the plaintiff of exclusive possession of their property. Under this broadened test, chemical drift, odors, and airborne particulate matter would constitute a trespass. Even with right-to-farm laws, farmers may become vulnerable to this attack (Bradbury 1986).

Acquisition of Development Rights

Recognizing that taxation and zoning programs are limited, if not often counterproductive, in their ability to preserve resource land, many local governments have sought to acquire development rights to such land, especially near urban areas. It is hoped that by placing development rights in the hands of local government or third parties, speculative value can be reduced and productive value increased. Three techniques are used to acquire development rights on resource land: (1) transfer of development rights; (2) purchase of development rights; and (3) conservation easements.

Transfer of Development Rights (TDRs). The cornerstone of the TDR concept is the recognition that the possibility of developing land is a fungible commodity distinct from the land itself. A TDR program typically permits owners of land in development-restricted areas called sending districts to sever the development rights from their property and sell those rights to property owners in specified receiving districts. Landowners who purchase development rights are then able to increase the amount of development that can be built on the receiver site. TDRs can be used to save historic structures from demolition, prevent urbanization of farmland, and preserve unique environmental areas and scenic vistas. TDRs offer communities a compromise between acquisition and regulation. Few programs, theoretically at least, seem to offer so much for so little—the community retains the critical resource, the property owner receives property tax relief and compensation, and the local government bears responsibility only for initial implementation of the program. Early TDR programs did not work well, however, largely because they were optional and because local officials had limited familiarity with how to operate them effectively. Second-generation programs have gone much farther toward fulfilling the original promise of the TDR concept.

Specific state enabling legislation is not necessarily required prior to utilization of a TDR program. At present, TDR programs exist in states that do not have legislation specifically allowing such programs. Broad enabling legislation, coupled with case law granting wide latitude to municipalities to zone for the public welfare, seem to allow TDRs as a legitimate use of a municipality's zoning powers (Bozung 1983). To be successful, a TDR program must recognize a viable market for development rights. Suitable receiver sites, capable of accommodating the

development to be transferred, must be identified. Receiver sites must be subject to sufficient growth pressure, and development regulations in the receiver area must be restrictive enough to provide landowners with an incentive to purchase development rights.

One serious limitation of TDR programs is that they do not assure maintenance of a critical mass of resource operations. Viable, commercial-scale agriculture in prime farmland regions requires very large areas of farmland on the order of thousands of acres (Lapping and FitzSimmons 1982). Random sales of TDRs will not prevent the scattered subdivision of farmland tracts to the acreage density allowed by zoning in all situations where TDR is used. Since subdivision and sale of farmland tracts into acreage rural residential sites is not prevented, it is possible that a regional farming economy can be so disrupted by such scattered development that it will no longer be able to support a commercial farming infrastructure (Furuseth 1980, 1981; Furuseth and Pierce 1982; Gustafson, Daniels, and Shirack 1983; Nelson 1983a, 1983b; Daniels and Nelson 1986; Daniels 1986).

Montgomery County, Maryland. Montgomery County adopted a farmland preservation program using TDR. The program was designed to reduce the effects of downzoning land in the agricultural reserve zoning district from one unit per five acres to one unit per twenty-five acres, the minimum size required to operate a profitable farm. Development in the agricultural district is further restricted by requiring a maximum lot area of 40,000 square feet, and requiring that all housing units be clustered within a confined area on the parcel. TDR is authorized by state statute in Maryland. That statute allows consideration of repurchase of development rights if, after twenty-five years, the petitioner for repurchase can demonstrate that farming is not feasible, and further provided that repurchase is authorized by the local governing body as well as by various state officials (Rose 1984). By the 1990s, development rights were fetching up to about $5,000 per unit.

Under the Montgomery County TDR program, landowners are entitled to sell the right to develop one housing unit for each five acres of restricted land, less the number of residences already on the property. Upon sale of all available rights, the development potential is extinguished through the placement of a restrictive easement on the sending property. In TDR receiving areas, maximum-density increases permitted with TDRs vary by residential district. This amount can be further increased if moderately priced dwelling units are included in the project. As an additional incentive, the provision of wastewater service is accelerated by at least four to five years upon purchase of the rights (Bozung 1983). An excess of available rights in sending areas has kept the price of a TDR too low for many farms to consider selling. Even though more receiving areas were added and the demand and utilization increased, the price of TDRs declined, indicating that more than simple supply-and-demand forces may have been at work. It appears that TDR entitlement based on acreage rather than land value makes it advantageous for landowners of lesser valued properties farther away from urban areas to sell. This helps keep the TDR price low and discourages those with more valuable land from entering the market. Despite these problems, however, the Montgomery County TDR program has been largely successful in preserving agricultural land and stabilizing farmland prices.

Purchase of Development Rights (PDRs). Another way to preserve resource land for the public interest is for local or state governments to purchase development rights outright. Purchase of development rights does not result in purchase of title fee simple. Rather, the rights to all future development are acquired. To date, the use of PDR programs is rare. One economic problem with such programs is that they involve taxpayers paying twice for those rights, first through infrastructure investments and development patterns that create development value and again for the value created. Another limitation is that since PDRs are voluntary programs, they suffer from the same limitations as TDRs in not assuring preservation of the critical mass of resource land needed to sustain the regional resource economic base.

King County, Washington. During the 1980s, King County purchased the development rights to about 13,000 acres of agricul-

Figure 3–5. This "choice" parcel on Big Pine Key in Monroe County, Florida, represents an example of how TDR systems can aid in preserving environmentally sensitive wetlands, as well as other resource lands. *Source:* Photo by James B. Duncan.

tural land east of Seattle (Spellman 1984). It is the only PDR program in place outside the northeastern United States. The rights were purchased from farmers who voluntarily negotiated the sale with the county. The county applies nonexclusive agricultural zoning on another 17,000 acres in the same area. The cost was over $50 million and it will cost the 1.3 million King County residents an average $9 per person for eleven years to retire bonds floated to purchase those rights. This will have the effect of ensuring permanent open space for urban residents in exchange for tax burden shifting (from farmland to urban landowners); without such purchase there is no guarantee that open-space land would not be developed at some point in the future. King County residents thus face up to the value of open space by internalizing its value through a tax arrangement. In effect, the program shelters future generations of taxpayers from subsidizing farmers in return for owning development rights.

Suffolk County, New York. In Suffolk County, on Long Island, New York, a similar program has worked to purchase a much smaller amount of farmland for much more money. For example, the development rights for the first 3,000 acres of farmland were purchased for more than $200 million (Klein 1978; NALS 1981; Rose 1984). Bonds financing the purchases are retired by an increment on the property tax.

Pennsylvania. The state of Pennsylvania offers funds to local governments to purchase development rights in their jurisdictions. Funds are appropriated from the legislature and then distributed to counties on a more or less first-come-first-served basis. The state has few guidelines for using the funds. Consequently, many purchases are not strategic and are not used to create the critical mass of land area needed to sustain agricultural operations. Indeed, the state actually works to undermine its own program by requiring counties to broadly advertise which development rights have been purchased and where. This results in developers subdividing land next to such farmland so as to build and sell at higher prices homes with exclusive farm views, but farmers become worse off because of urban spillovers.

Massachusetts. Under Massachusetts' Agricultural Preservation Restriction program, development rights to agricultural lands are bought and held by the Commonwealth, and future land use is limited to agriculture. The state also uses various land trusts to acquire and manage lands. Both of these programs, however, have been severely limited by state budgetary constraints and high land prices in recent years. Over the past decade, the state has spent $45 million to protect 22,000 acres of farmland. But this represents only 3 percent of Massachusetts' active farmland; the rest remains zoned for conventional development (Arendt 1990: 5).

New Jersey. In an effort to protect farmland, New Jersey voters passed a $50 million bond issue in 1981. It provided funding to two programs—an eight-year deed restriction program that allowed farmers to be eligible for state cost-sharing conservation programs and protected them from nuisance suits, and a permanent easement sale program, which paid farmers for the development rights to their property. While the development rights program was initially the most popular, both programs have been successful and in 1990 had protected a total of nearly 43,000 acres of New Jersey farmland from development (York 1989: 31).

Conservation Easements. Conservation easements involve the transfer of development rights from a property owner to a third party, such as the Conservation Foundation. Conservation easements enable landowners to retain title to an undivided tract and use it for resource purposes. The advantage to the landowner is reducing the value of land to its inherent value for resource activities. For many landowners, this enables them to continue living on their land without facing higher property taxes. It also gives them the altruistic opportunity to preserve resource lands as open space in perpetuity. Finally, since the easement is a gift to a qualified charitable organization, the difference between the market value of the land and its inherent resource land value becomes a deduction against taxable income.

Local government can play a role in facilitating conservation easements by putting third parties active in acquiring conservation easements in contact with potentially receptive resource landowners. Local planners can review the nature of current and anticipated land-use regulations and market conditions. This information will be needed by appraisers who must certify the value of the easement.

Agricultural and Forest Zoning

Agricultural zoning, including forest zoning, is the most common method of resource land preservation used by local governments (NALS 1981). Such zoning restricts land uses to farming and livestock, other kinds of open-space activity, and limited home building. It is sometimes used in tandem with regional urban containment planning (Nelson 1985b). Hawaii and Oregon require the use of agricultural zoning by all local governments that have prime agricultural farmland. The most

important element of agricultural zoning is the extent to which it restricts the intrusion of new, nonfarm uses into established agricultural areas. In its purest form, agricultural zoning intends to prevent nonfarm activities in resource districts. Many exclusive farm (and forest) use zones have very large minimum lot sizes that are calibrated to about the minimum size necessary to sustain a viable farming operation, taking into consideration the production characteristics of the region. Four general approaches to resource-land-use zoning are reviewed here: nonexclusive use zoning, voluntary agricultural districts, exclusive use zoning, and agricultural buffers.

Nonexclusive Use Zoning. Nonexclusive agricultural zoning usually includes (1) large minimum lot sizes, ranging from 10 to 640 acres and more; (2) entitlement to single-family home construction on any preexisting and newly created but conforming lot; (3) no requirement to demonstrate the effects on farm production of land partitioning at the minimum lot size; and (4) a wide range of uses allowed by conditional use permit, including commercial recreation, smaller than minimum lot size developments, patently nonfarm dwelling units, agriculturally related industrial activities, and planned developments (sometimes at higher densities).

There is evidence that nonexclusive zoning can have perverse outcomes (Archer 1977; Daniels and Nelson 1986; Nelson 1983a, 1983b). Families wishing to own one or two acres near urban areas are forced to buy entire farms and leave all but one or two acres untended. While the surplus land may be rented to nearby farmers, rental agreements are short term and typically do not involve maintenance of or investment in major improvements such as irrigation systems, tiling, and buildings (Daniels 1986). Viable commercial farming operations fall in number and the local agricultural support economy suffers (Daniels and Nelson 1986). Over time, large-acreage rural residential sprawl invades and succeeds in the region, resource land becomes underproductive or idle and more acres are taken out of production than would have been without such zoning (Archer 1977). As the agricultural economy is decimated, buyers of the large farm tracts should be expected over time to lobby for relaxing zoning restrictions to allow for smaller acreage development and perhaps low-density urban development.

Voluntary Agricultural Districting. Voluntary agricultural districting involves farmers within a defined area petitioning a state agency to collectively form such a district. Within agricultural districts, farmers are protected to some extent from (1) state and local land-use and building regulations on farming activities that do not threaten the public health, safety, and welfare; (2) special assessments for water, sewer, lighting, and other forms of utility districts; and (3) the use of eminent domain to acquire farmland for public uses (Berry and Plaut 1978; Geier 1980; Rose 1984; Bills and Boisvert 1988). Land within such districts receives differential property tax assessment, although such assessments are also available to outside landowners. Since the actual land-use restrictions are similar to those for nonexclusive zoning, these districts suffer from the same limitation.

New York State. In New York state, such districts are approved by local and state agencies and administered by the host county. Petitioners must own 500 acres or 10 percent of the land in the proposed district, whichever is greater. The state commissioner of agriculture may also create districts of 2,000 or more acres to protect "unique and irreplaceable agricultural lands," but so far none have been created by the commissioner. By the 1990s, more than 8 million acres of farmland (25 percent of the entire state land area) were in about 400 districts. The number of districts actually fluctuates, however, as district status can be changed by action of the county governing body (Bills and Boisvert 1988). Landowners can enroll in deferred taxation programs for which the tax penalty is five years' back taxes upon conversion. Many landowners eschew participation in this special tax program, although there is some evidence to suggest that participation increases in proximity to growing urban areas (Bills and Boisvert 1988).

Exclusive Use Zoning. Exclusive use zoning prohibits nonfarm activities in farming districts. Many exclusive use zones have very large minimum lot sizes that are calibrated to approximate the minimum size necessary to sustain a viable farming operation, taking into consideration the production characteristics of the region. When properly prepared and strictly administered, exclusive use zones show great promise for removing speculative value of resource land, thereby encouraging greater productivity of resource lands near urban areas than would be possible under speculative conditions.

California. In California, Madeira County has minimum lot sizes of 640 acres and Tulare County has an 80-acre minimum. Commercially viable agriculture in these areas requires large tracts of land.

Oregon. Oregon's growth management program requires that all lands with productive soils located outside of designated urban growth boundaries be classified as exclusive farm use zones. Many counties using exclusive use zoning initially had no explicit minimum lot size. Land partitionings are approved only when evidence shows that farming will be improved. Dwellings are allowed only if needed to support farming operations, although nonfarm dwellings are allowed on certain, low-production soils. Commercial recreation and industrial activities are restricted to the least productive soils or small areas most impacted by nearby urban development. In 1993, the Oregon legislature required local governments to adopt minimum lot sizes of 80 acres in western Oregon and 160 acres in eastern Oregon in exclusive use zones.

In addition, urban growth boundaries (UGBs) are used in Oregon to direct development into cities and preserve the countryside for agriculture and other open-space uses. Small-acreage homesites that cannot be ac-

Figure 3–6. Farmland within easy commuting range of downtown Portland and its edge cities is protected from urban sprawl by exclusive farm-use zoning. Farming has supplanted forestry as Oregon's leading resource industry, in large part because of extensive use of EFU zoning. *Source:* Photo by Arthur C. Nelson.

commodated within UGBs are directed to carefully restricted exception areas, which are areas of low resource productivity that are historically used for hobby farms or small woodlots.

Lancaster County, Pennsylvania. Does effective farmland preservation require state intervention as is seen in Oregon and Hawaii? Not necessarily. All the techniques used in Oregon are being applied in Lancaster County, Pennsylvania, albeit on a township-by-township basis. Through negotiations with local townships, Lancaster County is gradually installing urban service limits around cities and placing large areas of farmland into exclusive farm use districts. The county is successful because it uses state PDR funds in a strategic manner. Rather than using scarce PDR funds anywhere, it targets those funds in situations where they can be used to effectively create urban growth boundaries—by using conservation easements on farmland to create a ring around cities—and to create exclusive farming areas of such size as to achieve a critical mass of land area needed to sustain economic activity (Daniels 1991).

Agricultural Buffers. One method used to reduce conflicts between urban and agricultural land-use activities is to require urban development to buffer itself from agriculture or forest areas. Buffer schemes vary considerably from just a few feet to three miles. As a general principle, the larger the buffer, the more protected agriculture and forestry is from urban development.

California. The California Coastal Commission requires a 200-foot buffer between developments and commercial agricultural lands (Schiffman 1989).

Maine. Maine prohibits development and wells within 150 feet of any farm that is registered with a town government. The law also requires sellers of land adjacent to such registered farms to inform buyers of the buffer area (Schiffman 1989).

Oregon. Oregon requires that destination resorts be at least three miles away from prime agriculural areas, which are mapped as exclusive farm use districts on local comprehensive plans. Development outside urban growth boundaries is regulated by local governments, which usually require a minimum 100-foot setback and often as much as 500 feet.

Integrated Techniques Needed

The case for resource land preservation boils down to the need to intervene in the unregulated land market to offset or attempt to correct market imperfections and their outcomes. But resource land preservation policies work best in tandem with several other important policies. The package includes comprehensive regionally oriented plans, exclusive agricultural zoning, urban containment boundaries, restrictions on exurban or rural development, and, of lesser importance, farm-use tax deferral and right-to-farm provisions (Daniels and Nelson 1986). The individual techniques must reinforce each other: resource land tax deferral and right-to-farm laws create incentives for operators to keep operating; exclusive agricultural and forestry zones reserve resource land for resource uses in the long run; urban containment boundaries limit urban sprawl; carefully designed exurban districts accommodate new rural dwellers without harming commercial resource land operations; and comprehensive plans serve to legitimize the location and use of resource land districts, urban containment boundaries, and exurban districts. In economic terms, the objective of resource land

preservation policy is to prevent the speculation of such land for urban development and encourage greater productivity of such land, especially near urban areas.

SUMMARY DISCUSSION ON THE ECONOMIC BENEFITS OF RESOURCE LAND PRESERVATION

When successful, resource land preservation policies generate important benefits. Perhaps the most important benefit is in fostering economic diversification. In many areas, agriculture and forestry are important contributions to the local economic base. As resource lands are developed, the economic base is reduced. Over time, if the critical mass of land needed to sustain resource activities is eliminated, an entire element of the local economic base is needlessly eliminated. The result is reduced economic diversity. Although timely and well-planned conversion of resource land to urban uses may achieve other important growth management objectives, such as efficient accommodation of urban development needs or expansion of regional economic activities, we observe that most resource land conversion is premature and occurs in the absence of good planning. Instead, overallocation of land for nonresource uses leads to conversion in scattered, isolated, or low-density forms that undermines the economic contributions of resource land. The region is left economically worse off as such development forms are the most costly to serve, the least efficient in providing future urban services, and the most damaging to sustaining an important element of the region's economic base.

Effective resource land preservation not only helps keep the local economic base diversified, but it also improves productivity, principally by reducing the effects of the impermanence syndrome (Nelson 1992a). Another important benefit is the potential for resource land to help improve the nation's balance of trade. Recent passage of the North American Free Trade Agreement (NAFTA) and the revised General Agreement on Tariffs and Trade (GATT) will open significant world markets to American agriculture and forestry. Those areas that do a good job of preserving their resource land base may become front-line players in the global economy through the export of agricultural and forest products.

Lastly, there are important fiscal benefits. Because resource lands are the least dependent of all land uses on urban services, and because resource lands nonetheless contribute revenue to the local fisc, recent studies have found that resource lands generate net fiscal benefits to taxpayers. That is, resource lands contribute more to the local fiscal base than they cost in services. One recent study found that for every dollar in taxes received from resource lands, only 33 cents is returned for facilities and services (American Farmland Trust 1992). In contrast, resource land converted to one-, two-, or five-acre homesites results in a land use pattern that costs more to serve than it generates in tax revenue. One report synthesizing several studies shows that for every dollar such development generates, it costs local taxpayers $1.41 in facilities and services (American Farmland Trust 1986). While some may argue that converting farmland to acreage homesites will improve the local economy and the local fiscal base, studies actually show perverse effects. Not only are local taxpayers made worse off by subsidizing low-density development, but the local economic base is also made less diversified as the resource land base is undermined.

The benefits of resource land preservation are well known in all other industrialized countries, which consider resource lands to be an important element of national economic policy. As the United States becomes more competitive in the world economy, its resource land base increasingly will be viewed as a critical element of its economic development policy.

4

Special-Area Protection

PUBLIC-GOOD PROTECTION

Related to resource land preservation is the preservation of certain environmentally sensitive or otherwise significant landscapes. These are areas that, because of their many public-good qualities, defy adequate pricing in the market or behavior by landowners to preserve them. These public-good features can include (1) protecting urban development from natural hazards and disasters; (2) preserving endangered or threatened species habitats; (3) maintaining air, land, and water quality; (4) maintaining scenic views or vistas; (5) conserving historically or culturally significant areas outside urban development; and (6) protecting scientifically or ecologically significant areas. Important and emerging growth management techniques that are used to achieve these purposes are reviewed in this chapter.

Coastal Zone Protection

The federal Coastal Zone Management Act of 1972 provided planning funds to state governments for a limited number of years, followed by a larger sum to implement the state plans that were approved. Nine states had already adopted coastal management legislation prior to the federal program. Principal tools that have come to be used in coastal management are regulatory permit systems, comprehen-

sive planning, land-use designations through zoning and subdivision regulations, selective land acquisition and restoration, promotion of desirable coastal development, negotiation, and federal/state consistency requirements. Oregon has relied on local comprehensive planning as a means of coastal area resource protection from the start, although it is subject to rather elaborate state guidelines and review. Washington's program requires the preparation of local shoreline master programs for all land within 200 feet of shoreline along the coast, Puget Sound, rivers, lakes, and submerged lands. This local plan must be approved by the state's department of ecology. Upon approval, the program becomes state regulation and both state and local government must approve development permits (Bish 1982). The California program is also based on a state permitting system and is generally considered the most ambitious and among the most stringent of the state efforts (Healy and Zinn 1985).

California. The California Coastal Commission has been called the flagship of the national coastal zone management program. It is a well-funded, professionally staffed, comprehensive planning, management, and regulatory agency. It was established by the state's Coastal Zone Conservation Act of 1972, which resulted from the citizen initiative Proposition 20. All development within 1,000 yards

Figure 4–1. Atlantic coast barrier island development will eventually be destroyed by hurricanes, but taxpayers will subsidize reconstruction of homes owned by the affluent since the federal insurance program is not actuarially sound. *Source:* Photo by William J. Cleary.

Figure 4–2. High-density development along Florida's coasts have a high risk of being damaged or destroyed by hurricanes. Such development may be reconstructed at taxpayer expense—often by taxpayers who cannot afford to rent these hotel rooms—because of underfunded federal insurance programs. *Source:* Photo by Arthur C. Nelson.

of the shoreline required a permit from the commission.

The later 1976 Coastal Zone Act set forth policies to guide each city and county in preparing its own local coastal program for the portion of its jurisdiction that lay within the coastal zone. The width of the coastal zone in California varies from 1,000 yards in some urban areas to as much as five miles in rural areas. Public access to and along the shoreline was to be maximized; agricultural lands were to be protected; sprawling, leapfrog development was to be avoided; scenic areas were to

be retained; and coastal-dependent industry and port development were to be encouraged, especially in already developed areas. Each local plan would consist of two parts—the land-use plan and its local implementation program, which would include the necessary zoning, grading, architectural review, and subdivision ordinances. Once the coastal commission certified a local plan as fully meeting the requirements of the law, coastal permit authority would be returned to the local jurisdiction. The 1976 act eliminated the previous 1,000-yard permit area, requiring coastal permits for development in the entire coastal zone.

Approval of local coastal plans was delayed by a number of factors. A key factor was reluctance on the part of the commission staff to certify local plans that did not meet a very high standard. This reluctance was due to the fact that once approved, the commission lacked authority to require improvements or modifications to local plans. However, California's five-year evaluation procedure does not include recertification authority with an opportunity to require further improvements in the local plan. Had such a provision been incorporated in the Coastal Zone Act from the beginning, it would have enabled the commission to approve local plans without requiring that every foreseeable development proposal be addressed (DeGrove 1984).

Land acquisition programs, TDRs, and other alternatives to regulation have become particularly important in coastal areas since the U.S. Supreme Court's ruling in *Nollan* v. *California Coastal Commission* in 1987. In that case, the court struck down the coastal commission's longstanding practice of requiring dedication of a public-access easement along beachfront property as a condition of approval on virtually any building project. The ruling made it much more difficult for the coastal commission to achieve its public access goal through regulatory means.

North Carolina. During the 1960s and 1970s, many of North Carolina's coastal areas underwent considerable development for tourism and second homes, which led to water pollution, destruction of sand dunes—especially foredunes, which are important for hurricane protection—destruction of prime shell-fishing areas, and elimination of coastal marshes. In response to these concerns, the state legislature passed the 1974 Coastal Area Management Act. In part, this act was a response to federal coastal zone management legislation in that North Carolina lawmakers used the act to preempt federal regulation of its coastline. The act covers all twenty counties abutting ocean waters. Because of North Carolina's extensive barrier islands, the jurisdiction of the act is notable for its size, which extends up to one hundred miles in width. North Carolina's coastal management program is a unique blend of local governments and state agencies. Local governments, usually counties, prepare plans consistent with state guidelines, and the state coastal resources commission reviews those plans, albeit with nominal evaluation of their substance. Implementation is shared between local governments and the state. The state agency is charged with issuing development permits for "major" projects, such as natural resource exploration and exploitation, and large-scale projects. Local governments have jurisdiction in permitting all other kinds of development, called "minor" projects (DeGrove 1984).

Oregon. Within the rubric of Oregon's statewide land-use planning goals and policies are special requirements of coastal counties. Not only must those half-dozen counties comply with all planning goals and policies that the much larger inland, metropolitan areas comply with, they must also (1) prevent development in primary and sometimes secondary dune regimes; (2) protect the integrity of estuarine resources; (3) preserve waterfront and marine areas for marine activities such as boating, recreation, commerce, and natural aquatic functions; and (4) promote wise use of the continental shelf. Indeed, Oregon was the first state to apply planning goals and policies to the continental shelf, principally to regulate mining and other activities that may lead to pollution.

Critical-Area Programs

In attempting to balance conservation and development objectives, several states have designated critical areas in which innovative planning and management techniques are being applied. Built around seemingly opposing mandates to both protect environmental resources and encourage economic development, critical-area programs have been criticized by developers as being too proenvironment and by environmentalists as being too prodevelopment. Because sound growth management strategies require the maintenance of valuable ecosystems and the accommodation of reasonable economic growth, the basic challenge of critical-area management has been to ameliorate the traditional conflicts between these two objectives through a balanced technical review process. Programs have been developed for three general types of critical areas:

- *Generic areas,* such as North Carolina's coastal "areas of environmental concern" or Maryland's Chesapeake Bay "critical areas," where special state regulations are applied to all similar areas.

- *Geographic areas,* such as Florida's designated "areas of critical state concern," New York's Adirondack Mountains area, and New Jersey's Pinelands, where special local regulations unique to each area are applied under state oversight.

- *Potential critical areas,* which require negotiated solutions to avert problems, such as Florida's program for setting up committees to work out management plans that make critical-area designation unnecessary.

While still evolving, the critical-area concept has become an accepted tool for planning, growth management, and development review and permitting, especially in coastal states. By requiring public planners to clearly define necessary environmental impact mitigation measures in specific critical areas, it moves the professional debate beyond general environment/development conflicts to exact analysis of expected impacts, and consensus on proposed technical solutions (Godschalk 1987).

Florida. Florida's critical areas management program has evolved significantly, from the designation of individual critical areas to the identification of potential critical situations. A severe water crisis in the southern portion of the state led to the enactment of Florida's Environmental Land and Water Management Act in 1972. The act authorized the governor and cabinet to designate critical areas, establish principles for guiding development, and review local land development regulations and decisions for consistency with the guidelines. In 1979, the Florida legislature changed the critical-area law to require the establishment of an area resource planning and management committee prior to the designation of an area of critical state concern. This committee, made up of state, regional, and local officials and private-sector representatives, was responsible for organizing a voluntary, cooperative resource planning and management program.

During 1985 and 1986, two further variations on the critical-area approach were used. In the first, the legislature directly designated the Apalachicola Bay region as an area of critical state concern and devised applicable development management principles for the purpose of protecting the area. The second variation involved the use of intergovernmental growth management agreements. Two rapidly urbanizing counties north of Tampa were given the choice of entering into an agreement with the state to manage growth to protect their land and water resources or be included in a resource planning and manage-

Figure 4–3. This suburban subdivision outside of Pensacola, Florida, is on septic systems which, when they fail, will pollute these wetlands. In Florida, many "areas of critical state concern" affect wetlands. *Source:* Photo by Arthur C. Nelson.

ment committee. The two counties chose the simpler agreement process. Florida has shown a willingness to experiment with different forms of the critical-area approach, having learned from experience that a flexible process was needed to resolve conflict (Godschalk 1987).

Maryland. Maryland's Chesapeake Bay Critical Area Protection Law was one of thirty-four actions enacted by its general assembly in 1984 to address the decline of bay water quality and plant, fish, and wildlife habitats. The law asserts that the state has a critical and substantial interest in fostering more sensitive development activity along the Chesapeake Bay shoreline to minimize damage to water quality and natural habitats. The Chesapeake Bay critical area is defined as lands beneath the bay and all uplands within 1,000 feet of tidal waters or tidal wetlands. A critical-area commission was established and charged

with developing criteria to guide development in this area. The criteria, approved by joint resolution of the 1986 general assembly, are being used as guidelines by local governments in developing their land-use programs within the critical area.

• *Intensely Developed Areas.* Most new growth should occur in these areas. Development guidelines specify the improvement of water quality, the conservation of areas for habitat protection and resource conservation, and the addressing of existing stormwater and water-quality problems.

• *Limited Development Areas.* Within these areas, development can occur but it must not change the established density and prevailing land use and it must improve water quality and conserve existing areas of natural habitat.

• *Resource Conservation Areas.* Within these areas, development cannot exceed an overall residential density of one unit per twenty acres. Cluster development, transfer of development rights, and other means to achieve this density are encouraged.

Pinelands, New Jersey. The Pinelands area of New Jersey consists of over one million acres, one-quarter of the land area of the state, of agricultural and forest lands lying over an aquifer of exceptionally pure groundwater. Responding to threats to this resource from development pressures, the legislature in 1979 created the Pinelands Commission to develop a plan and regulate land use. The comprehensive plan, adopted in 1981, included the largest and most complex TDR program ever attempted.

Development rights, called Pinelands Development Credits, are assigned to landowners based on the development suitability of the land, ranging from 0.2 credits per thirty-nine acres for wetlands to 2 credits per thirty-nine acres for farmland. Each credit permits the development of four housing units in designated receiving areas. In all, about 6,500 credits were assigned to land in preservation areas (Mason 1992).

Endangered Habitat Preservation

The federal Endangered Species Act, administered by the U.S. Fish and Wildlife Service, prohibits the killing of any endangered or threatened species by any means, including the destruction of habitat through development. The act is potentially one of the strongest land-use mechanisms the federal government has. The act authorizes the secretary of the interior to designate areas of critical habitat for certain endangered or threatened species. It allows states, local governments, and special-interest groups to petition for endangered or threatened species status. Land designated as critical habitat may be developed, if at all, only with stringent safeguards in place. Moreover, the act prevents the taking of any endangered species. A *taking* means to harass, harm, pursue, hunt, shoot, wound, kill, trap, capture, or collect, or to attempt to engage in any such conduct. Taking can happen if development occurs on land even occasionally occupied by endangered species.

Congress amended the act to allow developers to engage in otherwise prohibited takings of endangered species under certain circumstances, if a habitat conservation plan (HCP) has been established that will ensure the continued existence of the species. The purpose of the HCP is to allow developers to submit plans that provide long-term commitments regarding the conservation of listed and unlisted species and long-term assurances to the developer that the terms of the plan will be adhered to and that further mitigation requirements will only be imposed in accordance with the terms of the plan. Habitat conservation plans are a relatively new regulatory device to reconcile development pressures with endangered species conservation.

Riverside County, California. In 1988, the U.S. Fish and Wildlife Service discovered in the western part of Riverside County, California, an 85,000-acre habitat of an endangered species, the Stephens kangaroo rat (SKR). Development proposals were held up until the federal government, the county, the cities of Perris, Lake Elsinore, Riverside, Moreno Valley, and Hemet, and the developers worked out a system of environmental mitigation fees. A joint powers agency, the Riverside County Habitat Conservation Agency, was established to receive the funds, which amount to $1,950 per acre on all construction within the habitat area, and implement an HCP. Some $25 million had been collected by the early 1990s, with another $25 million expected over the next decade. It will be used, along with state and federal funds (in amounts yet to be deter-

Figure 4–4. Riverside County, California.
Source: Photo © by Fred Emmert Air Views.

mined), to acquire up to 74,667 acres of SKR habitat in the county (Nelson, Nicholas, and Marsh 1992).

Bakersfield, California. A pay-as-you-go approach is being used in and around Bakersfield, California. Much of the land in the area is already developed for urban, agriculture, or oil operations. The Metropolitan Bakersfield HCP identifies potential reserves for a variety of species. In these potential reserves, developers are required to pay $1,000 per acre of land being developed. This money is put into a kind of bank, which then acquires potential reserves. Developers within these areas must also "enhance" habitat quality for the greater of (1) one acre of land for each acre of "open" but not natural land that developed (such as agricultural, pasture, or other disturbed land), or (2) three acres of land for each acre of natural land that is developed. The HCP anticipates the acquisition of 300 to 800 acres per year, depending on development pressures and location. (Nelson, Nicholas, and Marsh 1992).

Lee County, Florida. In 1989, Lee County enacted a protected-species ordinance that prevents development from encroaching on endangered and threatened-species habitat areas. The ordinance uses incentives, such as transfers of development rights and reductions in open-space requirements, to ensure protection of critical habitats. Property owners of sites that are likely to contain endangered species must prepare a survey that identifies the wildlife trails, feeding locations, and boundaries of the occupied habitat areas on the site. The ordinance requires that buffer zones be established around each occupied habitat. Habitats are then transferred to the county through the use of conservation easements (APA, November 1989).

Figure 4–5. Riverside County, California—kit fox. *Source:* Photo by Liz Snyder.

Clark County, Nevada. The desert tortoise was considered an endangered species by the U.S. Fish and Wildlife Service in 1984, but its formal designation lagged behind other, more critical, designation processes. The Fish and Wildlife Service later determined that the tortoise population was falling by 20 percent per year, and was also beset with a highly contagious upper-respiratory disease. In 1989, the tortoise was given emergency listing, and development in the Las Vegas area stopped. Using the HCP program, areas for protected habitat were delineated, while areas unsuitable for long-term tortoise habitat were allowed to be taken for development. To help pay for the HCP, developers agreed to contribute $2.5 million to the Desert Tortoise Conservation Center. For every acre of land developed and therefore taken from habitat, developers pay $550. The funds are used to acquire prime tortoise habitat outside the city. More than 400,000 acres of tortoise habitat (much of it already managed by the Bureau of Land Management) was set aside for habitat. Up to 22,000 acres of private land that is otherwise tortoise habitat is allowed to be developed. Tortoises living in the taken area are physically removed to the protected habitat.

Other Community Efforts. Austin, Texas, is currently in the process of developing a regional habitat conservation plan that might incorporate 123,500 acres for the black-capped vireo, an endangered songbird. And also in California, 17,000 acres are being set aside near Palm Springs to protect the fringe-toed lizard, and San Diego County is trying to determine how large a preserve will be needed for the least Bell's vireo (Collier 1990).

Scenic View Protection

Many communities today go beyond narrowly focused preservation efforts to a more comprehensive approach in protecting those special visual characteristics that give an area a distinctive sense of place, such as special vistas, scenic roadways, and community entryways. The concern over scenic roadways and vistas is not a new one, but like other aesthetic concerns, it has recently been rediscovered in many rapidly urbanizing areas of the country. Regulatory efforts to protect scenic views date back to the late 1800s. And in the 1930s, a scenic roadway movement swept the country and resulted in the creation of the Blue Ridge Parkway and Skyline Drive, ad-

ministered today by the National Park Service. Today, communities are relying on a combination of tools, including height and use restrictions, sign controls, and landscaping regulations, to protect scenic vistas and roadways (Duerksen 1986).

Austin, Texas. In 1982, Austin enacted special protective regulations for lands within 1,000 feet of Capital of Texas Highway, an outer loop highway that runs through the scenic Texas hill country west of the city. The regulations were oriented toward preserving natural terrain and vegetation and encouraging architectural compatibility. Subsequently, the city expanded the ordinance to include all other major hill country roads within its jurisdiction. Then, in 1984, Austin adopted a capitol-view protection ordinance that restricted new development from blocking views of the state capitol from twenty-six vantage points. Under the ordinance, height restrictions were placed on buildings within restricted-view corridors in the downtown area. Concurrent adoption of a similar ordinance by the Texas state legislature ensured that the height restrictions also applied to state-owned properties within the designated view corridors.

To attain transfer credit, property owners were given one year to have their affected sites certified by the city by submitting a volumetric study demonstrating what building heights and floor areas could have been achieved on their property had the capitol-view regulations not been imposed. Excess development rights could then be transferred from affected donor sites to one or more eligible receiver sites within three years of certification. While the view-corridor restrictions are still in place in Austin and remaining views of the capitol have been preserved, few properties were able to take advantage of the TDR provisions due to a severe decline in the local real estate market almost immediately after adoption of the ordinance.

Denver, Colorado. Denver's mountain-view ordinance, enacted in 1968 and upheld by the Colorado Supreme Court in 1986, was designed to maintain panoramic mountain views from parks and other public places. Both aesthetic and economic reasons were invoked to support the ordinance. Denver's basic approach was to create a series of overlay zones with special restrictions tailored to the area in which each applied. In the Capital/ Civic Center District, for example, the Denver ordinance creates five zones, each with its own height limit, designed to protect the view of the Rocky Mountains from the vantage point of the state capitol and the view of the capitol itself (Duerksen 1986).

Other Community Efforts. Most view-protection ordinances seek to protect mountain or hillside vistas. Monterrey County, California has adopted viewshed protection regulations for State Highway 1, a scenic two-lane road in the Big Sur area. Santa Fe, New Mexico has adopted very stringent building-height and setback regulations along five designated roadways (within 600 feet on either side) to protect views of the Sangre de Cristo Mountains. Cary, North Carolina prohibits any development within 100 feet of Interstate 40 and two other major highways within the community so as to retain the area's lush vegetation and natural beauty. Hilton Head Island, South Carolina has designated three major local arterials as scenic corridors and requires extensive landscape buffers and site planning in order to ensure that new development respects the environment. Albuquerque, New Mexico restricts de-

velopment along Coors Boulevard, a major local arterial, to protect views of the Sandia Mountains and Rio Grande River Valley (Bishop 1989).

Land Acquisition

Public acquisition of sensitive lands can assure absolute control over use. Although acquisition often requires significant financial outlays, a number of growth management and resource preservation programs involve the outright purchase of privately owned land. At least partially in response to the unwillingness and inability of government and public agencies to purchase land for the purpose of preservation, private land trusts have also worked to acquire private lands for a variety of public purposes. Most private land trusts are locally formed nonprofit organizations that acquire land for the purpose of public use or conservation. While less well known than national conservation organizations and federal and state land management agencies, these groups are an increasingly powerful force in the resource protection and preservation arena.

Although born in the late nineteenth century, real growth in the land trust movement did not occur until the 1950s, largely in response to increasing urbanization and land development pressures that were consuming large quantities of rural and natural areas. According to a 1988 survey conducted by the Land Trust Exchange, some 740 land trusts then operated in the country, compared to only 430 in 1981 (Land Trust Exchange 1989: 18). Land donations have traditionally formed the backbone of most land trusts' conservation programs, although changes in federal tax laws have reduced the financial incentive for wealthy landowners to donate valuable land. As a result, land trusts are increasingly focusing their efforts on limited projects in which a portion of a site is developed in order to finance the conservation of important resources on the remainder of the site.

Easement programs, which essentially involve purchasing some or all of the development rights from private landowners while allowing them to continue to use the land for farming and other low-intensity activities, have also grown in popularity as a means of preserving significant areas and resources. Easements are also attractive because, unlike outright fee simple acquisition by the public or tax-exempt organizations, such programs allow land to remain on the tax rolls (see Chapter 3).

California. In 1988, California voters approved a $770 million bond issue for parkland and open-space acquisition. Proposition 70, as the bond issue was called, was the first bond issue in more than seventy years to qualify for the statewide ballot via the initiative process. Proceeds of the bond issue have permitted various state agencies to make large purchases. For example, the Wildlife Conservation Board was able to buy 2,700 acres near Lake Tahoe, while the Santa Monica Mountains Conservancy was able to buy a 700-acre ranch, otherwise scheduled for development, in Glendale, adjacent to Angeles National Forest.

The most innovative and controversial aspect of Proposition 70 was the so-called park barrel approach. Local environmental groups around the state agreed to help gather signatures to place the initiative on the ballot, and in exchange received funding for their pet land-conservation projects. For this reason, Proposition 70 has, to a certain extent, taken the decision-making power away from state bureaucrats. On the other hand, it proved that public support for land-acquisition programs was widespread, encouraging many local governments to follow the same route (Fulton 1990).

Maine. Voters in Maine approved a $35 million bond issue in 1987 for the purchase of public open space and scenic areas. Nonprofit land trusts have also acquired land for preservation purposes. A total of forty-one local land trusts, including the Maine Coast Heritage Trust, have protected over 24,000 acres in the state (York 1989: 56–57).

Nantucket Island, Massachusetts. Nantucket's state-approved land bank, financed by a 2 percent real estate transfer tax on island land transactions, has fared much better in implementing open-space-preservation objectives than have traditional growth management mechanisms. The measure represents an attempt to preserve public access to the shores and moors. Critics, however, suggest that the program tempts the land bank commission to pursue fee simple purchases instead of searching for more creative, and possibly more economically viable, solutions (Klein 1986).

5

Rural Growth Management

IMPORTANCE OF RURAL GROWTH MANAGEMENT

Rural growth management is crucial to any overall growth management scheme. Since the early 1970s, millions of American households have chosen rural and exurban locations over urban and suburban locations. They appear to seek a particular lifestyle, one that is founded on the classically American, Jeffersonian ideal of a nation built not on urban development, but instead on a gentrified landscape that can now be characterized as rural or exurban sprawl (Daniels 1986; Daniels and Nelson 1986; Nelson and Dueker 1990). The most important factor stimulating rural and exurban sprawl is improving access to employment opportunities facilitated by decentralized employment, flexible commuting and work time, underestimation of the real costs of commuting through inefficient fuel and road-use pricing, and telecommuting (Nelson 1992e).

Unplanned and uncoordinated, this trend will lead to rural and exurban sprawl that will have far-ranging impacts on land use, transportation, regional fiscal structure, public services and facilities, and economic development. Moreover, as rural and exurban development spreads over much larger areas than suburban and urban development, coordination among affected local governments is exacerbated. The purpose of rural growth management is to properly anticipate the wide-ranging effects of rural and exurban development on rural resources and to address how such development can be properly integrated with urban areas.

This chapter presents a series of rural growth management techniques that preserve resource and other significant lands, improve the vitality of rural communities, and accommodate rural and exurban development needs.

Enhancing the Economic Vitality of Rural Places

Despite rural and exurban growth, many rural places have a difficult time improving their economic vitality. Large discount stores and shopping centers often locate so far away from Main Street that they entirely change shopping patterns and undermine Main Street vitality. Very low-density residential development located very far from rural places also undermines economic vitality. Rural places are more sensitive to decentralized shopping and residential activities than urban areas principally because rural market areas have so little disposable income with which to satisfy shopping, business service, and personal service needs. Mail-order purchases are higher among rural residents than among suburban and urban residents. What can be done? Here are two planning schemes.

Oregon. Oregon's statewide land-use planning program required all cities and urban areas, no matter how small or isolated, to accommodate the market area demand for commercial, industrial, and residential development within urban growth boundaries or carefully prescribed areas just outside small towns. The effect is that much new rural development is concentrated in small towns. This concentration creates important synergies that provide opportunities for retail trade, business, and personal services. Large discount stores are not allowed outside UGBs and are often directed to particular areas where the interaction between retail operations can be improved.

Manhattan, Kansas. After denying several zone changes from agriculture to commercial to build a shopping center in the outskirts of Manhattan, Kansas, the city used federal Urban Development Action Grant (UDAG), state, and special-purpose funds to acquire an abandoned lumber mill adjacent to Main Street (Poyntz Avenue) and underwrite the construction of a regional shopping center. The result is that Main Street has become intimately tied to the shopping center, which also benefits from the retail traffic that Main Street would generate in its own right. Residential areas are also confined to reasonably well-prescribed urban service areas. The overall effect on Main Street is increased retail trade, consumer opportunities, and employment.

Rural Cluster Development

Cluster development in rural areas is seen primarily as a means of preserving open space in rural areas near urban centers. Development is clustered through a density transfer scheme rather than evenly spread out at very low density. The approach is used to grant some development rights to areas where development is not encouraged, such as on steep slopes, wetlands, woodlands, floodplains, historically or culturally significant areas, or important habitats. An undeveloped preserve is thereby created that is either jointly owned by homeowners or, more commonly, sold as a very large tract to a single owner (Arendt 1994).

The cluster development scheme involves awarding farmland an underlying density that can only be exercised in a planned arrangement where residential units are clustered and a conservation easement is applied to the remaining large tract. The easement often assigns to the local government an interest in the property, thereby preventing the easement from being removed without governmental approval. The easement prevents further subdividing or construction of more than one home. In the best situations, the large tract is operated as a farm. The advantage to the original landowner is that the farm is substantially preserved as a very large tract while substantial income is received from the use of development rights in the cluster development.

However, there are important limitations to rural cluster development. First, the conservation easements often limit the use of the large tract. For example, they can prevent aerial or sometimes manual application of fertilizers, pesticides, and herbicides. Certain crops may be prohibited because of their odors, manner of harvesting, or obstruction of views. Farm animals may be limited, and livestock may be prohibited. Even without these restrictions, the cluster-home owners may act to prevent many activities. As a consequence, farmland often becomes less productive than before the cluster development. Long-term or intensive management as a farm may become economically infeasible. The large tract may become underutilized, harboring weeds, thistles, and native vegetation rather than crops.

Second, when farming regions become a series of clustered developments that effectively take land out of productive agricultural use, the critical mass of commercial farms needed to sustain the regional farming economy may disappear. Farming jobs are lost, along with the tax base commercial farms support.

Third, cluster development is actually a form of leapfrog development the pattern of which can result in more costly provision of public facilities and services than fiscal revenues generated by such developments (American Farmland Trust 1989, 1992). The American Farmland Trust has determined that for each dollar of local fiscal revenue generated by farms, only $0.33 is returned in public facilities and services. Farmland generates a net surplus in fiscal revenues. Yet, for each dollar of fiscal revenue generated by low-density developments such as cluster developments, $1.41 is returned in public facilities and services. Low-density and cluster developments generate a net deficiency in fiscal revenues that must be offset by other taxpayers.

Connecticut River Valley. Perhaps the best-known example of cluster development is the Connecticut River Valley, which passes through western Massachusetts. In the 1980s, much of the valley was designated for one-to-five-acre minimum lot sizes. To accommodate regional demand for housing, developers acquired farms and built subdivisions that met minimum lot size standards. To save farming in the region, the Center for Rural Massachusetts began working with several towns to change their land-use bylaws to allow for cluster development. The general scheme advanced by the center requires all new developments on farmland to be laid out in such a way that no more than 50 percent of the farmland would be developed and at least 50 percent would be preserved as a large tract intended for farm use. Typical lots would range from one-quarter to one-half acre. Provisions would be made for attached housing to accommodate lower-income and elderly residents. Lots would be located in a woodland fringe at the edge of fields, or screened from farms by newly planted trees that would serve as shelterbelts. Most cluster developments would be served by septic systems and wells. With smaller lots than the underlying zoning allowed, developers would save on road costs while townships would save on road maintenance costs. Farmers planning to use their farms for retirement income would still be able to do so, while new farmland owners would understand the limitations on dividing in the future (Yaro et al. 1990). The scheme is now widely applied throughout the valley. In the absence of a truly comprehensive regional urban growth management scheme, the approach used in the valley may be considered at least a stopgap to preserve farmland. However, there has been no long-term assessment of the extent to which the farming economy benefits from this scheme, or the extent to which local governments realize fiscal benefits.

Lancaster County, Pennsylvania. Lancaster County, Pennsylvania, is refining the rural cluster development approach to direct development into some small towns. In the areas surrounding these towns, agricultural land is limited to large acreage parcels. Higher density will be allowed on such land if the development rights are used in a cluster development locating near or adjacent to participating small towns. This approach shows promise to revitalize small towns, preserve agricultural land to sustain the regional agricultural economic base, and accommodate the regional demand for rural or exurban development.

Performance Evaluation

One of the more innovative approaches to rural growth management is the use of performance evaluation. McHenry County, Illinois, and Hardin County, Kentucky, are perhaps the leading examples of this approach. Both counties evaluate rural development proposals based on the Land Evaluation and Site Assessment (LESA) system developed by the U.S. Department of Agriculture, Soil Conservation Service. Under LESA, sites are initially evaluated for their soil quality in terms of suitability for cropland, forest land, and rangeland. This is figured on a scale from 0 to 100 points, followed by a site assessment resulting in up to 200 additional points after considering such factors as (1) percentage of land in agriculture in the area; (2) site economic viability factors such as farm size, land ownership, and investments; (3) impact of the proposed change in site use on agricultural, natural, historic, recreation, scenic, and other resources of the community; (4) compatability with relevant plans, zoning, and other resource land preservation measures; and (5) access to public infrastructure and necessary public, social, personal, and business services (Stokes et al. 1989). The community itself determines the land evaluation and site assessment factors it decides are appropriate.

McHenry County, Illinois. In 1979, McHenry County, Illinois, an exurb of Chicago,

applied A-1 (160-acre minimum lot size) zoning to about 200,000 acres or 75 percent of the county's best soils and A-2 (1-acre minimum lot size) zoning to the balance of the county's rural areas. These steps were taken after it became clear that between 1974 and 1979, when 5-acre minimum lot size zoning was imposed countywide, commercially viable farms were divided into unproductive 5-acre hobby farms. Rural development proposals involving A-1 land are evaluated using the county's adaptation of the LESA system. While there have been many rural development approvals since 1979, the LESA system effectively limits such development to areas adjacent to existing municipalities (Stokes et al. 1989).

Hardin County, Kentucky. The Hardin County, Kentucky, development guidance system (DGS) extends the LESA concept so completely that it virtually eliminates rural zoning. Any proposed development outside municipalities undergoes three separate evaluations: (1) a growth guidance assessment; (2) a compatibility assessment; and (3) a plan assessment. The growth guidance assessment includes both elements of the LESA system. The land evaluation component is weighted to discourage development of the highest quality soils and large farmland holdings; the more points up to 115, the greater the development suitability. The site assessment component is weighted to encourage development adjacent to existing municipalities and, to a lesser extent, established rural centers; the more points up to 200, the greater the development suitability. Proposals earning 150 points or more advance to the compatibility assessment while those scoring less go to the planning commission for probable denial. The compatibility assessment involves a meeting of the developer, neighbors, and the planning staff to identify unique development impacts that the growth guidance assessment would not detect. The plan assessment stage involves final site planning and review for consistency with recommendations coming from the compatibility assessment. While the process may sound cumbersome, in fact it is quite efficient since all decision-making is centralized within a single overall development review process that includes time limits within each stage. A development proposal can receive approval in as few as four weeks; proposals failing to earn 150 points receive denial in a matter of days. Table 5–1 shows the site assessment worksheet (which Hardin County actually calls the amenities assessment) (Stokes et al. 1989).

Rural Land Reassembly

What happens when unused and undeveloped rural land has been subdivided but, using modern planning and zoning practices, should never have been used for other than rural purposes? Many such rural "antiquated plats" cannot be used for farming or forestry because of multiple ownerships, nor can they be used for development because lots are too small to sustain wells and septic systems. Antiquated plats present two problems for rural growth management. First, such plats cannot

Table 5–1. Hardin County, Kentucky, Amenities Assessment Worksheet

Characteristic	Score 1–10	Weight Factor	Points Earned
1. Site size		1.2	
2. Percent of adjacent development		2.6	
3. Percent of surrounding development		2.2	
4. Agricultural use and classification		0.8	
5. Access road type		1.7	
6. Distance to: Incorporated city / Rural community		2.1	
7. Distance to public water		1.7	
8. Distance to public sewerage		1.5	
9. Distance to school facility		1.3	
10. Distance to fire department		1.2	
11. Distance to ambulance station		0.8	
12. Terms of ownership		0.7	
13. Relation to growth corridor		2.2	
14. Amenities points (add lines 1–13)			
15. Line 15 from Soils Assessment			
16. Growth guidance assessment points			

Source: Hardin County, Kentucky, 1987.

meet the demand for rural or exurban development because of antiquated platting, ownership patterns, and the uneconomical delivery of facilities. Second, the demand for such development is directed to unplatted areas including resource lands. Two states have worked to create solutions to this problem.

California's Coastal Land Assembly Program. The California State Coastal Conservancy was established in 1976 to deal with needs related to implementation of the state coastal plan. Under the terms of its legislative authorization, the conservancy can buy land, restore or resubdivide it, improve or develop it, own and manage it indefinitely, or sell/ transfer it to others. The conservancy's funds come from legislative appropriations, profits on its transactions, grants from the coastal commission, statewide bond issues, fines and settlements for violations of the Coastal Act, and in-lieu mitigation payments required by the coastal commission as conditions of development. With these funds, the conservancy undertakes a wide range of projects, including wetland restoration, acceptance and development of public access and open-space easements, management of several TDR programs, and the consolidation of old, small-lot subdivisions in scenic or environmentally sensitive areas. Through its land reassembly and resubdivision activities, the coastal commission generates sufficient revenue from many such ventures to show a profit that is then used for the next venture (Fischer 1985).

Growing Trees in Antiquated Plats, Oregon Style. Oregon planning policies have evolved in recent years to encourage developers to acquire through private means individual lots in antiquated rural plats, reassemble ownerships into buildable lots, and preserve areas within and adjacent to the plats for farming or forest use (Nelson and Recht 1988).

CONCLUDING THOUGHTS

There are two kinds of rural landscapes that need different kinds of planning. The first is the truly rural hinterland that has little direct contact with metropolitan areas, such as through commuting. In these areas, land resources are the mainstay of local and regional economies. These areas are also characterized as slow growing, and many are not growing but declining. In light of few growth pressures on farmland, forest land, and other kinds of resource land, land-use restrictions may seem irrelevant and perhaps they are. Instead, planning in the rural hinterland focuses on identifying opportunities for economic development and then arranging resources to exploit such opportunities. Growth management techniques would be used to preserve land for eventual exploitation and manage land use in a way that ensures production of maximum benefits from exploitation.

But there is another kind of rural landscape that is fragile and subject to development pressures that may undermine its character. It is called exurbia and it extends from the edge of built-out suburbs to the frontier of the rural hinterland, which is found in a range of about 50 miles from the center of a metropolitan area of less than 250,000 residents up to 100 miles from the center of a metropolitan area of more than 2 million residents and perhaps 150 miles from the center of a metropolitan area of more than 4 million residents (Nelson and Dueker 1990; Nelson, Drummond, and Sawicki 1992). The exurban landscape is complex, composed of farms, forests, and other forms of open space; small towns historically rooted in the natural resource economy; isolated pockets of settlements; and growing numbers of homes on acreage tracts and subdivisions of homes on tracts ranging from one to twenty acres.

Because exurbia is the next ring of development around metropolitan areas, it also has the largest volume of land. Unlike closer-in suburban areas that are built out, exurbia is unlikely to ever be built out because of the sheer volume of land involved. But the development of exurbia presents the most serious challenges to growth management. If left unmanaged, exurban sprawl will (1) adversely impact on the region's natural resource economic base; (2) result in scattered, low-density development that will raise the cost of providing public facilities and services (much of the cost of which we know from research and literature is not borne by exurbanites); (3) decrease the accessibility of households to jobs, services, and shopping—thereby also frustrating the regional economy as certain economic enterprises will lack the critical mass of population to survive; (4) increase air pollution as exurbanites need to travel longer and farther to work, services, and shopping; and (5) undermine, in some situations, the natural carrying capacity of the landscape.

The challenge to planners is to manage the growth and development of exurbia in such as way as to (1) preserve the critical mass of resource land needed to sustain the region's resource economic base; (2) direct exurban development to those areas that are most accessible to jobs, services, and shopping; and (3) organize exurban development to minimize public facility and service costs. A mix of growth management techniques presented throughout this book offers the solution to managing exurban development. Exclusive farm and forest use districts would preserve agricultural and forest land exclusively for farm and forest uses. PDR and TDR policies may be used in addition to exclusive-use policies to preserve these resource lands. Rural cluster development can be used to economize on the provision of public facilities and services, especially if they are located adjacent or near to existing small towns. Rural cluster development may also be used to create new hamlets and villages with a small range of services and shopping to accommodate everyday needs of cluster residents.

Nelson (1994) suggests an adaptation of Frank Lloyd Wright's template for *Broadacre City* to guide exurban development. Under this scheme, the exurban landscape would be composed of land-extensive resource preserves for farming, forestry, and other open-space activities, as well as pockets of Broadacre City developments. Each exurban Broadacre City would be a village composed of a variety of residential densities, a small commercial center, and public facilities and services scaled for a town of about 5,000 residents. The exurban Broadacre cities would connect various parts of the city with bicycle and pedestrian pathways. Individual Broadacre cities would be connected to each other and to urban centers with major highways, perhaps bus lines, and (in some instances) light rail lines. Short of realizing this scheme, however, planners working in exurban areas can nonetheless achieve many of its elements through the wise mix of rural and urban growth management techniques.

6

Urban Containment

Urban containment strategies represent an attempt to control the spatial pattern of development within a community or region. Unlike other planning and regulatory programs, such as environmental regulations, which also have the effect of controlling the location of development, urban containment plans are typically more comprehensive. The benefits of successful urban containment techniques can include greater predictability of the development process, more cost-effective provision of public services, encouragement of infill and redevelopment of existing urban areas, reduction of urban sprawl, and protection of agricultural land and environmental resources.

This chapter provides an overview of several selected urban containment–based growth management techniques and programs. Urban service areas or growth boundaries are a very direct technique for managing the location and timing of development. While growth boundaries may be intended to encourage compact and cost-effective development patterns, they are often part of a broader scheme to preserve agricultural land from inappropriate or premature development. If urban containment programs are to be effective and avoid negative impacts on the affordability of housing, they must be accompanied by strong programs that encourage infill and redevelopment.

URBAN CONTAINMENT PRINCIPLES

Urban containment planning has two basic purposes: (1) to promote compact and contiguous development patterns that can be efficiently served by public services and (2) to preserve open space, agricultural land, and environmentally sensitive areas that are not currently suitable for urban development. At the most basic level, an urban containment program consists of a perimeter drawn around an urban area, within which urban development is encouraged and outside of which urban development is discouraged. Urban containment lines are generally designed to accommodate projected growth over a specified future time period, typically ten to twenty years.

Land outside urban containment boundaries is generally restricted to resource uses and to very low-density residential development ranging from one unit per ten acres to one unit per twenty acres or more in prescribed and carefully restricted areas. The extension of utilities, especially wastewater service, is generally prohibited outside the boundary. Within urban containment boundaries, development is generally encouraged, often with density bonuses and, occasionally, with minimum density requirements. Land within an urban containment boundary, but outside the city limits, is often subject to contractual city/county agreements governing development standards and timing of annexation and utility extension.

Urban containment boundaries typically are complemented by urban service area plans, so that cost-effective delivery of public services can be accomplished by controlling the timing of utility extensions and infrastructure improvements. Land within the urban containment boundary may be subdivided into different categories for the phasing of services, depending on development suitability, proximity to existing public facilities, contiguity with existing development, and other factors. Enough land must be included within the boundary and urban service areas to provide sufficient land to accommodate projected market demand within the prescribed planning period, with additional land to provide for choice. If too little land of sufficient density and intensity is included, exorbitant increases in the cost of land and housing, legal challenges, and political pressure to prematurely extend the boundary may result. On the other hand, designation of too large an area or areas with insufficient density or intensity opportunities defeats the purposes of encouraging compact, contiguous development and usually results in excessive and premature capital outlays for public services and in urban sprawl.

The specific objectives of urban containment include the preservation of prime farm and forest land (see Chapter 4); the efficient provision of public facilities (see Chapter 7); the reduction of air, water, and land pollution; and the creation of a distinctly urban ambience. Local governments must include sufficient land within contained areas to meet the requirements for housing, industry and commerce, recreation, open space, and all other urban land uses. All land outside contained areas must be designated for nonurban uses to the end of a planning horizon, which is usually about twenty years. Specifically, urban containment programs must be based on the following seven factors:

1. Demonstrated need to accommodate long-range urban population growth requirements consistent with state, regional, and local goals and policies

2. Need for housing, employment opportunities, and livability

3. Orderly and economic provision of public facilities and services

4. Maximum efficiency for land uses in or at the fringe of existing urban areas

5. Environmental, energy, economic, and social consequences

6. Retention of farm, forest, and other resource land

7. Compatibility of the proposed urban uses with nearby resource activities

Urban containment planning aims to influence the regional market for urban land in several important ways. First, because land outside the containment boundary is restricted to resource uses or low-density residential development in exurban districts, the regional demand for urban development is shifted to the area inside the boundary. This should decrease the value of land outside the boundary and increase the value of land inside the boundary. If a gap in land values along both sides of the boundary is not seen, then either the boundary is too large in the near term or there is too much development potential remaining in rural areas regardless of any land-use restrictions.

Second, higher urban land values may signal more efficient land development patterns. Basic economic principles hold that if efficiencies are realized in the development of land, those efficiencies will be capitalized as higher land prices even when the price of a finished product such as a home remains unchanged. Such efficiencies can include (1) improved access to employment, shopping, and other services; (2) efficient delivery of facilities and services; and (3) preservation of the rural landscape for all urban residents to enjoy in a variety of ways.

Third, and of concern to developers, is that higher priced urban land may result in higher priced housing unless densities are increased. This may occur if planning fails to increase the supply of buildable land within the boundary. Peiser (1989) observes that urban containment boundaries are prudent land-use policies but only when accompanied by policies that increase urban development density and intensity. In the Portland, Oregon, metropolitan area, for example, local governments were required to increase residential development densities within the regional urban growth boundary. Thus, although land prices could rise, the finished house price would remain unchanged and conceivably the finished price could fall. Even if housing prices were to rise despite increasing densities, the increase itself might reflect savings and benefits realized by households because of urban containment.

From an efficiency perspective, urban containment boundaries and related policies provide information to developers about future development patterns that, if accurate, can improve the dynamic efficiency of the land market. If it is known that urban development will soon take place on agricultural land inside the containment area, then improvements in agricultural production are unlikely. Dynamic efficiency is enhanced as informa-

tion about future development is capitalized into land values and market participants can react accordingly (Knaap and Nelson 1992).

URBAN CONTAINMENT TECHNIQUES

When used in combination, several techiques help to achieve urban containment. It is important to use these techniques together; any single technique may not be effective without complementary techniques. For example, urban containment boundaries may not be as effective if aggressive urban infill and redevelopment techniques are not also employed. Some techniques could have perverse effects if not accompanied by other techniques. For example, urban containment boundaries can reduce the supply of buildable land in the long term, but upzoning and inclusionary zoning can offset potentially adverse supply effects. The general categories of techniques are reviewed below.

Urban Service Areas and Urban Growth Boundaries

Urban service areas (USAs) and urban growth boundaries (UGBs) are the principal means by which containment lines are drawn. Generally, USAs are more flexible in expansion because they are drawn mostly consistent with the economics of planned public facilities. UGBs, on the other hand, have many more policy objectives in addition to providing efficient services. Both conceptual forms of urban containment boundaries are reviewed in this section.

Oregon. Oregon's experience provides some of the best insights into the potentials and pitfalls of urban growth boundaries. One of the legally binding state goals (Goal 10: Urbanization) adopted pursuant to the state's 1973 Land Conservation and Development

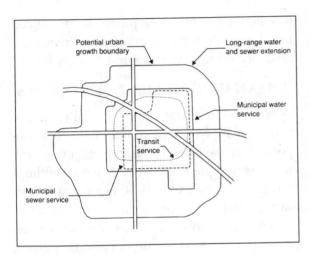

Figure 6–1. The urban service area can be derived by comparing the various maps of service areas and taking into account the desired level of service and available funding. *Source:* Drawing courtesy of V. Gail Easley, Henigar and Ray.

Act requires that Oregon cities take serious steps to discourage urban sprawl, including the delineation of urban growth boundaries. In 1977, the Oregon Supreme Court ruled that municipal land-use decisions, including annexation, must comply with the state goal of controlling sprawl, even prior to the adoption of an urban growth boundary. By 1986, all Oregon cities had adopted comprehensive plans that included an urban growth boundary. State guidelines prepared by the land conservation and development commission (LCDC) require negotiations between cities and counties to agree on the boundary lines, initially based on growth projections for the year 2000 but now those governments are designing boundaries out as far as the year 2040. If agreement cannot be reached, the issue is taken to the LCDC for resolution. In one instance, the LCDC ordered the approval of a city's proposed urban growth boundary after a three-year standoff between the city

and county (DeGrove 1984: 263). Even if local agreement is reached, LCDC reviews the plans for compliance with state goals, and periodic updates of comprehensive plans and urban growth boundaries are required every five years (Sharpe 1990).

Some observers argue that in spite of efforts to keep the boundaries tight, the state has approved boundaries that are quite generous in light of the state's overall growth projections. The Salem Comprehensive Plan, for example, was twice rejected by the LCDC for including far more undeveloped land within its urban growth boundaries than was considered necessary to accommodate projected growth. Under political pressure from legislators and the governor, the LCDC approved the Salem plan in 1982, only to have its decision overturned by the state court of appeals the following year for violations of state goals. Salem was eventually forced to redraw its urban growth boundary to exclude some 2,400 undeveloped acres (York 1989: 20). The state's most influential planning and environ-

Figure 6–2. The metropolitan Portland urban growth boundary runs along this street. *Source:* Arthur C. Nelson.

Figure 6–3. The separation between urban and agricultural land uses achieved by urban growth boundaries is clearly shown in the aerial view of the western portion of the metropolitan Portland UGB. *Source:* Photo © 1990 by Fritz Von Tagen.

mental watchdog group, 1,000 Friends of Oregon, claims that Portland's urban growth boundary also contains 21,000 excessive acres, although the local government contends that preexisting leapfrog development patterns had already committed the land to urban development (York 1989).

California. Because annexation is difficult under California law, and the formation of numerous special districts is relatively easy, the state has witnessed the proliferation of separate, overlapping, and uncoordinated governmental units, which sometimes even compete to provide the same services. Since 1963, the state has sought to "discourage urban sprawl and encourage orderly governmental boundaries" through the use of local agency formation commissions (LAFCOs) in each county. LAFCOs are technically state agencies, but they are made up mostly of elected officials from cities, counties, and special districts. Their staffs are technically independent, although they are often housed within the county bureaucracy.

LAFCOs are authorized, among other powers, to review and approve or disapprove all municipal incorporations, annexations, and special district formations. Under the California system, the local LAFCO determines each city's sphere of influence—an expected ultimate growth boundary that the city may begin planning for. Prior to a vote on incorporation, the LAFCO will conduct a fiscal analysis to determine whether the new city is financially viable. The rate of formation of special districts slowed by about half after LAFCOs were established (deHaven-Smith 1985: 72). While LAFCOs are more directly concerned with government organization and finance than with growth management, the coordination between local governmental entities has improved under the LAFCO system. Since the passage of Proposition 13, however, LAFCOs have been dealing more and more with fiscal issues, which has limited their ability to protect against urban sprawl. Because Proposition 13 virtually prohibits increases in property tax rates, cities and counties may increase their property tax base only by annexing new development. This has led to intense competition over newly developing territory, placing LAFCO in the role of mediator. Although these disputes are fiscally motivated, the LAFCO often helps to determine the future development pattern of a community by deciding which jurisdiction will control it (Fulton 1990).

Sacramento County, California. Sacramento County contains almost all of the Sacramento metropolitan area, including the city of Sacramento and a heavily populated unincorporated area to the east of the city. In 1973, the county adopted a new general plan designed to preserve commercially viable agriculture in the county and to provide for efficient service delivery. The plan contained an urban service boundary, which specified limits for water and wastewater extensions, and transferred 141,000 acres, more than one-fourth of the land under county control, from urban to nonurban land-use categories.

Land within the county's urban service area (USA) boundary was designed to accommodate projected residential development for eighteen years. Outlying lands were designated permanent agriculture, while land just outside the boundary was designated agriculture-urban reserve (to be kept in agricultural use until the county's population reached 880,000).

A last category, agricultural-residential, added in 1974, permitted residential uses on parcels of five acres or more, and represented a compromise in the southern area, where hobby farms were popular and scattered lot-splitting had already occurred. Minimum lot sizes in permanent agriculture areas were increased in 1977 from twenty to forty acres for Class I and II soils and to eighty acres for other lands, virtually excluding hobby farms from most of the area outside the USA boundary. From 1973 to 1977, the general plan was implemented largely through downzonings in the areas beyond the urban service boundary and through denials of subdivision requests on those open-space lands. Increased environmental awareness among the public, county staff expertise, high service costs in outlying areas, and California's general plan consistency statutes contributed to the county's success in implementing the plan during the first five years. From 1978 to 1981, density reductions inside the service area boundary, reflecting neighborhood opposition to the higher infill densities contained in the general plan, reduced the urban service area's planned population capacity (Johnston 1984). The Sacramento experience indicates that growth phasing is easier to accomplish than infill development, especially where multifamily projects threaten existing neighborhood character.

San Diego, California. In adopting a growth management plan, the city of San Diego divided the territory under its jurisdiction (lands within its corporate boundaries and sphere of influence) into three growth management tiers: urbanized area (UA), planned urbanizing area (PUA), and future urbanizing area (FUA). Within each area, the city adopted a series of policies designed to ensure orderly development. The FUA remained zoned for agricultural use, and property tax breaks were available to landowners under the state's Williamson Act program. The UA included areas already served by infrastructure. To encourage infill development in the UA, development fees for many facilities are waived. The PUA constitutes, in essence, the developable vacant land that will be opened up for urban and suburban development over the next generation. Because substantial infrastructure investments are required in the PUA, a mandatory and flexible "facilities benefit assessment" financing scheme was established.

Land is opened for urbanization in a staged, contiguous manner and landowners in each area opened for urbanization are responsible for paying part of the cost eventually, no matter when the landowner planned on developing the property (the financing scheme withstood a serious court challenge soon after its adoption). The urbanized area, which captured only 10 percent of the city's development prior to adoption of the tier system, captured nearly 60 percent of new development only four years later. In many years, the tiered approach worked too well and infrastructure in the urbanized areas showed signs of strain. The city subsequently revised the policy to generate some fee revenue from the urbanized area (Fulton 1990). In concert with several other referendum-adopted growth controls, the San Diego approach has been heavily criticized for contributing to other urban and economic problems (see Chapter 7).

San Jose, California. In 1976, the San Jose City Council established the San Jose Urban Service Boundary, a line beyond which essential public infrastructure would not be extended. New home development outside the boundary, even within city limits, was effectively prohibited. The measure was intended to slow the general rate of rural land conversion by promoting higher residential densities, and to redirect new home construction from outlying development areas to more developed infill areas. By any of those standards, the boundary has proven effective. Between 1975 and 1979, the number of acres converted from rural to urban uses declined from 1,840 to 1,360 per year. The urban services boundary was also effective in redirecting new construction. In the five years before the boundary was established, San Jose's developed planning areas accounted for 32 percent of residential permit activity. By the end of 1977, less than two years after adoption of the boundary, that share increased to 58 percent (Landis 1986).

Florida. While Florida has no specific state legislation governing the creation of urban growth boundaries or urban service areas, there has been considerable debate within the state over the past few years regarding the definition and application of the urban service area concept. Two Florida counties, Dade County (Miami) and Orange County (Orlando), have adopted UGB regulations in the absence of a statewide framework. Yet, to comply with Florida planning laws, local governments essentially create urban service limits or containment boundaries, in fact if not by name. State law is clear in requiring local governments to (1) encourage more compact urban growth patterns; (2) discourage urban sprawl; (3) ensure efficient transition of undeveloped land into developed land; (4) facilitate efficient infrastructure and services; and (5) protect natural resources and environmentally sensitive areas. These requirements are difficult to meet without creating something that looks like an urban containment boundary.

Larimer County, Colorado. In a joint city-county program, Larimer County and Fort Collins entered into an urban growth area agreement in 1980. The initial urban growth area, which encompassed the service areas of two water and wastewater utilities, comprised sixty-six square miles (forty of which were in incorporated Fort Collins). The agreement, which has since been revised several times, established an urban growth area review board, appointed by the city and county, to deal with land-use issues outside the city corporate limits, but within the urban growth area. The board reviews projects and makes recommendations to the county commission regarding development approvals. Guidance is provided by a county-prepared and city-reviewed plan. The agreement strengthened the role of county commissioner decision-making, and common development standards for both the city and county have been adopted. Relationships between city and county has improved significantly over the past several years. In 1993, a new program for the Fort Collins/Loveland corridor was initiated in cooperation with both the county and the cities of Fort Collins and Loveland. Other joint city-county efforts have included cooperation on a congestion management plan, a regional transportation plan, and a national heritage plan.

Thurston County, Washington. In 1988, the mayors of Lacey, Olympia, and Tumwater, and the chairman of the board of Thurston county commissioners signed a Memorandum of Understanding: An Urban Growth Management Agreement. While the document is nonbinding, it does establish a framework for a coordinated approach to managing growth within the county. The agreement creates a two-tiered urban growth boundary around the existing urbanized area. The short-term boundary is designed to accommodate growth for ten years; the long-term boundary is designed to accommodate projected growth for at least twenty-five years. The area outside the long-term boundary is limited to rural residential development and agricultural and natural resource uses. The agreement also outlines a joint planning process, including joint meetings of the individual planning commissions, to aid in the implementation. Although the agreement is voluntary, it is regarded as a success by officials throughout the state.

Lexington-Fayette County, Kentucky. The Bluegrass region around Lexington, Kentucky, is famous for its horse farms where thoroughbred racehorses are raised. The city of Lexington and Fayette County have had a long and successful history of managing urban growth to preserve this area's idyllic rural character. In 1958, an agreement between the two governments led to the adoption of one of the nation's first urban growth boundary pro-

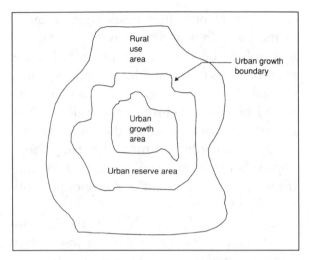

Figure 6–4. The urban growth boundary encompasses the urban reserve area and the urban growth area. *Source:* Drawing courtesy of V. Gail Easley, Henigar and Ray.

grams. The program was designed to protect productive agricultural and horse farm lands, while also encouraging efficient development patterns. The city and county consolidated to form the Lexington-Fayette Urban County in 1974, eliminating jurisdictional problems and increasing the effectiveness of the growth management program. Currently, land outside the urban growth boundary is limited to one unit per ten acres. An agricultural-urban zoning classification is used as a holding area for future development within the growth boundary. Density bonuses are provided to encourage redevelopment in older parts of the city. The program is generally viewed as having been successful in promoting contiguous development and providing some protection for agricultural uses, although only one horse farm remains within the city (York 1989: 96).

Urban Development Phasing

Urban areas are dynamic; land-use conversions occur and new land is often needed to sustain urban development. One function of growth management planning is anticipating future land-use needs and accommodating them over the long term. When urban development fills in and redevelops inner areas, outer areas must be prepared for future development. The Twin Cities region (Minneapolis-St. Paul, Minnesota) anticipates development needs over a ten-year period by redrawing its urban service limits every five years. Two other phasing approaches are used in combination with urban containment boundaries: intermediate growth boundaries and urban development reserves. These and related techniques are reviewed below.

Intermediate Growth Boundaries. Intermediate boundaries are, as their name suggests, short-term development boundaries within long-term containment boundaries. One example of this is metropolitan Portland, Oregon, where an intermediate growth boundary (IGB) limited urban development to certain areas within the long-term urban growth boundary (UGB) (Knaap and Nelson 1992). The IGB accommodated development from 1976 to about 1985, when the IGB was effectively removed and development could extend out to the UGB. Conceptually, IGBs are used to prevent the premature development of land located near the UGB before land inside the IGB is first suitably developed.

Urban Development Reserves. Urban development reserves are somewhat different than intermediate growth boundaries because development in the reserves requires formal urban containment boundary adjustments. There are two examples of these kinds of boundaries: metropolitan Dade County, Florida, and metropolitan Portland, Oregon. Metropolitan Dade County has a long-term urban growth boundary that is designed to

meet development needs to about the year 2010. The long term development plans anticipate the need to expand the supply of buildable land into particular areas located within an urban development reserve. This area has sufficient land to accommodate five to ten years' development when the UGB is filled in. The Oregon Land Conservation and Development Commission amended its urbanization goal in 1992 to require metropolitan Portland and some smaller urban areas throughout the state to create urban reserves adjacent to their UGBs. The urban reserves will include land that is currently used for small-acreage homesites pursuant to exception decisions made during the 1970s and early 1980s. The fear is that hundreds of small-acreage homesites encircling the UGB may prevent efficient UGB expansion when the need comes to increase the supply of buildable land. The urban reserves will be managed in such a way as to prevent low-density development that could preempt efficient UGB expansion.

Shadow Platting. In rural areas outside of urban service boundaries or urban growth boundaries, land that is not designated for exclusive resource use typically is allowed to be developed at densities ranging from two- to ten-acre lots. Such development is inefficient and severely constrains efficient urban expansion when needed to accommodate future urban development needs. One solution is to require *shadow* or *concept* plats of land outside urban service limits and especially of land within long-term urban growth boundaries or in urban reserve areas. A shadow plat is a proposed subdivision scheme showing prospective future lots consistent with anticipated future subdivision and density requirements. The homesite for a single residence is located on one of these lots. The shadow plat becomes a formal record of the local planning office and is used to guide review of future subdivision. Ideally, shadow platting should be undertaken at a scale involving more than 80 to 100 acres, which will normally involve all landowners in a particular area. At such a scale, shadow plats can lead to more efficient urban expansion when the time comes.

Zoning Approaches

Zoning is an important factor in growth management. Three of the most important uses of zoning are reviewed here, although there are certainly more forms and variations of zoning tools that are available for local use.

Upzoning/Downzoning. One of the principal outcomes of urban containment policies is the reallocation of land to achieve particular results. For example, if certain rural lands are intended to be used for farming and forestry but are zoned for one-, two-, five-, or even ten-acre minimum lot sizes, their ultimate use will not be farming or forestry but rather small-acreage homesites. The result is sprawl (Daniels 1986). Such lands should be downzoned to exclusive farm and forest uses with minimum lot sizes ranging from twenty to several hundred acres. This was done throughout Oregon during the 1970s and early 1980s. Some downzoning is also occurring in Florida.

On the other hand, urban land may be zoned in such a manner as to prevent more dense or intense development patterns. If a growth management scheme aims to limit the use of rural land for rural and resource activities, the regional demand for urban development must be accommodated in urban areas. Thus, upzoning must occur. This also occurred throughout Oregon during the 1970s and

1980s. Florida urban areas are also undergoing some upzoning.

Nontransitional Zoning. Many communities employ transitional zoning to buffer land-use activities from each other and to facilitate a concentric-ring urban form wherein uses farther away are at lower densities than closer in. Transitional zoning is not generally compatible with growth management, however. The result of transitional zoning is that low- and very-low-density land uses expand into rural areas and into resource lands, thereby perpetuating urban sprawl and undermining the long-term economic viability of resource production. Instead, growth management programs tend to employ nontransitional zoning strategies that, among other things:

• establish moderate to high-density and -intensity land-use categories throughout much of the urban area.

• facilitate nodal development especially along transit routes and major multimodal intersections that are themselves surrounded by moderate to high-density zoning.

• greatly reduce the scale of low and very low urban densities within urban areas.

• eliminate low- and very-low-density development in areas that are predominantly resource lands or other environmentally sensitive lands.

• restrict the size and location of low- and very-low-density development outside urban containment boundaries and away from resource or environmentally sensitive lands.

Oregon is perhaps the best-known example of the explicit attempt to use nontransitional zoning on a statewide basis. Florida's department of community affairs uses the presence of transitional zoning as one indicator of local planning policies that may not discourage the proliferation of urban sprawl. With few exceptions, nontransitional zoning has not yet become a substantial part of state and local growth management efforts.

Exclusive Use Zoning. Although the idea of exclusive use zoning was discussed in Chapter 3 in the context of resource lands, it applies as well to many other land uses. Traditional Euclidian zoning—so called after the U.S. Supreme Court's decision upholding zoning of the sort challenged in *City of Euclid, Ohio* v. *Ambler Realty Company*—involves a pyramid land-use scheme. At the top of the pyramid is residential land use; land zoned for residential is restricted to residential uses. Commercial zoning allows commercial and residential uses. Industrial zoning allows industrial, commercial, and residential land uses. Agricultural zoning allows all land uses. The problem is that many land uses allowed in some zones are incompatible with the primary purpose of that zone, such as a residential development in an industrial zone. The trend is now toward exclusive use zoning in which land is preserved for its primary purpose, or toward mixed-use zoning that results in mutually compatible land uses per se or is based on a design.

Inclusionary Zoning. Many communities use zoning strategies to exclude certain classes of residences such as low-income housing. A typical strategy is to zone the community for large lot sizes and large minimum floor areas. Low-income households will thus be unable to afford to live in the community. But many such schemes are considered unethical if not unconstitutional (Downs 1973). In New Jersey, the pioneering Mt. Laurel decisions require communities to avoid exclusionary zoning practices. Many communities now employ a variety of inclusionary zoning practices. They go beyond merely removing exclusionary barriers to require developments to have housing opportunities affordable to a wide range of households or contribute linkage fees to a fund to build such housing. The states of California, Florida, New Jersey, and Oregon require forms of inclusionary zoning in local plans.

Minimum Density Zoning. It is one thing to designate land for moderate to high density and give developers the impression that they have flexibility in meeting market demands; it is quite another to actually allow such densities. Unwary developers who propose high-density developments can get stalled in decision-making, often because existing residents oppose such developments (Advisory Commission on Regulatory Barriers to Affordable Housing 1991). Housing density is usually negotiated downward, but this defeats the purpose of growth management and urban containment policies. It also undermines the economical and efficient delivery of public facilities and services. Only the metropolitan Portland area has regulations in place that protect developers from this kind of behavior while also achieving administrative efficiency (see Chapter 9). Oregon administrative rules, promulgated by the land conservation and development commission, require all cities and counties (other than very small, mostly built-out cities) to designate sufficient land to allow for at least 50 percent of all new housing to be attached single-family or multifamily housing. The LCDC's Metropolitan Housing Rule specifically requires of local governments in metropolitan Portland:

• for cities with projected populations of less than 8,000, the overall housing density must be at least six units per net developed acre by the year 2000.

• for two suburban counties (Clackamas and Washington) and cities with projected populations between 8,000 and 50,000, the overall housing density must be at least eight units per net developed acre by the year 2000.

• for the urban county (Multnomah) and cities over 50,000 population (including Beaverton, Gresham, and Portland), the overall housing density must be not less than ten units per net developed acre by the year 2000.

These targets can be met only by minimum density standards that are either used formally by regulation or informally in review processes. In addition, developers have strong legal bases for securing approvals for higher density housing developments. There is the implied threat that communities that fail to meet these targets will have more onerous standards imposed on them by state and regional agencies, if not the courts. Combined with nondiscretionary review standards and permitting deadlines (see Chapter 9), the Metropolitan Housing Rule, with its minimum density implications, streamlines the permitting process that in some other parts of the nation would be especially problematic.

Jobs-Housing Balance

In the 1980s, planners and policy analysts began to cite job dispersal as one of the chief contributors to traffic congestion and overburdened roadways (Cervero 1986: 389). By attempting to balance the number and types of jobs with the amount and cost of housing, jobs-housing balance strategies seek to promote geographic equilibrium between employment and employee housing. Jobs-housing balance programs have been included in this chapter because they are crucial to effecting efficient urban development patterns as part of an urban containment strategy. Failure to improve jobs-housing balance will result in inefficient development patterns and fundamentally undermine the very purpose of growth management to direct development where it is appropriate and away from areas where it is inappropriate. In order to be effective, jobs-housing balance programs must emphasize not only a balance between employment and housing, but, perhaps more importantly, a balance between work and housing that workers can afford. Strategies used to achieve the desired balance include mixed-use requirements, linkage programs, affordable housing density bonuses, and public-private partnerships. California is generally recognized as the leader in the job-housing balance push, and New Jersey's state plan will consciously pursue the idea over the next twenty years. In both states, the concern is not only with commuting patterns and their effects on traffic congestion, but also on the air-quality effects of increased travel distances in bumper-to-bumper traffic.

Sacramento County, California. The primary objective of Sacramento County's jobs-housing balance program is to achieve a 25 percent reduction in the average length of a commuter trip by limiting 80 percent of such trips to eight miles or less. The goal of the program, which began in the early 1980s, was to be achieved by permitting manufacturing projects in and near residential areas in exchange for a requirement that such developments include housing units. The county reports little progress toward the realization of its trip-length reduction goal. This failure is believed to be the result of the fact that most industrial projects taking advantage of the policy were phased in a manner that added job-generating uses first. The required housing component of development plans has been slow to come and in some cases has not been built at all (APA, November 1989).

Costa Mesa, California. Like Sacramento's program, Costa Mesa's approach to jobs-housing balance permits commercial and industrial projects to locate in areas designated for residential development if they include a housing component. The city relies on individual phasing agreements to ensure that a balance between residential and nonresidential development is achieved throughout the build-out period. One recent study of a commercial project subject to the city's jobs-housing balance requirements showed that 18 percent of the projects residents worked within walking distance of their homes. The study also showed that 22 percent of the residents worked within a one-mile radius and an additional 22 percent worked within an eight-mile radius of the project (APA, November 1989).

Southern California Association of Governments. In 1989, the Southern California Association of Governments (SCAG) and the South Coast Air Quality Management District introduced a plan that directs local governments to make steady progress toward a balance of jobs and housing. The plan establishes a number of commutesheds within the region that are designated as either job-rich or job-poor; it calls for the adoption of implementation measures that will redirect new jobs from job-rich to job-poor areas and redirect new housing to job-rich areas. According to SCAG estimates, marginal shifts in the distribution of job growth could reduce the region's traffic congestion by up to one-third (APA, November 1989).

Durham, Oregon. Jobs-housing balance is not just for large and complex cities. Durham, Oregon, located in the southwest quadrant of the metropolitan Portland, Oregon, area, has a year-2000 population projection of just 1,600. However, it has designed its commercial and industrial land uses in a manner consistent with regional occupational trends to provide enough job opportunities for all employed residents of the city. This does not mean that all city residents would work in the city, but rather that there is a balance of jobs and housing based on occupation so that the opportunity exists for many residents to live and work within the same one-and-one-half square mile area.

Infill and Redevelopment

Infill and redevelopment can be viewed as both a cause and an effect of urban containment. No matter what the original goal of the program, stringent urban containment programs may have the effect of channeling growth and development back into existing urban areas. Communities frustrated with the failures of previous infill and redevelopment programs, on the other hand, may view the adoption of an urban containment strategy as the only effective means of assuring real success with their downtown and blighted area redevelopment efforts.

By themselves, urban growth boundaries or urban service areas will not necessarily result in the most compact or efficient development patterns. In order for these urban containment strategies to be effective without resulting in excessive housing costs and premature expansion of urban areas, a positive program to encourage higher residential densities and infill and redevelopment is necessary. For example, the lack of a positive infill strategy in San Jose's urban growth boundary program contributed to that program's negative effect on housing costs (Landis 1986).

A key element of a positive infill strategy is the promotion of higher densities in new residential development. Higher densities are not only more cost-effective in terms of providing public services, but they result in lower housing costs, thus offsetting higher land costs that result from containment. Higher densities can be promoted in a number of ways. Comprehensive plans and zoning can set aside a fair share of multifamily, attached single-family, and small-lot housing. TDR programs or density bonuses can permit higher densities in receiving areas than would be possible under existing zoning. Minimum density standards and reduced lot sizes can be incorporated into comprehensive plans and zoning district regulations. Performance zoning permit systems can award points for higher density and affordable housing.

The redevelopment of older urban areas and infill of small tracts should be encouraged as part of a comprehensive urban containment program. For example, land assembly through public acquisition or condemnation may be necessary where ownership is fragmented or where land titles are clouded. Flexible zoning provisions can ease site design problems on small or irregularly shaped lots. Improvements to infrastructure may also be needed to support infill or higher density redevelopment. Finally, reduction or waiver of development fees, or other economic incentives, may help compensate for the higher costs of infill or redevelopment projects.

Boulder, Colorado. While Boulder's growth management program focused more on limiting the rate of growth than encouraging compact development, it did include strategies to encourage the provision of affordable housing that is a reasonably agressive infill program. The Boulder permit system awarded points for the provision of moderate-priced housing. In addition, Boulder required that at least 10 percent of the units in all residential developments be affordable to households of moderate income. Because of these provisions, Boulder's growth management system, while it reduced the production of moderate-priced detached units, resulted in a dramatic increase in affordable attached housing (Miller 1986).

Palm Beach County, Florida. In 1986, the Palm Beach County Housing Partnership, Inc. was created by the county commission to address the shortage of low- and moderate-

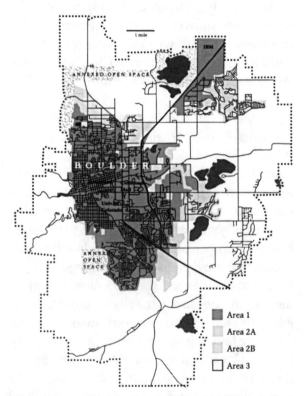

Figure 6–5. Boulder's urban growth boundary necessitated the adoption of infill development policies and guidelines to protect the character of the city's neighborhoods and commercial areas. *Source:* Dennis McClendon.

income housing in the county. The housing partnership is a nonprofit, public-private venture intended to promote infill and redevelopment in a "belt of blight" that runs through the county between Dixie Highway and I-95. It attracts start-up funds from various government and grant sources to buy land that is then offered to developers at reduced cost. Additional incentives include assistance in securing zoning changes, low-interest loans, and waiver of development fees (paid instead from other funds). Proceeds from land sales would be returned to the fund for future projects. The agency has used its authority to issue tax-exempt bonds to raise more than $30 million to develop multifamily units, new subdivision homes, and infill homes (York 1989: 260).

Urban Renewal, Missouri Style. Although there were many examples of urban-renewal abuse during the 1960s, today properly managed urban renewal is an important element of any growth management program. Simply stated, urban renewal facilitates the private redevelopment process to convert urban areas from lower to higher intensity uses. One of the impediments to efficient urban development is developers' inability to acquire sufficient amounts of land with adequate infrastructure to accommodate the market demand for higher intensity development. Although there are examples of successful efforts by developers to acquire entire neighborhoods, there are nearly always holdouts. The time it takes to acquire individual properties can pose problems. In many states, authorized urban renewal programs allow local governments to acquire land and buildings in blighted or underdeveloped areas, vacate streets and replat the land, install infrastructure, and market the package to private developers. The local government and developer will typically negotiate terms of lease or sale; taxes and fees to be paid during and after development; and the scale, phasing, and mix of development to occur.

Missouri uses a unique urban renewal approach. Under the state's urban renewal act, the city extends to a developer the city's power of eminent domain, which the developer then exercises to expedite land acquisition and development. The program works as follows: A developer approaches a city with a proposal to declare a section of the city a redevelopment area. The developer typically will have already prepared preliminary plans, market studies, and financial plans. The city then evaluates the proposed redevelopment plan against existing city planning policies and statutory criteria. Through negotiations between the city, the developer, and interested parties within the redevelopment area, a deal is struck. When approved, the city then extends to the developer the power of eminent domain. For its part, the city may commit to infrastructure financing and some long-term financing of certain elements of the development scheme. The result is an expedited land acquisition and redevelopment process that relies on the private sector to fulfill public policy. It has been used extensively in the cities of St. Louis and Kansas City.

Neighborhood Conservation

One of the most significant impediments to infill and redevelopment programs and urban containment efforts often comes in the form of political opposition from neighborhood residents who object to higher density development in or near existing neighborhoods. This was one of the major reasons that Sacramento County failed to achieve its infill goals. In some cases, state mandates, such as those used in Oregon, may be necessary to overcome local government resistance to infill and redevelopment activities.

Careful design of infill development standards to prevent excessive densities in close proximity to existing low-density developments, as well as to ensure the involvement of existing residents and community groups in planning for higher density infill, can also help to overcome community resistance to redevelopment activity. These and other types of neighborhood conservation programs have been used in communities seeking to implement infill and containment strategies.

Austin, Texas. Austin's neighborhood conservation program is implemented through special provisions in the city's zoning ordinance. The principal tools are compatibility standards and neighborhood conservation overlay districts. The city's compatibility standards are intended to ameliorate the negative land-use impacts associated with the location of higher density development near existing single-family areas. The compatibility standards impose setback, height, and buffer requirements on multifamily and nonresidential developments located within 540 feet of existing or approved single-family neighborhoods. General design and traffic impact provisions are also included in the standards.

While compatibility standards apply citywide, Austin's neighborhood conservation overlay district program is applied to older inner-city neighborhoods upon the request of neighborhood groups. Professional planning assistance is provided to those neighborhoods wishing to develop conservation plans. After development and adoption of a neighborhood plan, special zoning provisions may be put in place. The zoning requirements established as part of the neighborhood conservation process override the standard requirements that apply throughout the community. And unlike traditional overlay districts, the provisions may be less restrictive than those applied elsewhere. This has resulted in very specific design and development requirements that are applied in exchange for permitting uses within neighborhoods that would otherwise not be allowed.

Minneapolis, Minnesota. One of the impediments to urban containment is that older housing stock is occupied by empty-nesters who do not want to sell their homes and move out of their neighborhoods. Schools in the older urban areas become underused and expensive to operate, while new schools have to be built in newer areas. The result is frustration of efforts to revitalize older areas. Minneapolis addresses this problem in a unique way. It facilitates the construction of retirement homes and elderly-care facilities in older neighborhoods so that empty-nesters can sell their homes to young families (or to their own children) and move into smaller living units within the same neighborhood.

New Communities

Urban growth management policies should address the role of new communities—including variations on the concept such as new towns, neighborhood units, large planned unit developments, and neotraditional developments—in managing regional urban development patterns. Within a growth management context, new communities

• are developed under a comprehensive scheme controlling the timing, scale, and design of a long-term development process leading to build-out.

• follow principles of urban design including balanced land uses and specified population densities and nonresidential intensities.

• offer scale economies and fiscal viabilities for both the community and the host local government(s).

• have or achieve geographic and social identity

• provide a full housing mix; a primary employment and commercial base; and a full range of public facilities, community services, and cultural amenities.

• provide for local government and citizen participation throughout the development period.

There is no precise meaning of the term "new community." One definition is used by U.S. government agencies (Advisory Commission on Intergovernment Relations 1968: 64).

"[New] communities" are large-scale developments constructed under single or unified management, following a fairly precise, inclusive plan and including different types of housing, commercial and cultural facilities, and amenities sufficient to serve the residents of the community. They may provide land for industry or are accessible to industry, offer other types of employment opportunities, and may eventually achieve a considerable measure of self-sufficiency.

In the 1960s, new towns and communities were viewed as necessary to better manage urban sprawl and also to divert attention away from the many failures of urban renewal. The New Communities Act of 1968 underwrote development and financing costs up to 80 percent of the value of developed land or 75 percent of the value of the land before development plus 90 percent of the cost of development. New communities built under this act included Jonathan, Minnesota; St. Charles Communities, Maryland; and Park Forest South, Illinois.

The Urban Growth and New Community Development Act of 1970 significantly increased federal incentives to stimulate new community development. These included loans to cover interest charges on new community development debt for up to the first fifteen years; below market interest; supplemental grants (grants over and above those typically available for a particular type of facility) for federal aid programs to provide open space, water, and sewer facilities; and supplemental grants for urban mass-transit facilities, highway construction, airports, hospital and medical facilities, libraries, colleges, neighborhood centers, land and water recreation, urban beautification, and sewer treatment works. In addition to these capital grants, revenue grants would be made to public bodies responsible for providing certain essential public services to the residents of the new community during the initial development period. This would help during the time period before the area's tax revenues were sufficient to pay for educational, health, and safety services. Although about 100 applications were submitted for new community development assistance, only 13 private applications were approved for loan guarantees and other grants and assistance totaling about $372 million. In 1983, the framework for the national policy on new communities was repealed.

Federal involvement in new communities is largely considered a failure. However, the 1970 act did facilitate two famous American examples of new towns—Columbia, Maryland, and Reston, Virginia. These new towns are directly accessed by Washington, D.C.'s

Metrorail and, after thirty years of planning and development, can now be considered successes.

In recent years, the traditional neighborhood development (TND) has come to be viewed as a new community planning concept, even though it borrows features from ancient (preautomobile) town planning practices and organic (unplanned) town evolution (to borrow from cultural anthropology). It aims to create a sense of old northeastern or midwestern small town development. Elements include small streets, definable social places, moderate-density housing, and site planning allowing for easy pedestrian access. Interestingly, this is close to the neighborhood unit concept devised by Clarence Perry for the New York Regional Plan Commission (1929). The neighborhood unit would be home to about 3,000 to 4,000 persons and occupy 160 acres. Clarence Stein (1957) perfected this design; Radburn, New Jersey, was the result.

What distinguishes TNDs from Perry's 1929 concept? TNDs eliminate Perry's cul-de-sacs and result in higher intensity commercial centers as both shopping and social gathering places. TNDs also place greater emphasis on alleys, although Perry's design allowed for this as well. In theory, TNDs are less automobile-dependent than Perry's concept and are about twice as densely developed. While TNDs harken back to the preauto era, TNDs remain dependent on the automobile and autos are still allowed on streets and in garages. In order to achieve other objectives and still include some provision for autos, TNDs typically do not exceed ten units per net developed acre. TNDs merely reduce auto use but do not change the central premise of an auto-dependent design. This is the neighborhood unit design limitation as well.

The most promising reform to suburban community design may not be the TND but the pedestrian pocket (PP) (Kelbaugh 1989). In general, PP design doubles the density of the TND, emphasizes high-intensity commercial and employment nodes set amidst residential areas, and is consciously designed to fit into the larger urban context by being directly tied to the urban area by rail. Shopping, work, and leisure are all within easy walking distance. Commuting to major employment centers and high-level shopping is done by rail.

Types of New Communities. In practice, new communities fall neatly into four categories: self-contained, urban node, infill, and isolated resort.

Self-Contained. These new communities require about 3,000 or more acres. They are designed to be self-sufficient in terms of offering enough jobs, shopping, leisure, and housing opportunities for all residents. Miami Lakes, located north of Miami, Florida, built thirty years ago, is one such new community. Columbia, Maryland, and Reston, Virginia, are more recent examples. These communities are located within metropolitan areas and are most effective when linked to urban centers by rail and/or major highways.

Urban Node. Requiring 80 acres to 400 acres of land, these new communities are primarily residential and shopping areas with relatively little employment, although offices and business services are pursued. Residential density is about six to ten units per net developed acre. They are tied to rail lines either directly by locating near transit stations or indirectly by dedicated minibus service. Kentland in the Washington, D.C., area is one recent example. It is composed of 352 acres located in Loudoun County, Virginia, but it will be directly connected to Metrorail by the county Ride-On minibus service.

Urban Infill. These new communities are essentially high-intensity, mixed-use developments that nearly eliminate auto-dependency (although parking garages are found below grade). These communities can be built on as small as ten acres. Riverplace in Portland, Oregon, is an example of this type of community. It is an urban redevelopment and infill project on ten acres with more than 100 housing units, a hotel, several restaurants, and shops. In general, the urban infill new community can be located anywhere near or among downtowns, inner-city areas, and high employment centers. It can occupy land spaces of varying sizes.

Isolated Resort. These new communities are not intended to be residential communities but rather places for tourism and second-home use. One notable example is Seaside, Florida. It occupies eighty acres (including fourteen acres of beach) at a density of nine units per net developed acre. It retains auto dependency, but its scale allows tenants to move freely about the community.

General Criteria for Reviewing New Communities in a Growth Management Context. Some planners and developers misunderstand the role of new communities in the context of growth management. Sometimes, a developer will request a plan amendment or zone change to allow the development of a TND. Planners, not wanting to be viewed as standing in the way of a better way to do things, can be caught unprepared in evaluating properly the implications of the proposal in the context of growth management principles. It is for this reason that planners are advised to evaluate proposals for new communities for their consistency with growth

management principles. What follows are some criteria to guide this evaluation:

• Projections of population, housing, employment, and land-use needs that are prepared to justify a new community must be consistent with projections used by the local government. If the applicant for a new community relies on different projections, the local government must accept those projections before approving the new community. It must also revise its comprehensive plan to take into account the implications of different projections. This includes reassessing the capacity of existing land uses, land designated for urban development, and facilities and services to accommodate the revised projections. Further, such new communities should only be approved after the revised projections have been fully considered in the context of the existing plan's ability to be adjusted to reasonably accommodate the new projections. It must be proved that facility capacity exists or will exist to accommodate the revised projections.

• The location of the new community must be such that it will not alter the ultimate development pattern envisioned by the comprehensive plan. In particular, the new community cannot attract development away from areas where new investment is desired, such as downtowns and blighted neighborhoods; and the new community cannot introduce development that negatively impacts the integrity of nearby land uses, such as environmentally sensitive lands or commercially viable agricultural operations.

• The new community must not impede existing or anticipated capacity of local water and sewer services, roads, or other facilities in the accommodation of development that may otherwise be built closer in.

• Land-use patterns within the new community must not have the effect of increasing the supply of land otherwise allocated within the comprehensive plan for the community beyond that which is justified in the plan, unless the plan is revised to demonstrate that the additional supply is necessary at the new community location and during the time frame of buildout of the new community.

• Self-contained and isolated resort new communities are likely to have urban scale public facilities and services. Those facilities and services must not be allowed to extend beyond the projected development limits of such new communities; otherwise leapfrog or low-density contiguous urban sprawl will result. Moreover, such new communities must be connected to urban centers by limited access transportation systems so that there is no development between them and urban centers; otherwise radial urban sprawl will result.

• Isolated or self-contained new communities must be separated from nearby rural land uses. This is best accomplished by creating a large buffer around new communities. (Oregon requires a three-mile buffer.) The buffer should be an integral part of the new community, but it may be created through local government action. The buffer area must be sufficiently large and restricted in use to assure that the new community will remain isolated or self-contained, will not result in expanding the development limits of the new community, and will not adversely affect the present or future use of land in the region for natural resource, environmental, or open-space purposes.

PARTING COMMENTS

Unfortunately, we find that most cities and urban regions do not have the will to craft truly effective growth management plans that include the necessary urban containment component. Instead, inertia and the status quo rule the day as it is easier not to facilitate infill, redevelopment, and higher density mixed-use environments than to complain about declining tax bases, suburban flight, and urban sprawl. The techniques described in this chapter require courage and vision on behalf of public officials and the development community. These techniques require formation of a partnership between usually adversial interests: publicly elected officials, neighborhood preservationists, and developers. But when these interests merge to create growth management plans incorporating these techniques into a coherent vision, the benefits can be substantial. Downtowns become vital, neighborhoods retain if not improve their vitality as multidimensional residential communities, housing and employment opportunities are expanded, public facilities are more efficiently provided, local governments have greater fiscal capacity, and regionally important resources are preserved.

One of the main impediments to achieving urban containment and realizing its many benefits is the lack of regional cooperation, especially between central cities and their suburban neighbors. Central cities often view suburbs as robber barons, taking new investment away from them while, through a variety of exclusionary policies, leaving central cities with the region's most serious problems. Suburbs often view central cities as too large, impersonal, costly, and ineffectively managed. The trouble for suburbs is that they will face the same fate as central cities because of development cycles. As suburbs age, they decline much like central cities; but suburban decline can be more debilitating.

Despite their real or imagined shortcomings, central cities enjoy the many advantages associated with diversity of land uses, activities, and population. While parts of a central city may be in decline, other parts are being renewed. The same does not hold for suburbs, which are usually single-dimensional communities constructed during the same generation. When down cycles come, the entire suburb suffers.

Leinberger (1994) confirms these fears. He has found that many suburban "edge cities" are already beginning to suffer economic decline. With no real focal point, diversification of land uses and economic activity, and inefficient connections to much of the metropolitan area, many edge cities and their nearby suburbs are more vulnerable to down cycles than central cities. The trouble with suburbs, says Leinberger, is that "there is no there there."

The best solution is for central cities and suburban communities to work together to guide long-term regional urban development for the simple reason that if they do not work together, they will all suffer and perhaps many suburbs will, in the long term, suffer most despite any short term, seemingly intoxicating, gains.

7

Facility Planning, Adequacy and Timing

OVERVIEW

The regulation of land use and other development activities in the United States began in the early part of the twentieth century. Early efforts came primarily in the form of comprehensive planning and zoning controls; for nearly fifty years, the entire American land-use control experience revolved around those basic tools. Zoning and subdivision regulations did not, however, offer communities the ability to answer fundamental growth management questions—such as whether public facility capacities existed to absorb additional development and, if so, where that capacity existed within the community.

Clarkstown, New York, began to explore answers to those complex growth management and facility adequacy questions fairly early in the history of land-use regulation. The Clarkstown system, adopted in the early 1950s, imposed a requirement calling for basic public facilities to be in place before a development could be approved. The community's system was the model for the better-known system adopted by neighboring Ramapo nearly two decades later. Concerns about the adequacy of off-site public facilities increased greatly in the early 1970s for two

unrelated reasons. First, new federal water-quality laws resulted in the establishment of moratoria on the issuance of building permits in areas with overloaded treatment plants. Second, the impacts of rapid growth in some areas led to citizen uprisings against overcrowded schools, congested roadways, and other limitations on public services (Kelly 1993).

Not surprisingly, elected officials' interest in ensuring adequate provision of facilities and services stems as much from their keen understanding of the harsh political costs of allowing service levels to drop below locally acceptable levels as it does from a concern for public health, safety, and welfare. Few issues evoke the kinds of public outcry that accompany growth-induced traffic congestion and overburdened facilities. In some communities, such as Livermore, California, and Boulder, Colorado, growth limitations were adopted through citizen initiatives. In others, citizen concern prompted officials to adopt growth controls.

While the physical effects of growth most often dominate the headlines, the fiscal impacts of growth are equally important. Without adequate road, water, wastewater, and stormwater drainage systems, private development would be virtually impossible. Thus, most modern growth management programs must include policies designed to ensure the provision of adequate public facilities, as well as developer participation in funding the costs of new and expanded facilities needed to serve the new development. These techniques have obvious ties to sound growth management policy, and, in many cases, they represent the only possible means of accommodating new growth and development in an atmosphere of limited fiscal resources.

CATEGORIES OF SYSTEMS

Growth management systems vary in the degree of emphasis placed on the provision of adequate facilities. Local growth management programs in Florida, for example, rely more heavily on adequate public facility availability standards ("concurrency") than do programs in Oregon, where urban growth boundaries play a larger role. Growth management systems that emphasize public facility adequacy can be grouped into several categories: adequate public facilities standards, growth phasing systems, rate-of-growth systems, and carrying capacity systems. All attempt to balance the timing and amount of development with the capacity or willingness of a community to accommodate it.

Adequate public facilities standards require that, in addition to meeting applicable zoning and subdivision standards, new development demonstrate that facilities and services will be available to serve the project at the time that it comes on-line. Growth phasing systems are an attempt to address some of the shortcomings of performance-based adequate public facilities systems. Unlike adequate public facility requirements that are administered on a project-by-project basis,

growth phasing systems limit the amount of new development that can be approved over a certain period of time, typically one year. Rate-of-growth systems typically have annual development caps similar to growth phasing systems, but are less closely linked to public facility constraints. Finally, carrying capacity systems attempt to identify the upper capacity limits of the natural and built environment of a defined geographic area. These latter three techniques may be more properly characterized as "growth controls," since growth is limited or capped; growth management is more properly characterized as "growth accommodating." Nonetheless, these growth control techniques are important elements of an overall planning strategy for communities that have unique environmental limits or facility-capacity limits.

Adequate Public Facility Standards

Adequate public facilities standards require that, in addition to meeting applicable zoning and subdivision standards, new development demonstrate that facilities and services will be available to serve the project at the time that it comes on-line. Florida has adopted such a standard as state law and calls it concurrency management because it generally requires that needed facilities be available concurrently with impacts of the development.

Adequate public facilities controls are in one sense self-administering. A community adopts a level-of-service standard for each type of facility, and applications are denied if the service demands of a project cannot be accommodated at the adopted service level by existing or planned facilities. In practice, however, adequate public facilities systems are not nearly as simple as they might seem. If planned facilities are included in the capac-

Figure 7–1. Urban growth management programs attempt to provide adequate public facilities and services commensurate with development needs in a timely manner and in areas suitable for development. Here, urban expansion is facilitated by the installation of a regional wastewater trunk.

ity analysis, the timing of completion of those facilities must be related to the build-out of the project. On the demand side, development approvals must be tracked to estimate already committed capacity. Nonetheless, these are technical tasks and, once established, such systems can be administered with only periodic or perfunctory policy review, as in Broward County's highly automated traffic concurrency management system.

Known by a variety of names, concurrency and adequate public facility requirements are formal mechanisms used to enforce one of the most fundamental tenets of land-use planning—that development should not be permitted where it can not be adequately accommodated by critical public facilities and services. While land development regulations have historically been used as a means of ensuring that residents and end users of a development project can be adequately served

by community facilities, adequate public facility regulations go further, by ensuring that new development will not cause unacceptable reductions in service for existing area residents.

Due to the need for reliable data and the amount of monitoring required for the administration of adequate public facilities regulations, past efforts have generated limited service-level evaluation and enforcement programs. Recent innovations suggest, however, that adequate public facility programs and service-level maintenance requirements are becoming increasingly more common.

Florida. Under the provisions of Florida's concurrency doctrine, as set forth in its Local Government Comprehensive Planning and Land Development Regulation Act (chapter 163 of the Florida Statutes), cities and counties must adopt "adequate facilities" regulations requiring that all future development be served by infrastructure operating at or above adopted levels of service. According to the provisions of the act and its accompanying administrative rules (Florida Administrative Code chapters 9J-5 and 9J-24), no new development can be permitted unless it is first determined that public facilities are in place at the time they are needed to accommodate new development. Local governments are also prohibited from issuing development permits that would result "in a reduction in the level of services for the affected public facilities below the level of services provided in the comprehensive plan of the local government."

According to the Florida act, local governments may not issue development permits unless adequate public facilities for roads, water, wastewater, drainage, solid waste, parks, and, in more heavily urbanized areas, mass transit are available concurrent with the impacts of new development. The Florida Administrative Code sets forth the circumstances under which development permits may be issued:

• Adequate facilities are in place when development permit is issued.

• Adequate facilities are under construction when development permit is issued.

• Adequate facilities will be in place when development impact occurs, or adequate facilities are guaranteed in a development agreement.

State rules also allow transportation improvements called for in the five-year capital improvements program to be included in determining facility adequacy, if it can be demonstrated that the improvements will be available within three years of development permit issuance. (However, this requirement can be waived under special conditions.) For parks and recreation facilities, an additional one-year lag is permitted between the time of permit issuance and facility availability.

Florida's concurrency program has generated considerable controversy. A 1987 study indicated that the state needed to invest $53 billion in infrastructure improvements by the year 2000, but legislative actions, such as a $3 billion, five-year transportation appropriation in 1990, are falling far short of capital needs. While the system is not inherently growth limiting, the failure of the state government to adequately fund improvements to the state roadway network has lead to de facto development moratoria in some urban areas. Critics point out that the concurrency requirements, coupled with inadequate state funding for infrastructure, are encouraging development in rural and exurban areas where excess road capacity exists, contrary to state goals discouraging urban sprawl.

Broward County, Florida. Broward County has had adequate public facility (APF) regulations in place since 1981. Under the terms of the county's original program, development projects were required to demonstrate the adequacy of seventeen types of facilities. The original APF regulations amounted to a pay-and-play system under which permits were granted if the development paid impact fees or otherwise shouldered a proportionate share of the cost of system improvements needed to accommodate the development.

Broward County established its present concurrency management system in 1989 in response to the 1985 Local Government Comprehensive Planning and Land Development Regulation Act. Since the county's own APF system had been in place for ten years, compliance with the act simply required a few modifications to the existing system. The county land development code requires that an application for development approval comply with at least ten APF requirements. These include adequacy of regional roadway network, adequacy of major road rights-of-way, access to major and collector roads, surface water management, potable water supply, wastewater treatment, solid waste collection and disposal, regional and local parks, school sites and buildings, and fire and police protection. Inadequate roadways have historically posed the greatest practical constraint to new development in the county.

Under the Broward approach, applications for new development must satisfy two required determinations relating to the adequacy of regional roadways. First, they must meet concurrency standards within compact deferral areas (restricted trafficsheds that feed nearby overcapacity roadway links). Second, they must meet adequacy requirements (fee assessments) for all overcapacity systemwide roadways that will be affected by the proposed development. This essentially means that if a proposed development is located within one mile of an overcapacity roadway, it will not be approved until capacity is restored. If, on the other hand, it is not located near an overcapacity roadway, it may be permitted as long as an impact fee is paid to improve any overcapacity roadways that will be affected by the proposed development.

Traffic concurrency is measured by comparing the capacity of each roadway link on the regional network to the sum of current traffic on the road and projected traffic from approved but unbuilt development. If this total demand exceeds capacity, the roadway link is considered overcapacity, and a compact deferral area (CDA) is created. A CDA is an area extending for one mile on either side of an overcapacity roadway link, and for one-half mile beyond the end of the link. Within each CDA, no development permit can be issued for a project unless it is exempt from concurrency review. Moreover, a development permit will not be issued if a proposed development itself would create a CDA around the development site.

Development permits can be issued within a CDA only if it can be shown that (1) the project will not place any more traffic on the overcapacity roadway link creating the CDA; (2) the roadway link is not actually overcapacity (this requires a traffic engineering study); or (3) the property is vested. Projects that do not meet the criteria for permit issuance within a CDA have two options. They can wait until the overcapacity roadway link is improved or budgeted for improvement in the county's five-year capital improvements program, or they can propose and fund improvements to the county's transportation system that will mitigate the transportation impacts (on the overcapacity roadway link) associated with the proposed development. If mitigation is demonstrated prior to approval of the development, it is called a development agreement. If the application is denied, the subsequent study and mitigation proposal is called an action plan.

Broward County's traffic concurrency system introduces some degree of uncertainty into the development review process, because the status of roadway links changes frequently. Since a concurrency determination is not made until a final plat application is filed (at least six weeks after initiation of the platting process), new CDAs may be created during the plat review process that will affect the ultimate concurrency determination. The county publishes a monthly CDA map, but it is often out of date soon after its release. The maps provide a sharp illustration of the degree of the county's traffic problems. The April 1, 1994, map, for example, shows the majority of the county covered with CDAs. Roughly one-quarter of the area of the county not located within a CDA is in previously approved developments of regional impact, which are large-scale developments approved under state guidelines and exempt from traffic concurrency requirements. The Broward County approach is illustrated in Figure 7–2.

Transportation Demand Management. A variant of the adequate public facilities concept is transportation demand management (TDM), which is designed to increase the use of public transit, carpooling, bicycling, walking, and other modes of transportation that reduce single-occupant automobile commuting. TDM also encourages off-peak commuting and telecommuting. As a growth manage-

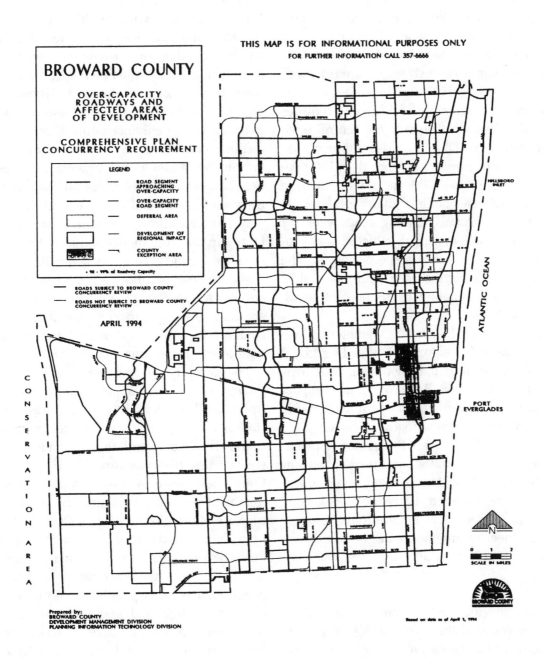

Figure 7–2.   Broward County, Florida, over-capacity roadways and affected areas of development. *Source:* Prepared by Broward County Development Management Division, Planning Information Technology Division.

ment tool, it increases the effective capacity of existing road networks, improves the economics of public transit, and facilitates higher intensity development in urban nodes and corridors. Some TDM strategies are reviewed below (Ferguson 1990).

Bellevue, Washington. Bellevue requires most developments outside the central business district (CBD) and all developments inside the CBD employing more than 150 people to engage in TDM incentives such as coordinating carpooling, giving preferential parking to carpools, paying employees for not using single-occupant vehicles, and providing guaranteed ride-home programs. The city hopes to increase the share of public transit and carpooling to 18 percent of all commute trips.

Minnetonka, Minnesota. Minnetonka requires TDM of developments exceeding 25,000 square feet or more than two peak-hour trips per 1,000 square feet. Based on a traffic impact study, the development must mitigate traffic impacts requiring new roadway capacity.

Pleasanton, California. Pleasanton hopes to reduce peak-hour traffic by at least 45 percent by the mid-1990s. All new and existing employers are required to reduce peak-hour traffic proportionately. Failure to make progress or meet requirements in good faith can result in a $250-per-day fine.

Growth Phasing

Growth-phasing systems are an attempt to address some of the shortcomings of performance-based adequate public facilities systems. Unlike adequate public facility requirements that are administered on a project-by-project basis, growth-phasing systems limit the amount of new development that can be approved over a certain period of time, typically one year.

Performance-based controls on public facilities work well with facilities such as arterial roadways, interceptor wastewater lines, and schools that serve particular regions and for which capacity must be measured in relationship to proximate demand. Through the addition of turning lanes, classroom additions, and other enhancements, these types of facilities can usually be expanded incrementally to serve new development. Some facilities, however, such as water and wastewater treatment plants and major commuter highways, serve entire communities and require large capital investments and long-term horizons to expand. Using such facilities as the basis for computation, some communities adopt growth-phasing systems designed to spread remaining capacity over the time period between the present and the probable date of facility expansion.

The capacity of a community to absorb growth is a measure that requires continual updating. The opening of a new mass-transit station, for example, may generate an increase in transit ridership and, thereby, an increase in surrounding highway capacity. The construction of new modules at water and wastewater treatment plans can dramatically increase the capacity of those facilities, as well. At the same time, the demand side of the capacity equation must be periodically reevaluated in light of new data. Dwelling units built in the 1980s did not contain as many people as the 1980 census might have suggested, and, consequently, water demand for such households was typically lower than anticipated. On the other hand, as the number of workers per household increased, peak-hour trips per dwelling unit in many areas increased significantly. For these and other reasons, the factors used to measure compliance with growth-phasing controls must be updated and reevaluated on a regular basis, even though the basic level of service standards by which conformance is measured remain unchanged.

Montgomery County, Maryland. Montgomery County uses a sophisticated and rather complex system to manage growth. The system includes an effective agricultural land preservation program, a coordinated set of functional and area master plans, and a sophisticated system of land development regulations. While recognizing the multifaceted nature of the existing program, the description here is limited to that part of the total system that deals with the capacity of public facilities to serve growth. Montgomery County's adequate public facilities ordinance (APFO) was added to the subdivision ordinance in 1973. Section 50-35(k) of the Montgomery County subdivision ordinance states:

> A preliminary plan of subdivision must not be approved unless the Planning Board determines that public facilities will be adequate to support and service the area of the proposed subdivision. . . . Public facilities and services to be examined for adequacy will include roads and public transportation facilities, sewerage and water service, schools, police stations, firehouses, and health clinics.

In recent years, the APFO has been implemented by a growth-phasing system. In 1986, the county council passed legislation requiring the planning board to prepare an annual growth policy (AGP) to be used as a guide in the board's implementation of the APFO. The AGP is adopted by the county council, on the recommendation of the planning board and county executive, before the beginning of each fiscal year. Among other things, the AGP must include

• current level of service conditions for major public facilities;

• an estimate of the service demands resulting from unbuilt but approved subdivisions (pipeline development); and

• recommended growth capacity (residential and employment) ceilings for each policy area, based on alternative scenarios of future public facility growth.

The AGP has become one of the county's real planning implementation workhorses. Besides relating the staging ceilings to factors closely tied to adequate public facilities, such as the capital improvements program and policies for promoting mass transit, the AGP has also been used as a tool to achieve land-use objectives outlined in sector plans, as well as jobs-housing balance and affordable housing goals. The focus of the AGP is the adoption of staging ceilings limiting the amount of new development that may be approved in each of twenty-two policy areas during the year. The amount of new development activity in new subdivisions is separated into two categories: residential, based on the number of dwelling units; and nonresidential, based on the number of jobs. This distinction allows the county to use the AGP as a tool to help achieve desired jobs-housing balance objectives. The council is also considering additional policy areas around some Metrorail stations. The major focus of the AGP has been on transportation facilities, although in some areas of the county, school capacities may be the primary constraint to growth. In other areas, staging ceilings may be set by the more restrictive limits included in adopted sector plans. For each policy area, one of six average roadway level-of-service (LOS) standards is adopted, based on availability of mass transit.

San Jose, California. San Jose has no formal citywide growth-phasing policy in place, although it has used such controls on an areawide basis since the early 1970s, when the area development policy was adopted. The only current use of the policy is in the Evergreen planning area on the city's east side, where a residential development permit allocation system is based on transportation capacity. Since there are no major employment centers within the Evergreen area (and none could realistically be developed under the city's land-use plan), it is believed that limits on residential development represent the only reliable means of ensuring adherence to adopted transportation LOS policies in the area. Available roadway capacity under the area development policy approach is determined after consideration of LOS standards, traffic counts, projected traffic from projects in the pipeline, and existing and planned transportation facilities. The overriding objective of the Evergreen area development policy is to maintain an average LOS rating of "D" for the six major screening intersections that bound the study area. Traffic impacts that are internal to the Evergreen area are addressed on a project-by-project basis during the development review process, at which time project impacts and any required mitigation measures, including impact fees, are identified by staff. To determine traffic capacity limits under the Evergreen policy, staff simply conducts annual traffic counts at all screening intersections and calculates LOS on a weighted-average basis.

The 1990 Evergreen area traffic analysis, for example, revealed that the weighted-average LOS at the six intersections was "D" (volume-to-capacity ratio [V/C] of 0.869). In order to provide an estimate of the maximum (theoretical) residential growth that could occur in the area while still maintaining an average LOS of "D," analyses for the six screening intersections were recomputed to identify the point at which LOS would drop to "E" (V/C = 0.899). The planning staff concluded that there was existing intersection capacity to serve an additional 830 residential allocation units within the area, over and above the 2,610 units given tentative approval in 1989. As a means of allocating the increased traffic capacity among proposed projects, new development requests are evaluated according to the following allocation criteria:

• The project contributes to an increased quality of development in the area.

• The project helps in balancing housing types and prices.

• The project can be implemented in a timely fashion.

• The project constitutes an infill site or completes a neighborhood.

• The project is served by existing or programmed public facilities.

While annual traffic analyses will continue to be conducted for the Evergreen area in the future, no further allocations will be available until such time as the city determines that intersection improvements or other factors have caused an increase in traffic capacity at the screening intersections. Two factors may help to explain why the area development policy concept has not been applied in other areas of the community: reliance on impact fees and other mitigation measures to address facility demands associated with new development and reliance on negotiated reviews and general LOS policies.

Westminster, Colorado. In 1977, Westminster, a northern suburb of Denver, adopted a long-term growth management program that limits the number of units for which building permits can be obtained to the number of service commitments held by the developer (one service commitment represents the immediate availability of water and wastewater service for one single-family dwelling unit). The number of new service commitments issued each year varies widely, depending on the availability of water and wastewater capacity. In times of capacity shortages, the system gives priority to the orderly completion of projects already underway, but it also allows for the initiation of new projects each year.

Westminster's growth-phasing system was designed to address capacity constraints in the community's water and wastewater systems that occurred in the late 1970s. In mid-1977, the city found that it had the capacity to serve only about 2,900 new dwelling units over the two and a half years before improvements would be completed to expand the wastewater system. The city had just issued 1,000 building permits for new dwelling units in the first quarter of the year, and estimated that an additional 28,000 dwelling units could be built in already approved subdivisions and PUDs. The city was also relying heavily on revenue from tap fees to help pay off its bonded indebtedness for previous water and wastewater improvements. Since the tap fees generated millions of dollars a year in revenues for the city, maintaining a steady rate of growth was a top priority for local officials. It was in this context that the city adopted its first growth management program. It was designed to phase development over the two and a half years that remained before new capacity would be available. The program established the number of water and wastewater service commitments that were to be granted each year. Both residential and non-residential developments are subject to the program.

Westminster's growth-phasing system does not involve estimates of pipeline development, since there are no exemptions and no building permits can be issued unless sufficient service commitments have been awarded to the project. Service commitments are, however, valid for up to two years and must be tracked. Despite the fact that parts of the community are served by two entirely separate sewage treatment systems (one belonging to the city and the other to a regional entity), the city decided not to establish annual service commitment allocations for geographic subareas. The centralized nature of the constraining facilities and the small size of the community may also have made location less important to Westminster's growth-phasing system.

Westminster's program accommodates other community goals with allocations for categories of project types and competition for those allocations within categories. Allocations to project categories give preference to projects already in progress and special categories such as affordable housing. Review criteria used to award allocations within categories give preference to projects completing line loops and critical collector roads. Those projects offering extra water conservation or otherwise helping the city to meet basic goals are given priority. In addition, the review criteria actively promote a diversification of the market—the addition of more jobs, an increase in shopping opportunities, and an increase in the variety of housing types. When the initial growth management program expired and was readopted in 1980, the criteria used for awarding service commitments in the competitive process were revised to place a greater emphasis on the design quality of projects.

Livermore, California. Livermore is located approximately fifty miles from the San Francisco Bay Area. Beginning in the 1950s, the city began to experience rapid population growth due to its emergence as a bedroom community for the larger Bay Area. By the 1970s Livermore was besieged by a host of growth-related problems. And in the mid-1970s, after passage of a slow-growth initiative and an EPA mandate to address growth-induced air quality problems, the city adopted its first growth management program. Until 1987, the foundation of Livermore's growth management program was a 2 percent annual growth rate cap. For most of that time the program was implemented by a fairly cumbersome points-based, competitive allocation system. In 1987, however, in response to difficulties associated with administering the system and widespread frustration with the program's constantly changing focus, the original growth management implementation system was replaced with a dramatically different approach.

Livermore's current growth-phasing system, known as the housing implementation program (HIP), involves three-year cycles of analysis and implementation. The first step in Livermore's three-year HIP cycle involves the planning staff's preparation of a background report that contains historical and technical analyses of the factors to be considered in the new HIP, such as water, wastewater, air quality, traffic, parks and open space, schools, and emergency services. The HIP preparation and adoption process takes about six months to complete and includes a detailed consideration of policy issues by a citizen committee, the planning commission, and city council.

While the Livermore system has not been driven by pure public facility adequacy concerns, difficult policy issues are addressed during the HIP adoption process. Those issues, however, are tackled within a growth management and community value context that can be characterized as slow growth, a context that is relatively intolerant of pay-as-you-grow philosophies. It is important to note, for example, that California's Proposition 13 virtually prohibits increases in property tax rates, which helps to explain some cities' reluctance to encourage growth that may require public expenditures to finance needed facility improvements. The Livermore system is illustrated in Table 7–1.

Table 7–1. Housing Implementation Program Priority Rankings, Livermore, California

Project Specific Review Ranking	HIP CATEGORIES		
	Reserved	Emphasized	Nonemphasized
Outstanding	1st Priority	4th Priority*	7th Priority*
Very good	2nd Priority	5th Priority*	8th Priority*
Good	3rd Priority	6th Priority*	9th Priority*
Average	**	**	**
Below average	**	**	**

*Not all emphasized projects must be granted allocations before nonemphasized projects in the same quality range.
**"Average" and "below average" projects do not normally receive any allocations even if units are left over after awarding allocations to "9th Priority" projects.

The HIP's growth-rate policy is its most important element. The city's general plan requires that the HIP's annual growth rate be set at from 1.5 percent to 3.5 percent. For the period from 1991 to 1993, the residential growth rate was set at 2.5 percent per year. Because small (less than four units) projects are exempt from the growth management program, actual growth typically exceeds adopted growth rates by 0.5 to 1 percent. The HIP's project-specific criteria are used as a means of ranking projects on the basis of site planning and design principles. Once a project's individual criteria have been evaluated, an overall ranking is assigned. Since project excellence is the goal, the process consists of evaluating the *overall* quality of a particular project, rather than simply adding up points or rankings in various areas. As a result of this big picture approach, a project that is extraordinarily successful in just a few categories could be ranked higher than a project that has good but not extraordinary performance in more categories. The following project-specific evaluation criteria are used:

• Siting (natural/unique features, grading, safety, compatibility)

• Street/lot layout (pattern, integration, pathways, layout, sensitivity)

• Open space (quantity, quality, access, facilities, integration, linkages)

• Landscaping (quantity, compatibility, integration, drought-tolerance)

• Architectural design (distinction, variety, scale, sensitivity, conformance)

• Solar access/energy efficiency (beyond state requirements, site design)

• Facility contributions (pedestrian, equestrian or bicycle trails, infrastructure)

• Innovation (distinguishing and unique design solutions)

• Location (infill, adequate facilities, environmental compatibility)

After staff reviews, projects are evaluated by elected and appointed officials during public hearings. While the lack of objective review criteria might suggest an approach that would be subject to criticism, the system has worked well. The system's know-it-when-we-see-it approach to design and project quality review has been praised by site planners, designers, and local public officials as being more flexible than systems that award points for specific project features.

Rate of Growth

Growth management systems that attempt to control the amount and rate of urban growth have been used primarily in communities experiencing very rapid growth and development. This section explores selected growth control strategies that have been employed as a means of slowing or reducing growth at the local level. Rate-of-growth systems typically have annual development caps similar to growth-phasing systems, but are less closely linked to public facility constraints. Despite some claims to the contrary, an analysis of the growth management systems of communities such as Boulder and Aspen, Colorado, and Petaluma, California, reveals that they were adopted with an eye toward locally desired rates of growth rather than on an analysis of facility availability. Facility adequacy may have been a consideration in determining desirable growth rates or in allocating development permits, but generally it was a secondary consideration.

Programs that seek to limit the amount and rate of growth within local areas might more appropriately be thought of as growth control, rather than growth management strategies. Growth management seeks to accommodate growth while directing the location and pattern of new development: growth control programs typically impose quantitative limits or quotas on residential and/or nonresidential development. Another distinguishing feature is that growth control systems can be adopted by communities with very little planning groundwork, while growth management programs almost always rest on a solid foundation of rational land-use, facility, and policy planning. Growth controls are usually applied where development pressures are so great that without controls congestion of facilities is imminent and costs of accommodating development in terms of facilities or pollution control are extraordinarily high.

Administering a rate-of-growth system is relatively simple. For example, Boulder computes the base number of dwelling units each year (based on the previous year's base plus new construction plus units in annexed areas) and multiplies it by 2 percent. In Aspen and Petaluma, the annual number does not change unless the fixed number of units is amended by the governing body. Consequently, unless a political decision is made to change underlying policy, such systems require no updating. When limits are placed on residential development, systems can have the effect of indirectly controlling the rate of population increase by sharply limiting the role of in-migration as a determinant of overall population change. The effects of nonresidential development caps or quota systems are less profound because they have little direct effect on the rate of population growth.

Development caps represent an attempt to set an absolute upper limit on development within a community or some portion of an area. Allocation systems, on the other hand, are a means of inducing phased or slower paced growth. Historically, caps and allocation systems have been enacted by communities experiencing rapid population growth and extreme development pressure. Many of the programs have been temporary, usually by design, and most have been used as a means of allowing communities to buy time for the development and adoption of more sophisticated and permanent growth management solutions, without resorting to outright building moratoria. Local officials in cities that have similar systems acknowledge that permit allocation systems tend to encourage developers to build large, expensive houses in order to generate greater profits. In an effort to mitigate potential exclusionary effects of allocation systems, some cities exempt low- and moderate-income housing altogether or set aside a percentage of available building permits for such projects. Table 7–2 compares development caps enacted by citizen referenda almost two decades and 3,000

Table 7–2. Development Caps, Boca Raton, Florida, and Seattle, Washington

	Boca Raton	Seattle
Problem	Rapid Growth	Tall Buildings
Action	Build-out Limits	Annual Limits
Adoption	1972	1989
Scope	Multifamily Citywide	Nonresidential Downtown
Enactment	Referendum	Referendum

miles apart in Boca Raton, Florida, and Seattle, Washington.

Boca Raton, Florida. In what is generally considered the first significant development cap measure to control growth, the city of Boca Raton adopted a population cap in 1972. The measure limited the total number of residential units that could ultimately be built within the community to 40,000 by reducing the number of multifamily units. Single-family units were exempted from this limitation. The cap was subsequently ruled invalid by the Florida courts largely because it was not based on rational planning studies. It is interesting to note, however, that several years later, the same Florida court (Fourth District Court of Appeals) ruled that a residential cap enacted by the nearby city of Hollywood for its North Beach area was legal and stated that, unlike Boca Raton, Hollywood did not follow an "Alice in Wonderland" approach in structuring its growth management controls. Hollywood's program was based upon detailed planning studies and was applied to all types of residential development, not just multifamily.

Seattle, Washington. Reacting to increasing urban growth and several new very tall structures (eleven over forty stories), Seattle citizens voted in 1989 to significantly restrict building heights and floor area ratios (FARs) within the downtown area and limit the overall amount of annual downtown construction. During the 1980s, office space in downtown Seattle doubled from about 13 million to 26 million square feet. The initiative imposed heights of 450 feet and maximum FARs of 14:1 in the primary downtown office area (permitted FARs had been 20:1). In the secondary downtown office area, height limits were set at 300 feet (down from 400 feet) and

FAR limits were rolled back to 10:1. In the downtown retail area, height limits were set at 85 feet (down from 240 feet) and FAR limits were cut in half from 12:1 to 6:1. An annual limit on total new floor space was also imposed as a result of the referendum. Through 1994, no more than 500,000 square feet of new downtown floor space could be built annually; from 1994 to 1999, the annual limit increases to 1 million square feet (Corr 1990).

Petaluma, California. The Petaluma residential growth control system is one of the best-known planning programs in the country. Petaluma is an exurban community in the San Francisco Bay Area. It became reasonably accessible to San Francisco commuters in 1956, when U.S. Highway 101 was widened. As housing prices in the Bay Area began to skyrocket, the community began to grow rapidly. The city had grown from around 10,000 people in 1950, to about 25,000 in 1970. It then experienced a rapid growth spurt, increasing by about 5,000 people (10 percent per year) in two years. Citizen concerns with the accelerating growth and its implications for their lifestyle led to widespread cries for adoption of growth controls by the late 1960s.

While the city was studying its growth control options, it first instituted a moratorium on rezonings and then on annexations. Both moratoria were adopted in early 1971. By mid-1971, the city had adopted new development policies that established a basis for a so-called environmental design plan. That plan then led to the adoption, one year later, of the city's first growth management ordinance. In 1972, Petaluma, California, established one of the nation's first growth allocation systems by imposing a limit of 500 residential building permits per year. Under the original scheme, the city held an annual competition to select development proposals to fill each year's quota for various city sectors and housing types. Borrowing from the next year's quota was allowed, as long as no more than 1,500 units were permitted within any three year period.

Under the current Petaluma system, housing projects compete with each other in two broad categories—public services and design/amenities. Under public services (worth a total of thirty points), projects receive up to five points each in various categories relating to the adequacy of public services. Under design and amenities (eighty points), projects receive up to ten points each for such qualities as architecture, bike paths, and infill development. The city council makes the final determinations on the award of development permits. There are exemptions for multifamily housing for the elderly, very-low and low-income units, and small projects. The small-project exemption applies to projects on less than five acres of land that contain less than thirty units, but the ordinance limits such a project to no more than fifteen units per year. Allotments to small projects are deducted from the available allocation pool for a future period through a borrowing process, but other exempt projects have no effect on the pool.

Although the system does not involve formal developer agreements, there is a provision that allows the city council to award reservations, which amount to advance allocations of dwelling units for the following year. The reservation provisions of the ordinance provide a developer with the opportunity to gain more certainty than would be possible with year-at-a-time allocations. The city is limited to granting a total of 250 reservations in any year. The annual growth limit was integrated with a capital improvements plan and revenue projections to finance it. As part of its growth management plan, Petaluma also adopted an urban limit line designed to limit the population of the city to 55,000 over the planning period. That stood in stark contrast to the city's own 1962 planning projection of 77,000 residents by 1985. The system was challenged in court almost immediately, and was struck down by the U.S. District Court. The Ninth Circuit Court of Appeals reversed the district court's decision.

Petaluma's was a first-generation growth management program, and it is really the only one that remains in effect in its original form today—even the number of residential units that can be constructed each year (500) remains the same as it was in 1972. Although the system was under great pressure in the early years, that pressure has not continued steadily; for instance, if the maximum 500 building permits had been issued each year, Petaluma's population would be approaching 65,000; instead its 1991 population was 43,500.

Boulder, Colorado. Boulder's residential growth control program is based on the Petaluma system. It is slightly more sophisticated than the Petaluma system in that it uses a 2 percent annual growth rate in residential units as the basis of its rate-of-growth concept, rather than the flat 500 units used by Petaluma. Although the Boulder system is not driven by adequate public facility concerns, it is part of a much larger (and longer) planning effort.

The city's first foray into the growth management arena occurred in 1958, when an imaginary "blue line" was drawn around the city at points averaging 400 feet above its 5,250-foot elevation. The blue line is some 100 feet below the city reservoir's mean water level and works to limit the provision of water service to an area below the line. Since Boulder's water flows from the mountains by means of gravity there was a very practical reason for limiting water service to lower elevations. The blue line also served the purpose of protecting the spectacular foothills from the clutter of development that might spoil the view from the city. The community took aggressive steps to control the water supply and eliminate competing providers, ensuring that no public water would be available in areas not served by the city. While the policy was effective in keeping development out of the mountains, it could not control growth on the lower elevations. Interest in planning and preserving the character of the community continued through the 1960s. In 1967, the community adopted a 1 percent sales tax, 40 percent of which was earmarked for open-space purchases and the rest for road improvements.

Over the years, the tax money has been used to acquire nearly 20,000 acres of open space, including a large greenbelt around the city. The open-space acquisition program was supplemented with another one-third-percent sales tax in 1989 that remains in effect today. At the beginning of the 1970s, the city tightened its land-use and annexation policies and adopted a policy requiring developers to pay for new public facilities. The city also entered into a joint planning agreement with Boulder County, resulting in the adoption of the Boulder Valley Comprehensive Plan in 1970. The Boulder Valley plan charted much of the basis for subsequent growth control efforts. Those included a charter amendment in 1971, imposing three tiers of height limits on areas of the city, and a 1972 agreement by the Chamber of Commerce to slow growth by curtailing

its industrial recruitment activities. Boulder adopted a separate ordinance in 1973, requiring construction of moderate-priced units. The ordinance required that no fewer than 10 percent of a project's units must be affordable by households of moderate income (Miller 1986).

It was the 1976 Danish plan, named for activist and council member Paul Danish and adopted by citizen initiative, that created the formal growth control framework in Boulder. The objective of that plan was to reduce the city's growth rate to a level below the 3 percent annual rate experienced in the early 1970s to the 1.5 percent to 2 percent range. In 1977, a growth management ordinance went into effect in Boulder that limited the number of new dwelling units to about 450 per year. The city's program worked by allowing competition among projects for the limited number of permits. The ordinance was structured to reward those projects built in the city's core and those that provided moderately priced and energy-efficient units. Twenty of the 100 points possible during the competition were available for the provision of moderate-priced housing.

Between 1977 and 1982, there were ten semiannual allocations under the plan. Competition in Boulder's periphery ranged from strong to mild, while competition in the core area of the city was nonexistent for five of the allocation periods. Whenever competition was intense, provision of moderate-priced housing made the difference between receipt of a full allocation and none at all. When competition was absent, fewer allocations for low-priced units were requested.

The Danish plan expired in 1982. A very similar program, adopted in 1985, remains in effect today. The 2 percent limit still applies.

The major change was the shift from a point rating system to a simple pro rata system. Under the 1985 ordinance, building permit allocation requests from each development are reduced proportionately to avoid exceeding the annual allocation. As a consequence of the city's move to a pro rata allocation system, the administration of the review process is now a simple mathematical exercise. The process is conducted quarterly, with application dates on the first days of February, May, August, and November. The calculation has been greatly simplified in recent years, because demand has been less than supply and no proration has been necessary.

Carrying Capacity

Carrying capacity is a term borrowed from the ecological sciences that describes the upper limit of population growth that can be supported within a particular area. Planning studies that use the carrying capacity concept fall into two categories—those directed toward developing land-use controls and those intended to provide regions with an early warning system concerning the cumulative impacts of population growth.

Because of its origins in the natural sciences, the term carrying capacity suggests an objectivity and precision that is not warranted by its use in planning. The notion of carrying capacity usually focuses on natural systems. Man-made systems, however, are also characterized by capacity limitations. Critical population thresholds can be identified that indicate when excess demand is being made on systems. Systems such as roadway networks, water and wastewater systems, and solid waste disposal, for example, can be particularly vulnerable to the increased demands caused by urban growth. Some studies also attempt to measure the capacity of social systems to withstand population growth, such as fiscal resources or school systems. As the particular systems analyzed become less physical, it is obviously more difficult to quantify capacity. Nevertheless, the concept provides a framework for analyzing resources of various kinds, and considers the impact of growth and its implications for future planning (Schneider 1978).

Sanibel, Florida.   The city of Sanibel is on a low-lying barrier island just off the western coast of Florida. In 1963, a 2.5-mile-long causeway was built, opening the island to development. The island was incorporated in 1974, and immediately set out to prepare a comprehensive plan. The planning process was based on Ian McHarg's environmental constraint mapping approach and is one of the earliest examples of applied carrying capacity planning. Based on environmental conditions, the character of the island, and existing and planned public services, the city determined that the ultimate number of residential and hotel dwellings on the island should be limited to between 7,000 and 9,000 units (Siemon 1989).

Chief among the limiting factors was hurricane evacuation, which was determined by the capacity of the causeway and bridge leading to the island and limited hurricane warning time. Other limiting factors included the island's roadway system, potable water sources, and a number of subjective quality of life measures. The city council reacted to the conclusions of the study by imposing a density limitation on development that ensured the population of the island would not exceed its carrying capacity. Supportable growth was then allocated throughout the island on the basis of environmental suitability and public facility availability. Limiting growth and development to an amount that did not exceed the carrying capacity of Sanibel's natural and built environments has helped to preserve the social, economic, and environmental character of Sanibel and has resulted in significant increases in land value. While the city's island geography provided an ideal setting for the application of carrying capacity analysis and while the analysis apparently did not address the potentially exclusionary effects of the growth limitation measures, Sanibel's experience illustrates the potential of the carrying capacity approach.

PARTING CONCERNS

Growth management systems are inherently growth-accommodating. Growth controls are used to deal with problems of short-term growth spurts or physical and facility constraints beyond the reasonable ability of some communities to manage. The problem with growth controls is their inherently exclusive tendency because of caps or quotas on development combined with uniquely attractive locations. Do these communities use their unique assets to foster exclusivity and shift regional burdens to other communities? In isolated communities, where (and how) do workers live who cannot afford to live where they work? Aspen and other Colorado mountain communities solve this problem by requiring that new developments provide housing for service workers or contribute money to a fund to build such housing. (Such housing has deed restrictions to preserve its availability to service workers.) Many communities have no such programs and as a result service workers must drive considerable distances to and from work. Some of these workers must live in substandard conditions to avoid unreasonably long commuting distances. In these cases, civic leaders and especially planners have a moral and ethical responsibility to find ways to accommodate a fair share of affordable housing for service workers within or near their communities, establish transportation services that connect service-worker neighborhoods to such communities, and in other ways find the means to fairly share the regional burden of accommodating the needs of lower income households.

8

Facility Financing

This chapter focuses on the financing and pricing of public facilities to accommodate growth. From the perspective of growth management, the choice of capital financing technique involves the issues of social equity and economic efficiency. Equity issues are related to how the costs of growth-related capital facilities are borne by new and existing residents. Efficiency issues concern whether charges to development reflect the actual costs to provide the facilities needed to serve them. The chapter begins with a review of the principles of efficient facility pricing and then reviews common approaches to facility financing.

Local governments regulate development to achieve certain outcomes that are in the general public interest. An obvious example is the need for public streets that line up with those of surrounding developments so that traffic can be accommodated safely and efficiently. Another example is the need for waste disposal facilities to guard against the spread of disease. In addition to its role as regulator of the development process, local government constructs and maintains the capital facilities necessary to support the development of land. Without adequate road, water, and wastewater systems, private development would not be possible.

The mutual interdependence between the private development process and the provision of public facilities is universally recog-

nized. Traditionally, however, the process of regulating and permitting new development has been divorced from the capital improvements budgeting process. The purpose of any financing program is to coordinate the development-permitting process with the provision of the capital facilities that will be necessary to serve the new development.

For most of the postwar period, the financing of facilities needed to sustain suburban development was heavily subsidized by the federal government with smaller amounts paid from locally collected, broad-based taxes. This has changed dramatically, especially since 1980. Now, the face of declining federal assistance and local voter opposition to tax and utility rate increases, cities and counties must turn to alternative techniques to finance growth-related capital facilities. These techniques include developer exactions, impact fees, special financing districts, and development taxes. Despite their differences, these funding techniques have a common theme: they shift the costs of new infrastructure from the general public to the new developments that create the need.

Still, it is important to remember that in financing facilities the method of financing involves a policy choice between two competing principles: ability-to-pay or benefit received. Taxation has a more advantageous effect on ability-to-pay, while user fees can promote more efficient allocation of resources. Since there is no clear way to compare these values, the appropriate balance between financing methods is a local policy decision. This chapter outlines a framework for such an evaluation and poses a range of financing options.

PRINCIPLES OF EFFICIENT FACILITY PRICING

Economic theory holds the view that efficient pricing of public facilities alone will make land-use patterns more efficient—thereby saving resource lands for resource uses and facilitating efficient urban development (Peiser 1989; Richardson and Gordon 1993). Frank's (1989a, 1989b) analysis, for example, demonstrates that it costs approximately $5,000 more per unit to provide capital facilities to a location ten miles from major central facilities than to a location five miles out (see Chapter 1). If public facilities were priced according to the costs of serving different locations, efficient development patterns would be encouraged.

The choice of facility financing method logically affects the pattern of urban development. For example, residential density and distance from a water or sewer treatment plant influences the costs of sewer facilities and services. If the true costs of providing water or sewer service are subsidized and new development does not pay its full share of those costs, inefficient development patterns will occur, characterized as urban sprawl.

Such average cost pricing occurs when local officials decide to charge everyone equally for the same service, regardless of the real cost to provide that service to a particular user. For example, sewer fees set on an average cost basis would charge connections to homes on one-acre lots five miles from the treatment plant the same amount as homes on 6,000-square-foot lots one mile from the plant. As a result of average cost pricing, outlying lower density developments are subsidized by closer in higher density developments. Urban sprawl is the result.

Table 8–1 illustrates this situation using actual figures from Loudoun County, Virginia. Notice that if all development is charged the same for service, some development pays

**Table 8–1. Annual Capital Facility and Service Delivery Costs
1,000 Housing Units Constructed at Different Densities, Loudoun County, Virginia**

Facility Cost Category	Rural Sprawl 1 du/5 acres	Rural Cluster 1 du/acre	Med. Density 2.67 du/acre	High Density 4.5 du/acre
Costs that vary with density	$4,052	$3,609	$2,621	$2,555
School operating costs	3,046	3,046	2,256	2,256
School transportation costs	187	153	67	33
Road maintenance costs	110	55	38	26
Water, sewer operating costs	709	355	260	240
Costs that do not vary with density	908	908	908	908
Public schools capital costs	243	243	243	243
Law enforcement	165	165	165	165
Fire/rescue services	58	58	58	58
Health/welfare services	295	295	295	295
General administration	147	147	147	147
Total Annual Costs	$4,960	$4,517	$3,529	$3,463

Note: Prototypical communities of 1,000 units each housing 3,260 people with 1,200 students.
Source: Smythe and Laidlaw: *Density Related Capital Costs* (The American Farmland Trust, 1984).

more for service and subsidizes other development. If subsidized development is occupied by households that are more affluent than development being overcharged, an inequity is created. Unfortunately, Loudoun County is not an isolated example of this kind of inefficiency and inequity.

Public finance economists advocate marginal cost pricing in the form of a three-part tariff as an alternative to average cost pricing. One part of the tariff would be a charge for the costs of the capital facility used to produce the good, such as the cost of building a water or sewer treatment plant. The charge is a flat fee per connection since the charge does not vary by density or distance, although the charge may vary by size of connection to reflect approximate variation in treatment-plant capacity that must be reserved for that use.

The second part of the tariff is a charge for the costs of delivering the service, such as the cost of extending sewer lines to the house. It is a flat rate per house based on the average cost of extending a sewer line to that and other homes in the same subdivision. The longer the line and the lower the density, the higher the charge.

The third part of the tariff is a charge for actual use based on the short-run costs of producing the service. It is a charge on the per-unit cost of providing potable water or processing sewerage. It could be based on the volume of sewerage passing out of the home and into the sewer line. More typically, it is based partly on the volume of water passing through a water meter into the home.

Planners argue that urban sprawl could be substantially reduced if facility use was charged based on the three-part tariff. More-distant and less-dense development would

only occur if its expected benefits to both developers and purchasers exceeded its additional or marginal costs to the public. Developers would not build and purchasers would not buy homes in inefficient developments since the charges would price such development out of the market. In theory, the primary task of planners is simply to determine the location of central facilities such as water and sewer plants and then price their use according to the three-part tariff. The market would then dictate appropriate land-use patterns. Although this discussion is simplistic, it does convey that marginal cost pricing can force developers and consumers to take account of all the fiscal costs and benefits of development before they try to have their plans approved.

Obstacles to Marginal Cost Pricing

Why is marginal cost pricing not being used? There are two primary obstacles. First, it is much more difficult a technical task to create marginal cost pricing systems. In a perfect situation, the marginal costs of each development and the characteristics of each facility used by each tenant would be calibrated and assessed. In practice, this is beyond the technical capacities of most local governments. A practical solution is calculating marginal costs by area, such as for neighborhoods or sewerage drainage basins.

One reason why communities choose not to employ marginal cost pricing is that they do not want to discriminate among members of the community. For example, if pricing is based on geographic service areas, boundary lines must be drawn, and it is often difficult to convince people near the boundary that their cost of service is significantly higher than their neighbor's on the other side of the line.

Many communities apply only a flat charge for residential water, no matter how far away a residence is from the supply source nor how much water is consumed. Such policy is fair on its face; all residents have equal access to the facility and are free to consume what they need. In such communities, it does not matter that some may use more or less than others. It also is the situation that in most communities taxes on commercial and industrial enterprises subsidize residential services. Marginal pricing would mean sharing this subsidy with new residents, thereby reducing the welfare of existing residents. Thus, technical, political, and social welfare considerations make average cost pricing the preferred financing approach.

Criteria for Selecting the Appropriate Facility Financing Mechanism

Because of dramatically changing times, local governments are increasingly looking for alternatives to average cost pricing. Here we discuss the criteria that should be used to determine the appropriate method of financing specific facilities and services. The criteria include marginal cost, scale economy, externality, price elasticity of demand, and administrative efficiency characteristics of specific facilities. We base our discussion on that offered by the City of Loveland, Colorado (1983), Lee (1988), and Fisher (1988).

Marginal Cost. The demand for facilities grows over time as a result of population increase and changing community preferences. Most capital facilities are added incrementally. It is not possible to construct one and one-half swimming pools or three and one-third fire stations. As a result, even if all capital improvements were made in a prudent and timely manner, the community will usually have either excess or deficient capacity of a particular facility at any point in time.

Certain services are likely to be more subject to this problem than others. For example, there may be only one library but thirty police officers. The relative impact of adding one new library is greater than adding one police officer. The library is more prone to excess or deficient capacity than the police department. Further, deficient capacity might be reflected in crowding or congestion of existing facilities.

Police service may require incremental additions to capital stock in the form of vehicles and equipment. New development needing one more officer than is presently serving may be assessed a fee to pay for the incremental capital cost. But what if the library is at capacity? Is the next new development project assessed the full cost of building a new library? This is a problem of lumpy investments. Whereas some facilities can be expanded incrementally, approximating smoothly linear increases in size, other facilities are lumpy and can only be built once in a great while. Examples of capital facilities that may be expanded incrementally include local roads, neighborhood parks, police, fire, and emergency medical—excepting of course for construction of new precinct headquarters or fire stations. Examples of facilities with lumpy investment characteristics include water and sewer plants (but not mains), schools, libraries, major roads, and major parks.

The financing of facilities with lumpy investment characteristics is best done through long-run marginal cost pricing. That is, the current cost of constructing facilities needed in the future is estimated but the cost is spread among all future users and not just the first new development needing access to that facility. For such facilities, average per-unit costs approximate long-run marginal costs. This average cost remains constant over different population levels.

Economies of Scale and Service Areas. Most facilities have efficient service areas. That is, a particular facility may be constructed and operated at least cost, provided it serves a particular geographic area at certain levels. Sewer systems typically operate at least cost within the same drainage basin. Fire stations operate at least cost if distributed roughly evenly across the community. Everyone within a service area mutually benefits, at least cost, from facilities designed to serve just that area.

For some facilities, service areas may be relatively arbitrary and are essentially designed to satisfy political or administrative criteria. Yet, if a facility is built to serve more people than will locate in the service area, the facility costs more money to maintain and operate than is efficient. More people might somehow be added to the service area, but this could cause congestion of other facilities. On the other hand, a facility built too small to serve all people that live within a service area may need to be replaced with a larger facility over time, or may become overused (congested). In either case, people in the service area pay in the form of additional capital costs or higher maintenance and operation costs or congestion costs than would have been the case had the facility been officially designed for the service area to begin with.

For some facilities, the larger the service area, the lower the unit cost of facility construction and operation. This is generally the case with water, sewer, and power generation facilities. Sometimes these facilities take on characteristics of natural monopolies since the larger they become and the more people

they serve, the lower their costs. These kinds of facilities are usually most appropriately managed by government since, by their nature, the average cost never equals the marginal cost and thereby they do not generate sufficient revenue. Most other facilities do not have these problems.

Externalities and Service Areas. The problem with many facilities is that people other than those living within the service area may use them. This is called the free-rider problem. For example, a Detroit suburb attempted to charge nonresidents for park use, arguing that since residents paid for the park they ought to have exclusive use of it. A federal judge voided the policy. Service areas for libraries, parks, and even schools are difficult to prescribe since people living outside those areas may still use the facilities. This is a problem inherent in any attempt to define users without charging them directly for their use.

Fire stations may have service areas, but if one fire station is responding, then equipment from other fire stations is moved to that station to provide backup. The same applies to police stations. Service areas for roads are very difficult to prescribe. For many kinds of facilities, service areas may be nearly the entire community, or may extend beyond community boundaries.

Therein lies one of the theoretical contradictions of many forms of facility financing. If a service area can be clearly defined, as it would be in the case of water and sewer facilities, that area exclusively benefits from the service being delivered by the facilities. It is therefore prudent to charge residents of the service area their proportionate share of the capital costs of facilities they use. This cost may be paid by property taxes. Water and sewer facilities are typically built for the long term, with bonds retired by revenues generated by property in the service area. But where service areas are not exclusive, it is imprudent to charge residents of the service area for benefits enjoyed by nonresidents. User fees are one possibility.

Price Elasticity of Demand. One of the functions of any facility financing mechanism is to force new development to use facilities efficiently. Where the price elasticity of demand for a facility is high, the most appropriate pricing mechanism is a fee based on metered use. This will tend to improve the efficiency of facilities. For example, the price elasticity of gasoline is relatively high. In order to improve the efficiency of road use, one solution is to charge more for gasoline. European and Japanese governments use high gasoline taxes to achieve this objective.

When the price elasticity of demand for a facility is low, however, the choice of financing mechanism becomes less clear since facility use is not likely to change much by charging more or less for actual use. When the price elasticity of demand is zero, the facility can be financed entirely by such mechanisms as impact fees since everyone must use the facility in roughly equal amounts. Water and sewer facilities have relatively low price elasticities of demand at low levels of use, but relatively high price elasticities of demand at higher levels of use. Everyone must flush the toilet and consume water for sustenance, although volume of use may be made more efficient by metering at some level.

Many public facilities seem to have price elasticity of demand coefficients of less than 1.0 (Inman 1979), thus implying that at some level, such facilities are candidates for impact fees or similar forms of lump-sum financing. Roads and recreation facilities have price elasticities of demand approaching 1.0. These facilities may be financed at least in part through user fees and other charges based on actual use. Facilities with price elasticities of demand approaching zero include education, police and fire, and parks. These facilities are better candidates for some level of broad-based financing such as general taxation.

Equity Considerations. Most financing mechanisms have the property of being relatively equitable horizontally. That is, all development of the same size and kind is assessed the same, no matter who lives there or what their income is. Some financing mechanisms, however, may violate principles of vertical equity since lower value developments pay proportionately more in fees than higher value developments of comparable community impact. For example, water-use fees may discriminate against low-income households because their basic need for water is the same as for higher income households, but lower income households must pay proportionately more of their income for the same water.

Site-Specific or Extraordinary Costs. No financing scheme can anticipate all impacts of all projects everywhere in the community. There is always the need to allow site-specific examination of development proposals in order to identify extraordinary costs that must be borne by the development; otherwise it will be borne by the community. For example, street and traffic improvements on or near the site such as traffic lights and turn lanes are more directly affected by the potential development and are therefore subject to site-specific standards. Site-specific standards should only apply to basic types of improvements, such as streets.

Summarizing Desirability of Financing Characteristics. Table 8–2 summarizes the

Table 8–2. Summarizing the Financing Characteristics of Major Public Facilities

Facility	Marginal Cost	Scale Economy	Externality	Demand Elasticity	One-Time Fee Capital-Based Suitability	O & M Method
Sewer	Lumpy for Plant	Large	Exclusive	Relatively Low	Good	Meters
Water	Lumpy for plant	Large	Exclusive	Relatively Low	Good	Meters
Drainage	Lumpy for Plant	Large	Exclusive	Relatively Low	Good	Periodic Charges
Parks	Lumpy for Major Parks	Small	Nonexclusive	Relatively Low	Fair	General Taxes
Recreation Centers	Lumpy for Most	Small	Can be Exclusive	Moderate	Fair	User Fees & Taxes
Library	Lumpy	Small	Nonexclusive	Moderate (Except for Lending)	Fair	Taxes
Fire	Lumpy for Stations	Small	Nonexclusive	Moderate	Fair	Taxes
Police	Lumpy for Stations	Small	Nonexclusive	Moderate	Fair	Taxes
Emergency Medical	Lumpy for Stations	Small	Nonexclusive	Low	Fair	Taxes
Schools	Lumpy	Moderate	Nonexclusive	Low	Poor	Taxes
Colleges	Lumpy	Moderate	Nonexclusive	Moderate	Poor	Tuition
Highways	Lumpy for Arterials	Moderate	Nonexclusive	High	Fair	User Fees
Transit	Lumpy	High	Nonexclusive	High	Fair	User Fees

Source: Adapted from Lee (1988).

nature of facility financing in terms of marginal cost, scale economy, externality, and price elasticity of demand characteristics. We also include our own determination of whether each facility is a good, fair, or poor candidate for substantial capital financing by one-time fees such as connection fees or impact fees.

FINANCING TECHNIQUES

In this section we review the major alternative sources of capital financing for new facilities needed to accommodate new development.

The techniques fall into the two major categories of developer exactions and special assessment programs.

Developer Exactions

Developer exactions are generally defined as the private provision of resources to serve public infrastructure needs created by new development. They are usually made a condition for development approval. In some states, private contributions must be volunteered by the developer and are known as proffers.

In most communities, developers are required to construct at their own expense and dedicate to the local government all public improvements within a development that are designed to serve only that subdivision. These internal improvements, which must be constructed to standards set by the local government, typically include local streets, sidewalks, water distribution lines, wastewater collection mains, and storm sewers.

Clearly, however, the improvements within a development are only a part of the total public improvements that are needed or affected by a new development. Such off-site facilities as schools and parks typically serve residents of a number of different developments. Streets in new developments will always connect to a network of collector and arterial roads outside the development. Similarly, most developments tie into larger networks of water, wastewater, and stormwater systems.

Typical exactions include the dedication of park land, school sites, and road rights-of-way. In addition to the dedication of land, developers may be required to construct public facilities, such as widening the portion of a substandard street on which the development has frontage or installing a traffic signal at a nearby congested intersection. Exactions may also take the form of monetary contributions, such as fees in lieu of dedication or developer participation in a pro rata share of the cost of installing a traffic signal.

In general, exactions fall into four broad categories: mandatory land dedication requirements, negotiated exactions, impact or linkage fees, and development taxes. A major limitation common to the first two types of exactions is that they tend to address only those public improvements that are either on-site or in close proximity to the development. Such needs as congested roadway systems or overloaded treatment plants are generally beyond the power of an individual developer to address through such exaction processes, hence the rationale for impact fees, linkage fees, and development taxes.

Mandatory Dedication Requirements. Mandatory park or school dedication requirements with in-lieu fee provisions typically apply only to residential subdivisions and are based on the number of dwelling units proposed for the total site area. Land dedication usually is required at the subdivision stage of the development process.

Land-dedication exactions have the advantage of being closely related to on-site needs created by new development. They have a long history of use and are generally accepted as legitimate exercises of local police power. They treat all residential subdivisions similarly and are relatively simple to administer.

A major drawback, however, is that they only cover the cost of land and make no contribution toward the cost of new capital improvements required by new development. In addition, since they are generally administered through the subdivision ordinance, developments not requiring land subdivision, such as apartments or previously platted land, are often exempted from the requirements.

Negotiated Exactions. Monetary or in-kind exactions are generally the result of open-ended negotiations between the developer and the local government, rather than from the application of a previously defined methodology. They may be imposed at any stage of the development process, particularly during requests for regulatory approvals, such as zoning, special permits, or planned unit developments, where the local governing body has broad discretionary authority. Such exactions typically involve public improvements in close proximity to the development.

While negotiated exactions are standard procedure in many communities, they are tightly regulated in some states. In North Carolina and Virginia, for example, the state governments have authorized two kinds of zoning districts, general use districts and conditional use districts. Local governments cannot require developer contributions as a condition of granting general use zoning, and can accept proffers only when conditional use zoning is requested. In Virginia, jurisdictions outside of northern Virginia and the Eastern Shore that have not been expressly granted conditional zoning authority are severely limited by the types of proffers that may legally be accepted.

In comparison with land-dedication requirements, negotiated exactions have the advantage that they may cover the capital cost of public facilities in addition to land costs. Since such exactions are based on the specifics of an individual development proposal, they can address public-facility improvement needs, such as driveway turning lanes, that are directly related to the development.

The amount of private contributions that can be negotiated with proffer systems should not be underestimated. Fairfax County, Virginia, for example, raised $86 million from developers in only thirty months through such negotiations (ITE 1988). Generally, however, funds raised in this manner are earmarked for improvements that reflect the needs of individual developments rather than the total community.

Another drawback of negotiated exactions is that they lack the attributes of predictability and equity that gained park dedications their early and wide acceptance. The amount of the exaction may depend on accidents of geography, such as the amount of land owned by a developer that happens to correlate with right-of-way needs, or on the political or bargaining skill of the applicant. Small developments, although they may cumulatively result in the need for significant capital improvements, often escape such exaction requirements because individually they are not capable of making significant contributions. Negotiations are often time-consuming and expensive for both the developer and the local permitting authority. Roadway exactions, for example, may be based on a traffic impact study required for each major development project.

A 1994 U.S. Supreme Court case, *Dolan v. City of Tigard, Oregon,* changes some of the ground rules for negotiated exactions. In that situation, Tigard required the dedication of a floodplain and a bicycle pathway as a condition of a variance to expand an existing retail store that may have increased stormwater runoff. The Court held that in the absence of a relationship between the dedication requirement and the impacts of the store expansion, the requirement was a taking. The Court went on to require local governments to demonstrate a "rough proportionality" between a dedication or other exaction requirement and the impact of new development. The potential legal problem with negotiated exactions is considerably offset by formal impact fee programs, which are discussed next.

Impact Fees. Impact fees (also known as development impact fees, system development charges, and the capital expansion component of connection charges) are assessments levied on new development to help pay for the construction of off-site capital improve-

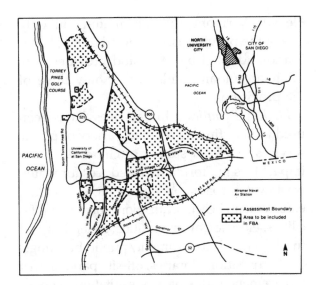

Figure 8–1. The North University Facility Benefits Assessment District was San Diego's first service area designed for impact fee financing. *Source:* Drawing courtesy of San Diego Department of Engineering and Development.

ments that benefit the contributing development. Impact fees are typically assessed using a fee schedule that sets forth the charge per dwelling unit or per 1,000 square feet of non-residential floor space. Impact fees are one-time, up-front charges, with the payment usually made at the time of development approval, although some jurisdictions allow extended payments over a period of years.

Unlike taxes, impact fees are a derivative of the police power and are a member of the regulatory family. Although eighteen states have thus far enacted specific enabling legislation authorizing impact fees, such fees generally have been legally defended as an exercise of local government's broad police power to protect the health, safety, and welfare of the community. The courts have gradually developed guidelines for constitutionally valid impact fees, based on a "ratio-

nal nexus" that must exist between the regulatory fee and the activity that is being regulated. The standards set by court cases generally require that an impact fee meet a three-part test:

1. The need for new facilities must be created by new development.

2. The amount of fee charged must not exceed a proportionate share of the cost to serve new development.

3. All fee revenues must be spent within a reasonable period of time and in proximity to the fee-paying development.

State Enabling Acts. Thus far, eighteen states have adopted impact fee enabling acts (see Table 8–3). Tennessee, North Carolina, and Hawaii have also adopted legislation authorizing impact fees in specific jurisdictions by special act. Texas was the first state to enact an impact fee enabling statute (SB 336) in 1987. While the Texas act resolved questions concerning the authority of its cities to use impact fees, it established complex procedural requirements. Most subsequent state

Table 8–3. State Impact Fee Enabling Acts

Texas	1987
Maine	1988
California	1989
Vermont	1989
Nevada	1989
Illinois*	1989
Virginia*	1990
West Virginia	1990
Washington	1990
Georgia	1990
Pennsylvania*	1991
Oregon	1991
Arizona	1991
New Hampshire	1991
Indiana	1991
Maryland	1992
Idaho	1992
New Mexico	1993

*Authorization for road fees only.

acts have streamlined such requirements, often based on the Georgia Development Impact Fee Act of 1990.

Conspicuously missing from the list of states with impact fee statutes is Florida, one of the states most closely associated with the rise of impact fees as a funding source. Although the Florida legislature has not adopted an impact fee act (primarily due to opposition from cities and counties), the Growth Management Act of 1985 sanctions the use of fees by including them in a list of recommended land-development regulatory techniques. In imposing impact fees, Florida cities and counties rely on home rule authority, the police power, and the extensive body of successful impact fee litigation.

Although no two state impact fee enabling acts are identical, all of them include a series of very similar technical provisions. These provisions generally relate to the following.

• Types of jurisdictions authorized to impose impact fees

• Types of development subject to impact fee assessment

• Types of facilities eligible for impact fee funding

• Rational nexus or reasonable relationship requirements

• Capital improvements plan (CIP)

• Level of service delivery

• System of tax and fee credits

• Exemptions

• Timing of fee payment or collection

• Separate interest-bearing account provisions

• Timing of fee refund

• Standardized methodology for fee calculation

Legislation in Idaho and Indiana addresses each of the above eleven provisions. Georgia,

Nevada, Vermont, and Washington omit only one of the provisions. On the other hand, legislation adopted by Maryland provides only minimal guidance, addressing only three of the provisions.

Eligible Facilities. Impact fees have been used to help finance a broad variety of public services. A recent survey of city and county impact fees in Florida reported fees for water, wastewater, roads, parks, fire protection, law enforcement, beach acquisition, correctional facilities, electric power facilities, general capital fund, general government/public buildings, land acquisition, libraries, off-site parking, tree replacement, rights-of-way, sanitation, schools, solid waste, streetlights, and stormwater drainage (Florida Advisory Council 1989).

In those states with impact fee enabling acts, the facilities that can be financed with impact fees are limited to those types of facilities specified in the statutes. All eighteen enabling acts authorize the use of impact fees for roads. Thirteen states permit water and wastewater fees, twelve allow stormwater fees, and eleven permit park fees. Fire and police impact fees are permitted in nine and eight states, respectively, and library and school fees are authorized in six. Solid waste, open space, and public buildings are allowed in five states. The impact fees authorized by these states are summarized in Table 8–4.

Benefits and Limitations. Impact fees are a conservative response to the notion that development should pay its own way. In some communities, impact fees are actually considered a progrowth tool because of their ability to defuse rising no-growth sentiments, ensure facility adequacy, and facilitate development approval. Payment of impact fees essentially establishes a contract between a developer and a local government. In return for the fee,

Table 8–4. Facilities Authorized under Impact Fee Enabling Acts

Facility	AZ	CA	GA	ID	IL	IN	ME	MD	NV	NH	NM	OR	PA	TX	VT	VA	WA	WV
Fire/EMS	✓	✓	✓	✓			✓			✓	✓				✓		✓	✓
Libraries	✓	✓	✓				✓			✓					✓			✓
Open Space	✓	✓	✓	✓			✓				✓				✓		✓	✓
Parks	✓	✓	✓	✓		✓	✓			✓	✓	✓			✓		✓	✓
Police	✓	✓	✓	✓			✓			✓	✓				✓			✓
Public Building	✓	✓					✓			✓					✓			✓
Roads	✓	✓	✓	✓	✓	✓	✓	✓	✓	✓	✓	✓	✓	✓	✓	✓	✓	✓
Schools	✓	✓					✓			✓					✓		✓	✓
Solid Waste	✓	✓					✓			✓					✓			✓
Stormwater	✓	✓	✓	✓		✓	✓	✓	✓	✓		✓		✓	✓			✓
Wastewater	✓	✓	✓	✓		✓	✓	✓	✓	✓	✓	✓		✓	✓			✓
Water	✓	✓	✓	✓		✓	✓	✓	✓	✓	✓	✓		✓	✓			✓

the local government promises to deliver public services.

Because they are typically used as a replacement for negotiated exactions, impact fees add speed and predictability to the development process. Impact fees are also more equitable than informal systems of negotiated exactions and are likely to generate considerably more revenue.

Impact fees can be used to fund a wider variety of services and types of facilities than is possible with exactions or special districts. Unlike dedication requirements that only cover land costs, impact fees can be used to cover the full capital cost of new facilities. Impact fees can also be structured to require new development to buy into service delivery systems with existing excess capacity, thus recouping prior public investments made in anticipation of growth demands. Recoupment of prior investments is generally not possible with other types of exactions.

Unlike many other financing options, impact fees can encourage efficient development patterns as well as raise revenue. Impact fee methodologies that reflect the actual cost of providing services based on location provide an incentive for development to locate in areas with already adequate facilities or where it is less costly to serve. Jurisdictions can use impact fees as a positive growth management tool by encouraging growth (through the use of lower fees) in areas already served by public facilities and discouraging growth (through the use of higher fees) in areas without infrastructure. San Diego is a leading example of this practice.

State enabling acts and court tests require a sound planning basis for impact fees, and impose a set of earmarking and accounting practices that limit the use of impact fee revenues to those facilities intended to be financed by the fees. The revenues from impact fees may not be used to pay for operating costs or to finance projects that relieve preexisting deficiencies not attributable to new development, although impact fee revenues can free other revenues previously used for eligible impact fee projects for such purposes. The requirement that impact fees be spent to benefit the fee-paying development is typically met by earmarking revenues for expenditure in the zone, district, or service area in which they are collected.

Some jurisdictions face initial problems in gaining developer and builder acceptance of impact fees. Problems have also occasionally arisen from technical difficulties associated with the newness of the technique, such as determining demand levels, calculating construction costs, establishing accurate fee levels, and keeping proper accounting records. Probably the most important limitation of impact fees, however, is that they cannot address existing infrastructure deficiencies. In other words, they are not a panacea for all local financing problems.

The primary strengths of impact fees include applicability to a wide range of public services, ability to promote efficient development patterns, predictability for both the public and private sectors, and acceptability due to a clear linkage with the needs of new development. Their limitations include inability to fund operating costs, lack of expenditure flexibility, dependence on construction cycles, and lack of bonding capability (since the fees are usually not a stable revenue source required by the bond market).

Facility Reservation Fees. An unusual variant on impact fees are facility reservation fees. Although calculated in the same manner as impact fees, reservation fees involve developers paying up front for their proportionate share of the cost of new or expanded facilities needed to serve their future developments. What is unusual is that such fees are paid sometimes years in advance of development permits and the facilities are built only when enough funds are collected.

The village of Chardon, Ohio, offers an example of how this program may be used. In 1995, Chardon had just under 5,000 residents but its sewer plant was at capacity. Growth projections called for another 4,000 residents

by about 2010. Since the plant was at capacity, Chardon faced issuing bonds for $10 million to double the existing plant capacity to accommodate new development. But bond debt service in early years would be paid only from higher rates assessed on an existing, smaller base of taxpayers. Impact fees assessed on new development to pay its proportionate share of the cost of plant expansion would eventually offset some but not all of the higher rates. Preliminary estimates showed that existing taxpayers would see up to a doubling of current rates used to retire debt solely to accommodate new development.

The solution considered was to have developers pay the city about $5,000 for every equivalent residential unit they wished to reserve in new system capacity to accommodate development plans several years into the future. A developer who decided not to exercise the reservations could sell or assign the reservations to other developers. Although developers would prefer to pay impact fees when building permits are issued, the village could hardly justify raising everyone's rates to retire wastewater bonds issued solely for the benefit of new development.

Linkage Fees. A variant of impact fees are linkage fees. Linkage is a form of development exaction requiring nonresidential development projects to contribute to the funding of affordable housing and other social programs, the need for which can be linked to the new development. Linkage works by requiring that a portion of the value created by private investments and development activity be redirected to provide affordable housing, day-care facilities or job training opportunities. During the 1980s, various forms of linkage programs were adopted in several cities in the northeastern United States

(Boston, New York, Chicago, Jersey City, Hartford, and Cambridge) and on the West Coast (San Francisco, San Diego, Santa Monica, and Sacramento). Linkage fees have been criticized from both sides. Housing advocates argue that the fees are too low to finance construction or rehabilitation of affordable housing. Business advocates argue that linkage fees discourage office construction. Nevertheless, linkage fees are growing in popularity.

Impact Taxes. A development impact tax, also called an improvement tax, is a tax on new construction, usually assessed at the time of application for a building permit. Impact taxes are generally based on the value of new improvements, and tend to be more popular than other kinds of taxes because they are levied on new construction rather than existing development. However, reroofing, remodeling, and alterations to existing structures are also subject to such a tax. Even in a high-growth community like San Jose, California, over one-third of total building permit valuation is for such remodeling activities.

Unlike impact fees, impact taxes need not be based on the cost of facilities needed to serve the development, and the special studies required to justify impact fees are not required. In addition, revenues from such taxes may be spent in any way the local jurisdiction sees fit, subject to the provisions of state enabling legislation.

However, impact taxes may be perceived as inequitable if the tax revenues are not earmarked to provide facilities necessitated by new development. In practice, such earmarking often occurs for political reasons, somewhat diluting the flexibility of revenue expenditures.

A further consideration is the constitutional question of taxation without representation, which can arise when a city attempts to impose development taxes outside its corporate limits but within its planning jurisdiction. This was a major factor in 1984 when the city of Raleigh, North Carolina, decided to seek authorization from the state legislature for impact fees rather than impact taxes.

California. In the 1960s, home rule cities in California became the first in the nation to assess impact taxes. Impact taxes are an exercise of the taxing power, rather than the police power from which impact fees derive their authority. Because of this, impact taxes must be specifically authorized by state law, and such general enabling legislation currently exists only in California and Arizona (Frank and Downing 1988). However, outside of these two states, impact taxes have been enacted with specific state enabling legislation.

Franklin, Tennessee. In 1988, Franklin, Tennessee, adopted an improvement tax, called a facilities tax, under a special 1987 state authorizing bill (HB 1308). Franklin was authorized to enact an excise tax on new development based on the size of new development improvements, rather than on the assessed value of the property. Taxes are paid at the time of the issuance of a building permit. The bill provides maximum tax rates of one dollar per gross square foot of new residential development and two dollars per gross square foot of new nonresidential development. Adoption of a capital improvements program that identified public facilities needed to serve new growth was required prior to imposition of the tax. Further, all tax proceeds were required to be used "for the purpose of providing public facilities, the need for which is reasonably related to new development."

Real Estate Transfer Taxes. Real estate transfer taxes are levied on real estate transactions. While impact taxes are generally based only on the value of new improvements, real estate transfer taxes are assessed on sales price, which includes the value of both land and improvements. As with all taxes, real estate transfer taxes cannot be adopted by local governments without state enabling legislation. Real estate transfer taxes are not dependent on new development, but rather on an active real estate market. Transfer tax revenues are more predictable than revenues from impact fees or exactions and hence more suitable for bond financing. On the other hand, transfer taxes lack the political appeal of impact fees.

San Jose, California. San Jose's real estate conveyance tax, adopted in 1972, assesses a value-added tax on every sale or transfer of real property. Revenues are earmarked for the acquisition and development of parks, libraries, fire stations, and emergency services. Under the current allocation formula, a minimum of 48 percent of conveyance tax revenues must be spent on parks within the district of origin; up to 16 percent may be expended on parks outside the district of origin; and a maximum of 36 percent can be spent for specified nonpark uses. The majority of San Jose's conveyance tax revenue results from turnover of developed property, rather than from new development (Schoennauer and MacRostie 1988).

Nantucket, Massachusetts. In 1983, Nantucket Island received special authorization from the Massachusetts legislature to collect a 2 percent tax on real estate transactions. Revenues are used by the Nantucket Land Bank to purchase environmentally sensitive land and ensure public access to the shoreline.

Even though 35 percent of all transactions are exempted, including divorce proceedings, inheritances, and the first $100,000 of first-time home purchases, the tax generated over $6 million during the first two and one-half years, a sizable sum for a small resort community with a peak season population of 35,000 (Klein 1986).

San Francisco, California. In 1981, San Francisco began to require developers of large office buildings (50,000 square feet or more) in the downtown business district to provide new or rehabilitated housing or pay a five-dollar-per-square-foot in-lieu fee. The Office-Housing Production Program did not require, however, that the housing provided by the program meet affordability guidelines. Between 1981 and 1985, developers committed to subsidize 3,793 residential units through the city's linkage program. In 1985, the city revised its linkage policy, adding require-

Figure 8–2. With 240 units, Centennial is one of the largest affordable housing developments in Aspen, Colorado. It is financed in part from linkage fees. *Source:* Photo © 1994 by Design Workshop, Inc.

ments for affordable housing. If developers built the housing themselves, 62 percent of the units had to be set aside for low- and moderate-income units. If developers paid an in-lieu fee (raised to $5.34 per square foot), then 100 percent of the units subsidized with the money had to be set aside for low- and moderate-income units (Keating 1986).

Boston, Massachusetts. Boston instituted its affordable housing linkage policy in December 1983 with an amendment to its zoning code. Under Boston's housing linkage law, developers of large commercial projects are required either to build affordable housing or contribute money to build such housing. This amount is calculated at five dollars for every square foot over 100,000 square feet. By 1990, developers had committed to pay over $76 million in housing linkage fees through the 1990s, with over $28 million in linkage fees already committed to create over 2,900 housing units, 80 percent of which were targeted for low- and moderate-income residents (Counts 1989: 1).

Jersey City, New Jersey. Jersey City developed an affordable housing linkage program in 1987 in response to both the New Jersey Fair Housing Act of 1985 and the community's lack of affordable housing for low- and moderate-income families. The program is voluntary and based on guidelines and incentives rather than ordinances. As with most linkage programs, it seeks to link market-rate housing and commercial and office development to the provision of inner-city affordable housing. There are three avenues available to developers under the program: they can build or rehabilitate housing, finance housing elsewhere in the city, or contribute to a housing trust fund. For residential projects, developers are asked to meet an across-the-board 10 percent set-aside for low- and moderate-income housing (APA, May 1987).

Special Assessment Programs

While developer exactions may be gaining popularity, they do have their limitations. Such exactions are only one-time assessments usually dedicated to capital improvements. As such, developer exactions have little relationship to maintenance and operating expenses, and they do not aid in the process of getting existing development to contribute its proportionate share of capital improvements. Special assessment techniques reviewed here help solve this problem. Many local governments will use both developer exactions and special assessment programs.

Special Districts. Special districts are geographic areas within which fees or taxes are collected (in addition to jurisdictionwide general taxes) to fund capital investments or special services that clearly benefit properties within the district. The distinctive feature of special districts is the very close and visible tie between the facility constructed or maintained and those who benefit from and pay for it. Unlike other financing options that target new development to pay for a share of communitywide improvements, special districts assess and tax all properties in a defined area, developed and undeveloped alike.

Special districts are attractive for a number of reasons. They shift the burden of infrastructure finance from the general public to properties receiving direct benefit, while avoiding the short-term time horizon of purely private infrastructure provision. Property owners are assured that their additional taxes or fees will be spent in a manner that will benefit them, with a more single-minded focus than is characteristic of general-purpose government activities.

There is a bewildering variety of special districts, with very little uniformity among different state enabling legislation. California alone has more than twenty different enabling acts authorizing various types of special districts. Special districts may be temporary creations of local government strictly designed to raise revenue for a specific improvement, or they may be independent special-purpose governmental entities. Assessments may be in the form of user fees or ad valorem taxes. Special districts may be within a local government's jurisdiction or they may cross jurisdictional boundaries. Most special districts are limited to one major facility that obviously benefits a distinct geographic area. Over 90 percent of all special districts perform only one function (U.S. Census 1992).

Most states permit the creation of special districts with the approval of the majority of property owners within the district. In most cases, once the district is created, participation is mandatory for all property owners. An exception is Colorado, which permits the creation of special districts with voluntary participation of property owners within the district.

Tax or fee assessments within special districts are based on attributes of property— such as property value, parcel size, street frontage, or use—assumed to be directly proportional to benefits accruing to property owners. However, the basis and level of assessments may vary within the district, depending on the needs of the district and the preferences of participating landowners. For example, the Elk Grove school district in the Sacramento, California, area proposed, although unsuccessfully, a special district to finance improvements to existing schools and construction of new schools, which would have assessed senior citizens only 30 percent

of the tax, and new homeowners two and one-half times the tax paid by existing residents (APA 1987: 1–2). In Denver, the benefits of a transit mall special district were assumed to be related not only to the size of the property, but also to proximity to the improvement, and thus zones of benefit were defined with different assessment rates for each zone (Apogee Research 1987: 32). These examples illustrate how the flexibility of special-district fee structures can be used to link charges very closely to benefits received from district improvements. However, it should be noted that complex assessment structures are more likely to generate controversy than uniform assessments.

In contrast to the temporary special-purpose districts just described, some special districts are quasi-governmental entities that have ongoing functions and are independent of local government. This type of special district has seen the most rapid growth of any governmental entity in the United States. Between 1962 and 1987, the number of special districts (excluding school districts) increased from 18,323 to 29,532, a rise of 61 percent (U.S. Census 1984). Most of the new districts, formed to provide such services as water supply, wastewater disposal, fire protection, and flood control, are in newly developing areas and independent of the general governments that spawned them.

Special districts have the ability to assess both existing development and vacant land in the immediate vicinity of the capital improvement. Particularly in special districts with a considerable amount of existing development, revenue streams are more predictable than those of impact fees, development taxes, and developer exactions, which are dependent on development cycles. One concrete advantage resulting from the greater predictability of the revenue stream is that bonds can be issued by pledging to levy assessments necessary to repay the bonds.

Once established to provide a single service, special districts usually operate outside the public spotlight that is focused in most communities on elected general governments. The proliferation of special districts can weaken the authority of general governments to deal effectively with growth and to govern in the comprehensive way that they should. For example, the North Carolina legislative provision that created the Research Triangle Special District, which provides services to that unincorporated area, will not allow the area within the district to be annexed, even if annexation and integration into municipal facilities might be more economically efficient (Miller 1987: 8). Widespread use of such districts can create a confusing hodgepodge of overlapping, independent taxing jurisdictions that lack the visibility and accountability, as well as the ability to coordinate different activities, that characterize general-purpose governmental entities.

Special districts also can be abused if there are not built-in procedures and safeguards. In some cases, developers can use special districts to finance internal improvements that lower initial prices in their development, while the costs of infrastructure or special amenities show up later in the form of higher tax bills. If assessments are based on the value of improvements, early developers may bear an excessive burden. If such disparities are accompanied by recession, assessment levels may force some landowners, or even the district itself, into bankruptcy.

Due to the diversity of special district approaches, generalizations about this flexible

technique should be viewed cautiously. Yet it would seem relatively safe to conclude that, while special districts may be appropriate for selected areas, this technique has much more specialized applications than other financing options such as impact fees or development taxes.

Montgomery County, Maryland. Montgomery County has pioneered several variants of the special-district approach. One approach is for the county to provide front-end money for improving a state highway, and then to create a participation fund that requires buyers of new homes in benefiting subdivisions to pay a fee at closing. Road clubs, another approach used by Montgomery County, require payments at closing or amortization of the tax bill over five or ten years (Casella 1990).

Texas. The Texas approach to special-district infrastructure finance is notorious for its abuses. Texas law freely permits the formation of municipal utility districts (MUDs), which can issue revenue and general obligation bonds for water, wastewater, storm drainage, parks, fire protection, and solid waste collection facilities. MUD bonds are particularly attractive to developers because they can be used to pay advance interest on bond debt as well as construction finance interest charges (Butler and Myers 1984). The bankruptcy of several MUDs following Texas' economic recession in the mid-1980s generated support for substantial reforms to the state's MUD legislation. These failures also led to several Texas S&Ls being bailed out at taxpayer expense (see Chapter 1).

Tax Increment Financing. Tax increment financing (TIF) districts differ from other special financing districts in that no special fees are assessed in addition to jurisdictionwide taxes. District revenues consist of a diversion of that portion of tax revenues attributable to new development within the district to retire bonds that finance the initial improvements that stimulated the new development. It is this internal financing, or bootstrap redevelopment, approach that accounts for much of the popularity of the TIF technique.

TIF is particularly attractive to cities because other taxing authorities, such as counties and school districts, may be required to contribute to the redevelopment fund, and that fund is ordinarily under the control of the city or its redevelopment agency. In theory, the other jurisdictions do not lose revenue because there would be no growth in the tax base in the TIF district's tax base without the stimulating public investment. Even if this were true, however, the development attracted to the TIF district might have otherwise occurred elsewhere in the region, although its location may be more consistent with local growth management plans.

Unlike the other financing options discussed in this chapter, TIF is not a method for the private financing of public improvements; rather, it is a sophisticated method of shifting the cost of public improvements among taxing entities. An analysis of TIF projects undertaken by nine municipalities in Milwaukee County, Wisconsin, found that taxpayers in some communities pay more in tax increments for the use of TIFs throughout the county than they would have paid financing their own development projects solely through local taxes (Huddleston 1986).

The 1986 federal Tax Reform Act made a number of changes in rulings about what bonds are tax exempt that will influence the way that local government use TIFs. The effect of these changes is that many bonds that would have been tax exempt will now be considered private-activity taxable bonds. Because the TIF bonds will be taxable, they will require a higher interest rate to be marketable. The tax-exempt bonding component of the TIF subsidies constitutes between 10 and 20 percent of the total value of the financing assistance (APA, September 1988).

Portland, Oregon. The primary financing mechanism for urban redevelopment in Portland is TIF (Nelson and Milgroom 1994). TIF was originally used as a means of providing local matching funds for federal urban housing projects. The Oregon state legislature expanded the use of TIF in 1979 to include most economic development and urban renewal projects, thus opening the door for a much wider scope of funding. One crucial element of TIF, as mandated by the legislature, is that an urban renewal district and plan for that district must be established in order to enjoy the benefits of TIF. Central city revitalization financed through TIF has proven to be a successful means of initiating private development in blighted areas. These areas, however, must be carefully defined and planned for as demanded by state law. All of the urban renewal areas defined in the 1988 city plan were created as qualified TIF zones. TIF is used to leverage private investment. The result has been an onslaught of new downtown development. Two of the largest projects, Pioneer Place and RiverPlace, totaled over $240 million in private and public investment from 1987 to 1990. Since 1970, more than $1.5 billion in public and private funds have been invested in Portland's downtown.

California. Tax increment financing is one of the most common methods used by California cities and counties to deal with the fiscal constraints imposed by Proposition 13 and federal cutbacks. The biggest attraction of

TIF in California is that it allows the issuance of revenue bonds and circumvents Proposition 13 restrictions on general-obligation bonds. The city of Los Angeles has made effective use of TIF, particularly in its downtown area. And recently, the city's community redevelopment agency has expanded its use into 14 other areas. Since California law requires 20 percent of all TIF revenue to be used to build or refurbish affordable housing, Los Angeles has invested some of its TIF money in housing programs for homeless people who frequent downtown's skid row.

While Los Angeles has had success with TIF, other localities should be certain of the economic situation before declaring an area blighted. Los Angeles' first TIF site became successful only after the city began to emerge as a regional financial center. A report by the California Debt Advisory Commission also cautioned that TIF districts can depress the local tax base. In the mid-1980s, about 3.5 percent of the property value in California was channeled into TIF districts, souring relations between TIF and other taxing entities such as state and county governments and school districts (Arana 1986).

Transportation Utility Fees. Many local governments face a transportation financing dilemma. Growth places increasing demands upon transportation system expansion, which is dealt with in a number of ways including various forms of developer exactions, general obligation bond issues retired from property taxes, federal and state grants, and impact fees. Meanwhile, funding for operations, maintenance, and repair fails to keep pace. Since often there are no revenue sources dedicated for operations and maintenance needs, one solution being developed is the transportation utility fee.

Orlando, Florida. Orlando meets its operations and maintenance shortfall by implementing a variation of a user fee—a transportation utility fee designed to charge the users of the transportation system based upon trip generation rates and ridership for different land use categories. The transportation utility fee covers operations and maintenance costs, freeing up general revenue funds and gas tax revenues for capacity improvements. The fee varies from year to year as costs vary. The fee is collected once a year and is included on the property tax bill. (The city also collects its stormwater utility fee in this manner.) Orlando assesses each property for its proportional share of transportation costs based on the trips each land use generates based on national and regional studies (York 1991).

LaGrande, Oregon. LaGrande has a flat rate street fee of $2.50 per month for all residences and businesses. The revenues generated by the street fee are dedicated to a street fund to be used only for construction, reconstruction, major maintenance, and repair of streets within the city. Opposition has been minimal, in part because of the low fee and the fact that the idea was recommended by a citizen organization (York 1991).

Fort Collins, Colorado. Fort Collins has adopted a transportation utility fee calculation based on trip generation rates and street frontage. It is used in combination with a one-fourth percent sales tax also earmarked for transportation (Ingemon 1990).

Medford, Oregon. Medford's street utility is based on trip generation rates reduced by a percentage that reflects the estimated percentage of passerby-trips. Revenues from the street utility are earmarked for the street utility fund for maintenance and operations (York 1991.)

Table 8–5 reviews the major policy considerations affecting selected facility financing techniques principally incurred by new development.

THE FINANCIAL SMORGASBORD

Local governments are inventing new ways to cope with the problem of financing growth in a climate of dwindling federal and state resources and local taxpayer opposition to paying higher taxes. The trend is away from liberal financing approaches to conservative ones. It was, after all, President Ronald Reagan who called for the privatization of government services and the financing of services based on the benefit principal. The result was sweeping federal government retrenchment from financing local facilities during the 1980s.

For their part, local governments are increasingly looking to those who create demands to pay up. The result is a new era of more responsible attribution of facility costs to the sources of demand. Ironically, it is the

Table 8–5.
Facility Financing Techniques: A Comparative Analysis

	Impact Fees	Impact Tax	Real Estate Transfer Tax	Negotiated Exaction	Special District
Study Required?	Yes	No	No	Yes[1]	No
Time of Assessment	Building permit	Subdivision or permit	All land sales	Rezoning conditional use, or other discretionary action	All district property
Calculation Basis	Net cost	Per unit	Percent of sale	Negotiated	Assessed value
Initial Payer	Developer	Developer	Owner	Developer	Owner
New Development Affected	100%	100%	Sales and resales	Usually large developers	Varies
Limitations	Rational nexus required	Arbitrary	General fund	Usually large developers	Limited off-site role
Requirements for Calculation	Rational nexus	None	None	Rough proportionality	Formula
Finance Policy	Earmarked	Unrestricted use	Unrestricted use	Negotiated	Ad valorem
Legal Assessment	Enabled by many states but not necessary in most states	Requires enabling legislation	Requires enabling legislation	Except for a few states, authorized under police power	Requires enabling legislation
Political Framework	Conservative	Liberal	Liberal	Conservative	Conservative

[1]Prior to *Dolan v. City of Tigard, Oregon,* studies showing the relationship between exactions negotiated and the impacts of new development were not clearly required. Subsequently, findings showing at least a rough proportionality must be undertaken by local governments to justify exactions that are not otherwise exercises of taxation authority.

usually politically conservative development community that harks back to the liberal approach to accommodating new development through general taxpayer financing of improvements.

This change in financing philosophy has much to do with growth management. As the costs of facilities must be borne increasingly by local taxpayers and developers, local governments are finding that such costs can only be reduced through more efficient land uses and squeezing more capacity out of existing facilities. By bringing unit costs down through more efficient urban patterns, both taxpayers and developers are sheltered from potentially high costs of facility expansion and long-term maintenance. Indeed, the low-density suburban communities that were subsidized by generous federal wastewater grants—75 cents of federal money for every 25 cents of local money—are now finding the costs of upgrading, maintenance, and operations nearly prohibitive.

As local governments face ever-rising costs of facility expansion and as local taxpayers continue to be unwilling to shoulder much of the financial burden on behalf of new development, local governments will turn ever more to selecting from a smorgasbord of financial techniques based on the general principles and practices presented in this chapter. In our view, those local governments that combine these financial principles and practices with sound growth management efforts will be those who do the best job of keeping total facility costs down. In our view, the result will be more responsible management of taxpayer resources.

9

Administrative Responsiveness: The Key to Effective Growth Management

Despite all the benefits of growth management, one of its features can be the disruption of the private sector decision-making process. The problem can be characterized by vague standards for approving development proposals, coupled with linking development approval to discretionary standards that are determined on a case-by-case basis, in ad hoc settings. This creates uncertainty and unpredictability, and increases the risks of project infeasibility. Sometimes, there may be outright prohibitions against constructing particular kinds of developments, even if they do not result in environmental damage. Examples may include manufactured housing and high-density housing prohibitions.

Even in the best of growth management programs, however, there can be unusually lengthy review processes that delay projects that meet all relevant criteria. This can occur when planning bodies delay, table, or defer decisions to successive meetings. One reason for delay may be land-use restrictions that are behind the times in terms of market realities, technology, or evolving legal principles. Another reason may be uncoordinated permitting by several agencies that must be involved in permit review.

One of the potentially unfortunate effects of the administration of growth management programs can be frustrating desirable development from occurring, which makes communities with growth management programs unattractive. This can have the perverse effect of shifting such development into more distant areas at higher social, environmental, or economic cost. Moreover, by frustrating the development process, prices for developments, especially housing, go up. The solution is to make growth management systems administratively efficient. The purpose of this chapter is to pose the principles of administrative efficiency and then review various approaches to achieving it.

PRINCIPLES OF
ADMINISTRATIVE EFFICIENCY

In the absence of efficient administration, growth management will fail in its purposes (see Chapter 1). How can growth management systems be efficiently administered? Some basic principles should be followed.

Streamlined Permitting

Despite the seeming desirability of streamlined permitting, it is difficult to achieve. Various schemes have been attempted across the country with perhaps the most popular approach being one-stop permitting. The problem with typical one-stop permitting systems is that they often add one more layer of government procedures to the permitting process. For example, under the typical one-stop system an official convenes an initial meeting of all relevant permitting agencies or departments. Often information requested after that meeting is directed to this lead official, who coordinates information gathering with other officials. Those officials send their responses back to the lead official, who assembles all responses in a report to the developer. The developer must then respond back to the lead official, who passes the responses back to the other officials, and the process recycles. Ironically, the multistop system can be more efficient than the one-stop system simply because developers can work directly with each permitting agency to solve problems face-to-face and one-at-a-time. One-stop systems usually work best when all relevant permitting is centralized under one permitting agency, otherwise one-stop permitting adds complexity rather than simplifies processes.

What works? Schiffman (1989) offers several suggestions. First, local governments can facilitate permit gathering by making all permits available in one place. The developer therefore knows what permits may be needed and can go directly to the permitting authority. Although a central person or agency can inform the developer of the status of permits, the developer is free to communicate directly with the permitting authorities.

Second, local governments should convene preapplication meetings involving the developer and the permitting authorities. This allows the developer to become acquainted with the permitting authorities and establish channels for direct communication.

Third, local governments should prepare and make available, free or at low cost, material that will aid the developer in understanding what is required to secure permits. The material may include checklists and flow charts. It should include findings-of-fact forms. This will clarify to the applicant what is required and what the decision-making criteria are. All forms should be designed to expedite staff review. To guide the developers work, the material should include sufficient detail on discretionary issues.

Fourth, the planning department should become the central permit-coordinating agency within local government. Although other departments within local government may have more expertise in certain areas than planning staffs, planners tend to understand processes better and are better able to manage the work of other departments. Sometimes other departments will prefer that planning staffs manage their permitting process.

Fifth, special and streamlined processes should be created to facilitate innovative, mixed-use developments such as planned unit developments and new communities. All too often a PUD proposal is more trouble and more time-consuming than a cookie-cutter subdivision proposal. To remedy this problem, the city of Durham, Oregon, for example, requires all developments to be processed as PUDs and further restricts the processing time to fewer than four months (consistent with Oregon law). By removing the option for cookie-cutter developments but sticking to an accelerated review process, the city's entire decision-making process is made more efficient, and developers are rewarded for innovative designs.

Finally, local planning offices should establish a continuing education program for planning and public officials and perhaps developers. This will provide everyone, especially new players, with knowledge of current laws, trends, and issues. It should also expedite their decision making.

Promising approaches to streamlined permitting include permitting deadlines, exemplified by California and Oregon, and special permitting processes, exemplified by one Orlando, Florida, case.

California. The California Subdivision Map Act and the Permit Streamlining Act establish maximum time limits for local government processing of permits that do not require plan amendments, zone changes, conditional use permits, or other discretionary action. A local government has thirty days from the time it receives a tentative subdivision map to determine its completeness. Where the local planning commission can only review and recommend action but the governing body acts, the planning commission has thirty days in which to make its recommendation and the governing body has another thirty days in which to act. Where the

planning commission is delegated approval authority by the governing body, it must act within thirty days' receipt of a completed tentative map. Failure to meet these deadlines results in the tentative map being "deemed to be approved" (Schiffman 1989).

Oregon. Oregon law requires local governments to act on development proposals within 120 days' receipt of the formal application. If the requested permit is not issued during that time, state law presumes the permit to be approved. In practice, however, the situation is different. If a local government finds it difficult to process the permit within the time frame required, it will often ask the applicant for an extension. Unless the application is uncomplicated and requires few if any negotiated terms—in which case an extension is probably not needed anyway— the developer is obliged to offer an extension. The veiled threat is that the local government will act unfavorably on the permit. Despite this practice, there appears to be consensus in the development community that permitting is accomplished faster under this arrangement than without it (Nelson 1991; Hales 1992). The downside is really felt by citizen activists who typically like to use delaying tactics to force major compromises with a developer, or so delay development as to force the developer to rescind the application.

Orlando, Florida, and the Timberleaf Development. The city of Orlando has approved a 188-acre mixed-use housing development to be built out in phases over two decades. It is called Timberleaf (York 1991). It is expected to build out at about 1,800 units. The city and Timberleaf negotiated all the major questions of scale, timing, facilities, and density in one master plan that is implemented by a development agreement between the developer and the city. Build-out will occur in stages. The agreement calls for flexible designs that respond to specific site conditions and changing market demands. Specific guidelines assure unity and quality within the development. The program anticipates an average density of about ten units per acre. Single-family homes are being built at up to seven units per acre.

Although the initial negotiations for the development took more than one year, individual approvals for stages of the development occur within thirty days. In contrast, the average subdivision in urban Florida takes up to eighteen months. The streamlined permitting process is managed by a design review committee (DRC), which is given specific authority to permit development in Timberleaf, that includes local bankers and developers. The purpose of the DRC is to find ways in which to optimize savings design in some design standards, streamline the permitting process, and coordinate development requirements. The process generally works as follows: The developer submits a preliminary plat, which is based on the overall design standards established on the development agreement. During the same week the plat is distributed to planning, transportation, drainage, water and sewer, and other permitting departments. A DRC meeting is convened. Department heads or their representatives attend. The meeting is not a public hearing, although it is open to the public. The meeting ends with agreement on all details of development among all departments, the developer, and the DRC. The final plat is filed, often within thirty days of the original submittal, and construction begins.

The developer is thus able to build houses as the market demands. House prices range in the low $50,000s to the middle $70,000s. Not only are the house prices affordable by most standards, the developer also pays over $5,000 in impact fees. The combination of certainty in development approval and certainty in infrastructure availability allows the developer to provide lower cost housing in shorter periods of time than competitors.

Nondiscretionary Standards

Another way to achieve administrative efficiency is to remove discretionary standards and replace them with nondiscretionary standards. Other than Oregon, no state, regional, or local planning program does this. In Oregon, once land has been designated for a range of land uses consistent with state planning goals and policies, development *must* be allowed. If certain kinds of developments are subject to conditional uses, special permitting, floating zone restrictions, or other forms of decision-making that are usually discretionary outside of Oregon, the conditions for approval must be specified. Thus, if a developer demonstrates consistency with the nondiscretionary criteria, the permit must be granted. The standards themselves must be clear and objective so that there can be little dispute as to compliance. Finally, the standards must be reasonable and not have the effect of preventing development. In this and other important ways, Oregon is able to effectively discourage development in rural areas and encourage it in urban areas.

Rational Review of Urban Development Expansion

The litmus test of growth management effectiveness is the extent to which petitions to expand urban containment boundaries or develop rural and resource lands are allowed. Certainly efficient accommodation of development requires expansion of boundaries, eventually, and development of some rural lands—although perhaps not resource lands and lands of environmental significance—may be necessary. The problem is that if urban areas are expanded without regard to urban infill and redevelopment objectives of growth management, such efforts may be undermined. To some extent, development must be induced—through strict enforcement of urban containment boundaries—to infill and redevelop to the maximum extent reasonable. What are the appropriate criteria by which to determine whether a boundary expansion is justified? This is fairly new ground, but some insights can be gained from Florida and Oregon policies.

Florida Criteria. Expansion of urban land in Florida is based primarily on the adequacy of facilities and the fulfillment of infill and redevelopment policies. Principal criteria include the following.

Currency. Florida's concurrency principle requires that urban expansion and urban development are allowed only when facilities needed to accommodate development are in place concurrent with the demands of development.

Facility Capacity. Preservation of facility capacity to accommodate urban infill and redevelopment must be assured according to Florida planning policies. In particular, urban area expansion cannot result in reducing or eliminating facility capacity necessary to accommodate infill or redevelopment closer in.

Oregon Criteria. In Oregon, boundary expansions are relatively difficult, especially if substantial amounts of undeveloped or underdeveloped lands exist within urban growth boundaries. As a general proposition, UGB expansion is not allowed unless the following criteria are satisfied.

Resource Lands. There is no incursion of urban development into resource lands un-less such lands are already substantially impacted by development along most sides.

Needs. There is insufficient land within the UGB to accommodate development. However, this criterion does not necessarily mean that the UGB should be expanded if the owners of vacant or underdeveloped land are unwilling to develop their land or sell to developers. This caveat is considered when there are substantial amounts of vacant or

Figure 9–1. This subdivision of two-acre lots requires individual septic systems and water wells. This makes future expansion of urban facilities very difficult and expensive. All too many local governments allow such developments, arguing that since urban facilities and services would not be available within a near-term or even long-term planning horizon, such rural development is acceptable. *Source:* Photo by Arthur C. Nelson.

underdeveloped land; it is not considered in situations where only a very small amount of the area inside UGBs remains undeveloped and the owners of such land essentially exercise monopoly control over the land.

Infrastructure. The expanded area will be provided with infrastructure needed to accommodate development. On this score, Oregon law has evolved a particular adequate-public-facilities standard that will not allow boundary expansions where even one set of public facilities is unable to accommodate development of such additional land. School capacity particularly has been a problem.

Congestion. Development of land added to the UGB will not result in congesting facilities.

Judicial Review: The Wildcard of Administrative Efficiency

Land-use decisions requiring plan amendments, zone changes, conditional use permits, special permits, or other kinds of discretionary approvals are prone to legal challenge beyond the level of local government decision-making. Developers aim to meet market demands while neighborhood, environmental, and other interests aim to either prevent change or alter development patterns to achieve particular objectives. Yet, except for fulfilling execution pursuant to the death penalty, land-use decisions as a class of decisions take longer to resolve through judicial processes than criminal cases.

From beginning to end, the typical process generally works as follows. A developer proposes a project that requires a discretionary action. Assuming that the proposal meets all technical specifications of the local government, the earliest a hearing is held is thirty days from submittal but it is quite often sixty or ninety days. The first hearing is before the planning commission, which may defer its decision over one or more meetings each of which may be one month apart. At the hearing, the planning commission affords opportunity for all sides to present their case. The developer usually provides experts. Within about three to six months the planning commission decision is rendered. In many situations, the decision can be appealed to the local governing body, which often will conduct its own hearing (at which time all parties present their case again). Within about three to six months the local governing body renders its decision. The losing party can appeal to the state trial court and demand a trial. At the trial, all parties again present their case. At this stage, however, the developer can offer new and more detailed evidence for consideration by the judge. This stage of the judicial process is considered de novo. About a year or two from filing, the judge (or jury) renders a decision. This decision can be appealed to state appeals courts, and state supreme courts, in a process that can take another year or two. All totaled, the permit may take two to four years to resolve, assuming there are no remands at any level for further review.

The judicial process added on top of lengthy local processes can frustrate developers, putting some out of business or otherwise making the risks of development so high as to prevent them from meeting marginal housing or other development needs of a community. The process can also frustrate interest groups as it can bleed them of resources, ultimately causing despair and resignation. A comprehensive growth management system must consider the judicial decision-making process. But few states or local governments have done so. Figure 9–2 summarizes the lengthy process typified by most state land-use judicial decision-making processes.

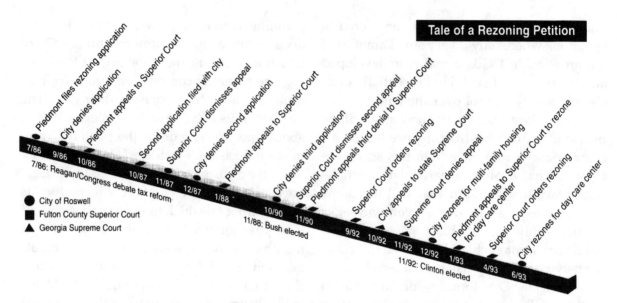

Figure 9–2. This seven-year story of Piedmont Capital Investments' request to rezone land abutting single-family housing for multifamily housing and a day-care center in Roswell, Georgia, shows the time and expense required of all parties when controversial local land-use disputes are resolved in the courts. *Source:* Illustration by Annie Bissett. Reprinted from *Land Lines,* © 1994, Lincoln Institute of Land Policy.

Florida's Evolving Judicial Review System. As in most states, the decretionary land-use decision-making process usually starts at the planning commission and goes to the local governing body. Hearings are held at both levels, at which time all parties can present information, including new information, before the governing body. Unlike most states, however, appeals of local government planning decisions go the the state department of administrative hearings (DOAH), which must schedule a hearing before a hearings officer within ninety days of its receipt of a petition. The hearing itself runs similar to a trial court in which all parties can offer witnesses who may be cross-examined. Newer and more detailed information than was offered at the local level can be introduced in the hearing. Hearings usually consume one week but often stretch over two or three weeks, sometimes divided over several months. After the hearing, the hearings officer has 120 days in which to render an opinion and prepare a recommended order. The order is sent to the governor and state cabinet for official action. There is no time limit on the governor and state cabinet. That decision, however, can be appealed to state trial court, the decision of which can in turn be appealed to the state appeals courts and supreme court. Any local government decision challenged through DOAH but not beyond the governor and state cabinet will take about two years from initial filing to final order. More time would be added if the case moved into state courts.

New Jersey's Affordable Housing Review Process. New Jersey takes a different approach when it comes to housing development decisions. The New Jersey Supreme Court has created three "Mt. Laurel" judicial districts throughout the state and assigned one justice to each district to hear fair-housing cases pursuant to the Mt. Laurel doctrine. Simply stated, this doctrine requires all municipalities to accommodate their regional fair share of low- and moderate-income housing. The judges also hear cases involving challenges to the certification or denial of certification of a municipality's master plan housing element, which is submitted to the state council on affordable housing.

The three judges may appoint a special master, usually a professional planner, to undertake fact finding when a trial court finds that municipality's zoning ordinance must be revised because it does not satisfy Mt. Laurel criteria. The master conducts hearings, prepares a report, and presents that report together with specific recommendations for making local ordinances consistent with Mt. Laurel criteria. The recommendations are not binding on the Mt. Laurel judges, but they tend to influence judges' final orders.

The process works as follows. An application for a housing project must be denied or conditioned by a local government. If the developer believes the denial or conditions are inconsistent with Mt. Laurel principles, the developer can appeal to state trial court in a de novo proceeding. This can take six months to one year. The developer must win at the trial court for the relevant Mt. Laurel judge to consider the developer's petition to convene the special master. Once appointed, the special master has ninety days within which to determine how the local government's ordinance may be revised to remedy deficiencies. The Mt. Laurel judge may then order those revisions or some variation of them. The developer may then apply for a permit consistent with the final order for revising the ordinance. The entire process, from initial application to final order, usually takes about two years but can sometimes take longer. The process applies only to residential developments.

Oregon's Streamlined Judicial Review Process. Rather than focus only on reforming judicial review processes, Oregon has reformed the entire discretionary decision-making process from application to final order. Local governments have only 120 days in which to render their final decision on a permit or land-use application. This period includes all actions by local governments. Because of the limited time to process applications, many local governments delegate final local decision-making authority to the planning commission or a local hearings officer. Appeals of local government decisions are made not to state trial courts but to a special state court, the land use board of appeals (LUBA). LUBA operates much like tax courts in many states. Its purview is narrow and its judges are specialists in land-use law. LUBA must hear cases within thirty days' receipt of a petition and must render a decision within 120 days of the petition. LUBA reviews the case only on the locally assembled record. That means there is no trial. The record of the case that was constructed by the local government is the only basis on which LUBA decides. LUBA hears oral arguments, but restricts those arguments to legal issues. LUBA can remand the case back to local government for further findings, or it can accept or reject a petition. Appeals from LUBA go to the state appeals court, which must hear and decide the case within ninety days, and then to the supreme court.

Most land-use cases are resolved in less than one year.

Considerable pressure is put on local governments to establish efficient decision-making processes. Because review by LUBA is only on the record, the record must be complete. All parties interested in the case must make their full presentation before the local planning commission or local hearings officer, since this is their only opportunity to have their arguments put into the official record. Local staffs must assemble records, and planning commissions or hearings officers must efficiently manage quasi-judicial proceedings. But the rewards include greater respect for local decision-makers, more competent staffs and commissioners, much less time in the process, greater responsiveness to market needs, and better fulfillment of growth management principles.

CONCLUDING OBSERVATIONS

Special-area protection programs are most effective when done in a growth management context. The benefits of special area protection may be lost if development near or adjacent to such areas is not properly managed. Equally important is that oftentimes the benefits of special area protection can be lost if not enough development occurs nearby. For example, to enhance the local property tax base, growth management plans may target certain kinds of development to take advantage of scenic views when properly designed. The effect may be improved economic activity and higher property values. Special-area protection programs can be used in tandem with exclusive resource land preservation policies to create large open spaces that define the edges of existing or future urban areas. When used within a growth management context, special area programs will generate many more benefits than if such programs were used incrementally or in isolation.

To work properly, growth management systems must provide predictability, certainty, and timeliness to the development community and citizens. This requires efforts to streamline review and appeal processes. But above all, it requires the preparation of thoughtful and thorough plans from the beginning. Plans that are fraught with vague phrases and criteria, and plans that fail to account for the community's legitimate development needs over the planning horizon, will lead to lengthy delays in permitting, court challenges, and frustration among all people affected. An efficient administration process must be part and parcel of any effective growth management program.

10

Pulling It All Together

This chapter has three sections. The first section reviews the significant factors required to adopt and implement growth management systems whether at the state, regional, or local level. The second section presents all of the growth management techniques reviewed in Chapters 3 through 9 in terms of an effectiveness continuum. The concluding section tries to tie everything together.

INGREDIENTS OF EFFECTIVE GROWTH MANAGEMENT POLICIES

What are the elements of effective growth management policies? In our view there are nine critical elements, which we have derived from analysis of successful efforts at the state and regional level.

Consensus for Growth Management

There must first be a consensus for growth management. Consensus is often but not always reflected in politicians' calls for growth management combined with the favorable disposition of the mass media with active citizen interest groups. The consensus for growth management is often based on visible degradation of natural resources such as development of farms, forests, beaches, other open spaces, and sensitive lands. It is also often based on concerns about the effect of rapid growth on public facilities. In Oregon

and Maine, land-use planning programs were initially rooted in the desire to preserve important open spaces from development and only recently on providing adequate facilities and services to sustain development. In Florida and Georgia, statewide planning policies reflect a fundamental desire to provide adequate public facilities concurrent with demands of growth but only to a lesser extent the preservation of open spaces. In all cases, however, there was substantial public consensus on addressing visible problems created by rapid growth.

Executive Leadership

Once consensus for growth management has been achieved, a single major actor is usually needed to galvanize that consensus into action. It is usually not a legislator or a local elected official, even though many may be acknowledged for their leadership. Rather, consensus is galvanized through an executive, such as a governor, mayor, county executive, or regional executive. In Oregon, Governor McCall championed legislative formation of a statewide land-use planning policy. In Florida, Governors Askew and Graham championed statewide growth management planning. In North Carolina, the successful coastal planning program was championed by Governor Hunt. In Georgia, Governor Harris focused support for planning at critical times during the legislative process. In all cases, it was those key players who were able to bring the need for statewide planning policy to bear on recalcitrant legislators. We do not know of a successful growth management planning process that lacked executive leadership. However, once plans are put into place and properly administered they become less dependent on executive leadership.

Goal Setting and Visioning

At some point early in the design of growth management policy there must be a formal goal-setting process, ideally one that leads to a shared vision. In Florida, this was done through statewide legislative hearings. Those hearings elicited proposals by citizens and interest groups, as well as local public officials. Additional hearings were held at the state capitol. In Oregon, those goals were outlined by the same legislative hearing process, but they were only legitimized after a year of statewide land conservation and development commission (LCDC) hearings. Those hearings were conducted in every region and in every major urban area of the state. They elicited responses from virtually every pro- and antiplanning interest group. The objective of such a goal-setting process is to define growth management consensus in terms that most can agree on and perceive as being implementable. In Georgia, a series of hearings was conducted throughout the state by the governor's growth strategies commission to both elicit concerns about planning and development and to create consensus around specific planning goals and objectives. In all cases, individuals and groups involved in the goal-setting process have been given a stake in planning.

Consensus on the Desired Urban Form

Perhaps the most significant consideration in the design of growth management policy involves the question of the kind of urban form desired as a product of the process. Only five states set forth to achieve an ultimate urban form—Florida, Maine, New Jersey, Oregon, and Washington. Only Oregon pursues the textbook example of an idealized urban form involving containment of urban development behind urban growth boundaries (that are difficult to move) and preservation of all other land for environmental, open space, or resource use. Yet, all states involved in state-enforced growth management pursue an urban form whether explicit or not. For example, in most states there are policies to protect critical lands, focus development where urban facilities exist, and preserve rural lands until needed for urban uses. Many regions are effecting their own urban forms, such as the Association of Bay Area Governments which is involved in planning greenbelts throughout the San Francisco Bay Area. Other regional examples include San Diego, Sacramento, the Twin Cities of Minneapolis and St. Paul, Cape Cod, and parts of the Washington, D.C., area. The effect of these policies is an urban form that at minimum aims to separate urban and rural land uses, achieve more compact urban development, and sustain or improve the productivity of resource lands. It would be better, however, if the urban form desired would be made explicit as part of the policy-making process. This would help to focus planning and implementation.

Citizen Involvement

The cornerstone of any effective growth management policymaking process is citizen involvement. Only through high-profile citizen involvement can local concerns be placed into appropriate context within the framework of planning goals. While the form of citizen involvement varies depending on the planning jurisdiction, a general model is set forth below.

Within each community there are a series of community goal-setting sessions. At those sessions problems and opportunities are identified and subsequent planning is based largely on accommodating those concerns. Community planning goals are set. Drafts of plan elements addressing those goals are openly shared with citizens in formal hearing processes held by the local planning commission, broad-based citizen advisory committees, and the local governing body. In addition, there are a number of formal written review periods through which people can respond to proposals. The outcome of this level of citizen involvement is a local land-use plan that has consensus and legitimacy.

There will be problems when local plans based on such citizen involvement become inconsistent with state or regional planning goals. For example, some Oregon communities desired to exclude or severely restrict low-income housing. The state housing goal explicitly requires communities to provide for the housing needs of all households likely to live in those communities. The state LCDC returned many plans to communities for redrafting. Also, in Oregon, citizen involvement extends all the way from the local to the state level. For every level of planning there is a broadly constituted citizen advisory committee. Thus, there are citizen planning advisory committees for the state and for every city, county, and regional government.

In Florida, Georgia, and Maine, citizen advisory committees are established at the local

and regional government levels, although the visibility of such committees varies dramatically by local government.

Perhaps the most important long-term role of citizens is during plan implementation. Citizens should become watchdogs, making sure that growth management plan policies are properly applied and decisions about changing those plans are made consistent with overall plan goals. The best way to assure citizens of adequate access to the implementation process is to give them adequate standing to challenge the application of policies in local public hearings and later at appeal. Only when citizens have legitimate access to the implementation process will they maintain their stake in the overall aims of growth management. For example, in Florida citizens can challenge plan amendments, but this usually limits citizens to only the largest or most controversial development proposals. In Oregon, citizens have the ability to challenge all land-use decisions, which are generally those involving discretionary approval such as plan amendments, zone changes, conditional use permits, and variances.

Financial and Technical Support

Planning done at state or regional levels is successful only with considerable support. Over the course of ten years, Oregon spent over $100 million to complete statewide planning. Most of that money went to local government planning agencies. Florida has spent less than half that amount, but most of that has also gone to local governments to support planning. In Georgia, staff at regional development centers was added primarily at local government expense. Those staff members were trained by the state and universities in how to provide local land-use planning coordination services. Cities and counties also received some financial assistance.

Technical assistance is provided by virtually all state planning agencies, including those in Oregon, Florida, Georgia, Maine, New Jersey, Connecticut, Rhode Island, and Washington. In Florida and Oregon that technical assistance usually takes the form of model planning elements and procedures, and recommendations for plan improvements. In Georgia, technical assistance includes setting up local geographically based electronic information systems that use state-generated data on natural resources, roads, and census tabulations.

The cost of good planning and administration may at first appear high, but if such planning leads to even small percentage savings in public facilities costs or more efficient land-use patterns, the savings will overwhelm the costs.

Intergovernmental Coordination

In addition to local and regional governments, many state and federal agencies make plans. State and federal agencies plan highways, airports, drainage projects, and so forth. Thus, one dimension of growth management is the coordination of state and federal agencies' plans with local and regional planning processes. In Florida, the state plan incorporates plans of state and federal agencies, and local governments must plan within those constraints. In Oregon, local governments have had some formal voice in how state and even federal agency plans impact them. The Oregon legislature required all state agencies to coordinate their plans with the LCDC. This made the LCDC or its administrative arm, the department of land conservation and development, a kind of mediator between state and local agencies where state agency planning and local planning were at odds.

Local plans must also take into account their impact on nearby communities. In Florida, regional planning agencies coordinate local planning, and also coordinate among other regions. In Oregon, local plans had to be formally coordinated by both regional and other nearby local governments. Failure to have local government sign-off meant that a local plan was not yet ready for LCDC approval. Disputes among local governments were settled either by regional planning agencies (where they existed) or by the LCDC itself. Usually, even the most bitter of local government disputes were settled by the local governments themselves.

In Georgia, coordination of all planning by all agencies is done at the regional level. Regional development plans are then coordinated among regions to iron out inconsistencies, especially in border situations.

In New Jersey, local governments were involved in a "cross-acceptance" process resulting in one, fully coordinated, state growth management plan.

These coordination mechanisms can be considered forms of dispute resolution. They should be recognized as such and future legislation could provide general guidance on the procedures to follow in resolving disputes involving these kinds of coordination processes.

Streamlined Review Processes

There should be an institutionalized, yet streamlined, structure for reviewing appeals to local planning decisions that is sensitive to needs of local government, citizens, and developers.

We have already reviewed some of the more innovative alternatives to the standard model of local government and judicial review processes. In our view, the California and Oregon approaches to streamlined local review of development proposals—in California applying only to subdivisions but in Oregon applying to all land-use decisions—are perhaps the nation's most efficient formalized structures, while Oregon's special judicial approach, with its land use board of appeals and judicial review based only on the record built at the local government level, being clearly the nation's most efficient judicial process. In the absence of legislative mandates, local and regional governments can impose time limits and streamline review processes on their own. The use of hearings officers familiar with land use and real estate law is one option larger local governments have to expedite discretionary decision-making. But even in the absence of state land-use appeals boards like Oregon's, it may be possible for local governments to prevent de novo proceedings (trials) in court if they create trial-like (quasi-judicial) procedures at the local decision-making level. In such situations, it may be possible to preempt court challenge through summary judgment if it is clear that the decision made at the local level conformed with constitutional due process and other constitutional concerns, while also being consistent with locally adopted growth management plans.

Adequate Administrative Support

Effective growth management plans require adequate administrative support. This often means larger and more professionally trained planning staffs than some local or regional governments are accustomed to. But the ben-efits of adequately provided, professional staffs to both the public and private sectors are tangible. Well-managed growth management plans lead to more efficient land use patterns, less costly delivery of public facilities and services, greater fiscal capacity, greater local exchange of currency as people are more accessible to goods and services, more viable alternative transportation modes, and preservation of regionally important resources. For developers, well-managed growth management systems result in facilities being in place or planned concurrent with the impacts of development, clear and objective standards in development review, greater certainty on project feasibility, and proper signals on the appropriate times and places to plan new development. These outcomes are not wishful thinking; areas with well-managed growth management plans are being found to provide these and other benefits.

EFFECTIVENESS OF GROWTH MANAGMENT TECHNIQUES

This section discusses and then presents, in tabular form, all the individual growth management techniques reviewed in Chapters 3 through 9. Let us first summarize the practices that, based on our professional work and analysis, we consider most effective in achieving growth management objectives, and why.

Urban containment boundaries with interim development boundaries, urban reserves, and urban service limits. These techniques direct urban development into areas intended or needed for urban uses and away from areas intended or needed for rural and resource areas. Boundaries create a clean break between potentially inconsistent urban and rural land uses, thereby protecting rural land from urban spillovers while also providing important environmental and economic benefits to urban development.

Appropriate capital and operational pricing of public facilities. The choice of appropriate financing technique is crucial for the equitable and efficient provision of public facilities and services. For many facilities, this is possible through user fee approaches, improvement districts, and various forms of impact fees.

Capital improvements programming and adequate facilities standards (concurrency). These techniques ensure that public facilities will be available concurrent with demand and that development farther away does not deprive infill and redevelopment because of inadequate facility capacity. Moreover, when properly configured these techniques give important signals to developers on what can be expected when and where intended.

Preservation of lands for resource production and environmental protection through exclusive use designations. These techniques remove subsidized or inefficient speculative value from resource lands and are part of an overall strategy to direct development into urban areas and away from resource areas; help sustain the economic contributions of productive resource lands while also generating important environmental benefits to urban areas; and protect the critical mass of resource lands needed to sustain long-term economic vitality of resource areas.

Minimum density standards. This technique ensures that developers of minimum development expectations and that development will make efficient use of public facilities and services.

Infill and redevelopment. Efficiently facilitated infill and redevelopment is needed to ensure that urban areas remain vital, to respond to changing needs when and where needed, and to help dampen urban sprawl pressures. The most efficient infill and redevelopment technique appears to be Missouri-style authority.

Transfer/purchase of development rights. When properly used, these techniques can protect the critical mass of resource lands needed to sustain long-term economic vitality of resource areas.

Rural land reassembly. This technique helps correct for bad decisions of the past by reassembling rural land for resource uses through the use of rural cluster techniques to help finance the reassembly.

All forms of special-area protection. These techniques direct development away from special areas to areas intended for urban uses.

Streamlined permitting. Streamlined permitting facilitates development, redevelopment, or infill development in urban areas in a manner that is responsive to market needs.

Nondiscretionary (clear and objective) standards. Conversion of vague and uncertain standards to reasonable, clear, and objective standards affords developers maximum certainty while assuring that development is consistent with growth management goals, objectives, and policies.

Expeditious development review. Time limits for permit review, record building strictly at the local level, and special land-use judicial review provides developers with greater certainty, predictability, and direction in investment decision-making while at the same time elevating local public-sector policy- and decision-making to a higher and more responsible level.

Table 10–1 indicates the effectiveness of these techniques in achieving particular growth management purposes using a con-

Table 10–1. Technique Effectiveness Continuum
(Effectiveness of Individual Techniques without Combination with Other Techniques)

Technique	Preserve Resource Land	Urban Containment	Efficient Public Facilities	Meet Market Demands
RESOURCE PRESERVATION				
Differential Tax Assessment	−	−	±	−
Restrictive Agreements	−	−	±	−
Circuit Breaker Taxes	−	−	±	−
Capital Gains Taxes	−	−	±	−
Right-to-Farm	−	−	±	
Transfer Development Rights	±	+	+	+
Purchase Development Rights	±	+	±	±
Land Acquisition	±	+	±	±
Nonexclusive Zoning	−	−	−	−
Voluntary Districting	−	−	−	−
Exclusive Zoning	+	+	+	±
Agriculture/Forest Buffers	+	+	±	
SPECIAL-AREA PROTECTION				
Coastal Zone Management	+	±	±	±
Critical-Area Programs	+	+		
Endangered Species Protection	+	+		
Scenic View Preservation	+	±		
Conservation Easements	+	±		
RURAL GROWTH MANAGEMENT				
Small Town Focus	+	+	+	+
Rural Cluster Development	±	±	±	+
Strategic Cluster Development	+	+	+	+
Performance Evaluation	+	+	+	±
Rural Land Reassembly	+	±	±	+
URBAN CONTAINMENT				
Urban Containment Boundaries	+	+	+	+
Intermediate Boundaries	+	+	+	+
Urban Development Reserves	+	+	+	+
Upzoning/Downzoning	+	+	+	+
Nontransitional Zoning	+	+	+	+
Exclusive Use Zoning	+	+	+	+
Inclusionary Zoning	+	+	+	+
Minimum Density Standards	+	+	+	+
Jobs-Housing Balance	+	+	+	+
Infill and Redevelopment	+	+	+	+
Housing Linkage	+	+	+	+
Neighborhood Conservation	±	±	±	±
New Communities	±	±	±	±
FACILITY ADEQUACY, TIMING, AND PLANNING				
Adequate Public Facilities	+	+	+	±
Transportation Management	+	+	+	+
Growth Phasing	±	+	+	±
Rate of Growth	−	−	±	−

(continued)

Table 10–1. (continued)

Technique	Preserve Resource Land	Urban Containment	Efficient Public Facilities	Meet Market Demands
FACILITY ADEQUACY, TIMING, AND PLANNING *(continued)*				
Carrying Capacity Limitations	+	+	+	
Interim Development Controls	±	–	–	–
FACILITY FINANCING				
Mandatory Dedications			+	+
Negotiated Exactions			+	+
Impact Fees	+	+	+	+
Impact Taxes	±	±	±	–
Improvement Taxes	±	+	+	+
Real Estate Transfer Taxes	±	±	±	±
Special Districts	±	±	+	±
Tax Increment Financing	+	+	+	+
ADMINISTRATIVE RESPONSIVENESS				
Streamlined Permitting	+	+	+	+
Nondiscretionary Standards	+	+	+	+
Review of Urban Expansion	+	+	+	+
Expeditious Judicial Review	+	+	+	+

tinuum from most to least effective. Each technique is assessed for its effectiveness in achieving specific growth management purposes. In review, those purposes are:

• Preservation of agricultural, forest, and other resource land and land that is environmentally, historically, scientifically, or culturally significant (see the "Preserve Resource Land" column in Table 10–1).

• Urban containment, or containment of development to areas most suitable for development (see the "Urban Containment" column in Table 10–1).

• Provision of infrastructure to accommodate efficient development (see the "Efficient Public Facilities" column in Table 10–1).

• Accommodation of market demand for development, with consideration of natural and man-made carrying capacities (see the "Meet Market Demands" column in Table 10–1).

Each technique is given the following assessment:

+ Mostly Positive or Positive

± Neutral or Possibly Positive

– Mostly Negative or Perverse

If there is no assessment of a technique's effectiveness with respect to a specific purpose of growth management, it means that the technique does not directly apply to that purpose.

A CHALLENGE FOR PLANNERS

The new vision of planners is one in which they are simultaneously the protector of taxpayers and advocates of the public interest. These roles may be at odds. Local taxpayers, who may have short-term interests, do not necessarily consider long-term social and economic consequences, which are the public-interest concerns of planners according to the Code of Ethics of the American Institute of

Certified Planners. If planners can influence short-term, parochial interests to consider long-term, societal interests, future generations will enjoy a higher quality of life. These are noble aspirations. We believe that growth management principles, and practices implementing those principles, is where everything begins. Chapter 1 and the introduction to several other chapters review the principles of growth management and offer many practices—some of which are more effective than others.

At the beginning of this book, we cited the challenge offered by William K. Reilly. In our view, planners who create growth management systems that embody the principles and practices offered throughout this book will meet this challenge.

References

Advisory Commission on Intergovernmental Relations. 1968. *Urban and Rural America*. Washington, D.C.: U.S. Government Printing Office.

Advisory Commission on Regulatory Barriers to Affordable Housing. 1991. *Not in My Backyard: Removing Barriers to Affordable Housing*. Washington, D.C.: U.S. Department of Housing and Urban Development.

Alonso, William. 1960. A Theory of the Urban Land Market. *Papers and Proceedings of the Regional Science Association* 6: 149–57.

Altshuler, Alan. 1979. *The Urban Transportation System: Policies and Policy Innovation*. Cambridge, Mass: Joint Center for Urban Studies.

American Farmland Trust. 1992. *Does Farmland Protection Pay: The Cost of Community Services in Three Massachusetts Towns*. Washington, D.C.: American Farmland Trust.

American Farmland Trust. 1986. *Density-Related Public Costs*. Washington, D.C.: American Farmland Trust.

American Farmland Trust. 1986. *Fiscal Impacts of Major Land Uses in the Town of Hebron*. Washington, D.C.: American Farmland Trust.

American Farmland Trust and Cornell University Co-operative Extension of Dutchess County. 1989. *Costs of Community Services Study: Dutchess County, New York*. Washington, D.C.: American Farmland Trust.

American Planning Association. November 1989. Solving Traffic Woes by Balancing Jobs and Housing. *Zoning News*. Chicago: American Planning Association.

American Planning Association. November 1989. States Mandate Local Planning for Growth. *PAS Memo*. Chicago: American Planning Association.

American Planning Association. September 1988. Tax Reform Means Changes in the Use of TIF. *Public Investment*. Chicago: American Planning Association.

American Planning Association. December 1987. Cannibalism in Minneapolis! *Public Investment*. Chicago: American Planning Association.

American Planning Association. September 1987. The Community Facilities District. *Public Investment*. Chicago: American Planning Association.

American Planning Association. May 1987. Affordable Housing Linkage Program. *Zoning News*. Chicago: American Planning Association.

American Planning Association. March 1987. Water Supply and Growth Limits. *Zoning News*. Chicago: American Planning Association.

Apogee Research, Inc. 1987. *Financing Infrastructure: Innovations at the Local Level*. Washington, D.C.: National League of Cities.

Arana, Ana. 1986. Doing Deals. *Planning* 51, 2: 30–33.

Archer, R. W. 1977. *Policy and Research Issues in Subdivisions for Rural Residences, Hobby Farms, and Rural Retreats*. Paper prepared for the 48th ANZAAS Congress.

Arendt, Randall. 1994. *Rural by Design*. Chicago: American Planning Association.

Arendt, Randall. 1990. Open Space Zoning: An Effective Way to Retain Rural Character. *Michigan Planning* 3, 1: 1–7.

Bahl, Roy W. 1968. A Land Speculation Model: The Role of the Property Tax as a Constraint to Urban Sprawl. *Journal of Regional Science* 8, 2: 199–208.

Baltimore Regional Council of Governments. 1992. *Impact of Land Use Alternatives on Transportation Demand*. Baltimore: Baltimore Regional Council of Governments.

Barron, James C., and James W. Thompson. 1973. *Impacts of Open Space Taxation in Washington*. Washington State University Agricultural Experimental Station Bulletin 772. Pullman, Wash.: Agricultural Experimental Station, Washington State University.

Barrows, Richard, and Kendra Bonderud. 1988. The Distribution of Tax Relief Under Farm Circuit Breakers. *Land Economics* 64, 1: 15–27.

Batie, Sandra, and Robert G. Healy. 1983. The Future of American Agriculture. *Scientific American* 248, 2: 45–53.

Baumol, William J., and Wallace E. Oates. 1975. *The Theory of Environmental Policy*. Englewood Cliffs, N.J.: Prentice-Hall.

Beaton, C. R., J. S. Hanson, and T. H. Hibbard. 1977. *The Salem Area Urban Growth Boundary: Evaluation of Policy*

Impacts and Recommendations for the Future. Salem, Ore.: Mid–Willamette Valley Council of Governments.

Berry, Brian J. L., and Donald C. Dahmann. 1980. Population Redistribution in the United States. In *Population Redistribution, and Public Policy,* edited by Brian J. L. Berry and Lester P. Silverman. Washington, D.C.: National Academy of Sciences.

Berry, David. 1978. The Effects of Urbanization on Agricultural Activities. *Growth and Change* 3: 2–8.

Berry, David. 1976. *Idling of Farmland in the Philadelphia Region, 1930–1970.* Regional Science Research Institute Discussion Paper Series No. 88. Amherst, Mass.: Regional Science Research Institute, University of Massachusetts.

Berry, David, and Thomas Plaut. 1978. Retaining Agricultural Activities Under Urban Pressures: A Review of Land Use Conflicts and Policies. *Policy Sciences* 9: 153–78.

Berry, David, Ernest Leonardo, and Kenneth Bieri. 1976. *The Farmer's Response to Urbanization.* Regional Science Research Institute Discussion Paper Series No. 92. Amherst, Mass.: Regional Science Research Institute, University of Massachusetts.

Bills, Nelson L. 1975. Extent of Local Efforts to Form Agricultural Districts in New York State. *Journal of the Northeastern Agricultural Economics Council,* occasional series, volume 4.

Bills, Nelson L., and Richard N. Boisvert. 1988. *Information for Evaluating Land Retention Programs: The Agriculture District Approach.* Paper presented to the Resolving Rural Conflicts Symposium. Mt. Allison University, New Brunswick, Canada.

Bish, Robert L. 1982. Shoreline Management. In *Governing Puget Sound.* Seattle, Wash.: Puget Sound Books.

Bish, Robert L., and Hugh O. Nourse. 1975. *Urban Economics and Public Policy.* New York: McGraw-Hill.

Bishop, Kirk R. September 1989. Designing Urban Corridors. *Planning Advisory Service Report No. 418.* Chicago: American Planning Association.

Blewett, Robert A., and Arthur C. Nelson. 1988. A Public Choice and Efficiency Argument for Development Impact Fees. In *Development Impact Fees,* edited by Arthur C. Nelson. Chicago: American Planning Association.

Blumenfeld, Hans . 1983. Metropolis Extended. *Journal of the American Planning Association* 52, 3: 346–48.

Boal, Frederick W. 1970. Urban Growth and Land Value Patterns. *Professional Geographer* 22, 2: 79–82.

Boehm, Thomas, and Joseph McKenzie. 1981. *The Investment Demand for Housing.* Washington, D.C.: Office of Policy and Economic Research.

Bolen, Richard. 1979. *Building Moratoriums—Impacts and Alternatives.* Portland, Ore: Home Builders Association of Metropolitan Portland.

Bollens, John C., and Henry J. Schmandt. 1982. *The Metropolis.* New York: Harper and Row.

Bollens, Scott A. 1992. State Growth Management: Intergovernmental Frameworks and Policy Objectives. *Journal of the American Planning Association* 58, 4: 454–66.

Bourne, Larry S. 1980. Alternative Perspectives on Urban Decline and Population Deconcentration. *Urban Geography* 1, 1: 39–52.

Bozung, Linda J. June 1983. Transfer Development Rights: Compensation for Owners of Restricted Property. *Zoning and Planning Law Report* 6, 6.

Bradbury, Dana Ann. 1986. Suburban Sprawl and the Right to Farm. *Washburn University Law Review* 22: 448–68.

Brown, H. James, and Neal A. Roberts. 1978. *Land Owners at the Urban Fringe.* Cambridge: Harvard University.

Brown, H. James, Robyn Swaim Phillips, and Neal A. Roberts. 1981. Land Markets at the Urban Fringe. *Journal of the American Planning Association* 47, 2: 131–44.

Bryant, William, and Howard Conklin. 1975. New Farmland Preservation Programs in New York. *Journal of the American Institute of Planners* 41, 6: 390–96.

Burgess, Ernest W. 1925. The Growth of the City. In *The City,* edited by Robert E. Park, Ernest W. Burgess, and R. D. McKenzie. Chicago: University of Chicago Press.

Butler, Kent S., and Dowell Myers. 1984 Boomtime in Austin, Texas: Negotiated Growth Management. *Journal of the American Planning Association* 50, 4: 447–58.

Buttel, F. H. 1982. The Political-Economy of Part-Time Farming. *GeoJournal* 6: 293–300.

Callies, David L. 1992. Dealing With Scarcity: Land Use and Planning. In *Politics and Public Policy in Hawaii,* edited by Zachary A. Smith and Richard C. Pratt. Albany, N.Y.: State University of New York Press, 130–45.

Capozza, Dennis, and Robert Helsley. 1989. The Fundamentals of Land Prices and Urban Growth. *Journal of Urban Economics* 26: 295–306.

Carbonell, Armando J., and Dan Hamilton. 1992. Creating a Regional Constituency on Cape Cod. In *State and Regional Initiatives for Managing Growth: Policy Issues and Practical Concerns,* edited by Douglas R. Porter. Washington, D.C.: Urban Land Institute.

Casella, Sam, AICP, Casella and Associates. 1990. Clearwater, Fla.: personal communication, February 13.

Casella, Sam. December 1984. What Is TIF? In *Tax Increment Financing,* Planning Advisory Service Report No. 389: 1–10. Chicago: American Planning Association.

Catanese, Anthony J., and Arthur C. Nelson. 1988. *The Buying of America's Neighborhoods: The Planning Policy Implications of Neighborhood Buyouts.* Atlanta, Ga.: Center for Urban Planning and Development, Georgia Institute of Technology.

Catanese, Anthony J., and James C. Snyder, eds. 1979. *Introduction to Urban Planning.* New York: McGraw-Hill.

Center for Urban Policy Research. 1992. *Impact Assessment of the New Jersey Interim State Development and Redevelopment Plan.* New Brunswick, N.J.: Center for Urban Policy Research, Rutgers University.

Center for Urban Studies at Portland State University and Regional Financial Advisors, Inc. 1990. *Local Government Infrastructure Funding in Oregon.* Salem, Ore.: Land Conservation and Development Commission.

Cervero, Robert. 1986. Unlocking Suburban Gridlock. *Journal of the American Planning Association* 52, 4: 389–406.

Chapin, F. Stuart, Jr., and Edward J. Kaiser. 1979. *Urban Land Use Planning.* 3d ed. Urbana, Ill.: University of Illinois Press.

Clawson, Marion. 1971. *Suburban Land Conversion.* Baltimore: Resources for the Future.

Clawson, Marion. 1962. Urban Sprawl and Land Speculation. *Land Economics* 38, 1: 99–111.

Collier, Bill. February 8, 1990. A Little Bird, A Lot of Real Estate. *Austin American-Statesman,* A1.

Committee of the Regional Plan of New York and Its Environs. 1992. *New York Regional Survey of New York and Its Environs.* New York: Regional Plan Commission.

Congressional Budget Office. 1992. *The Economic Effects of the Savings and Loan Crisis.* Washington, D.C.: Congress of the United States.

Conklin, Howard, and William Bryant. 1974. Agricultural Districts: A Compromise Approach to Agricultural Preservation. *American Journal of Agricultural Economics* 56: 607–13.

Connors, Donald L., and Anne Richard Jackowitz. 1992. Summary of Cape Cod Commission Act. In *State and Regional Initiatives for Managing Growth: Policy Issues and Practical Concerns,* edited by Douglas R. Porter. Washington, D.C.: Urban Land Institute.

Corr, O. Casey. January 1990. Seattle in CAPtivity. *Planning* 55, 1: 18–21.

Correll, Mark R., Jane H. Lillydahl, and Larry D. Singell. 1978. The Effects of Greenbelts on Residential Property Values. *Land Economics* 54, 2: 207–17.

Coughlin, Robert C., David Berry, and Thomas Plaut. 1978. Differential Assessment of Real Property as an Incentive to Open Space Preservation and Farmland Retention. *National Tax Journal* 31, 2: 165–79.

Counts, Rick, ed. November-December 1989. Affordable Housing In Spite of State and Federal Cutbacks. *City Planning and Management News,* 1–2.

Courant, Paul N. 1976. On the Effect of Fiscal Zoning on Land and Housing Values. *Journal of Urban Economics* 3: 88–94.

Currier, Barry A. 1978. An Analysis of Differential Taxation as a Method of Maintaining Agricultural and Open Space Land Uses. *University of Florida Law Review* 30, 5: 821–42.

Curtin, Daniel J. 1994. *California Land Use and Planning Law.* Point Arena, Calif.: Solano Press.

Daniels, Thomas L. 1991. The Purchase of Development Rights: Preserving Agricultural Land and Open Space. *Journal of the American Planning Association* 57, 4: 421–31.

Daniels, Thomas L. 1986. Hobby Farming in America. *Journal of Rural Studies* 2, 1: 31–40.

Daniels, Thomas L., and Mark B. Lapping. 1984. Has Vermont's Land Use Control Program Failed?: Evaluating Act 250. *Journal of the American Planning Association* 50, 4: 502–8.

Daniels, Thomas L., and Arthur C. Nelson. 1986. Is Oregon's Farmland Preservation Program Working? *Journal of the American Planning Association* 52, 1: 22–32.

Daniels, Thomas L., Robert H. Daniels, and Mark B. Lapping. 1986. The Vermont Land Gains Tax. *American Journal of Economics and Sociology* 45, 4: 441–56.

Dantzig, G. B., and T. L. Saaty. 1973. *Compact City.* San Francisco: Freeman.

Davis, Judy S. 1990. *Commuting Patterns of Exurban Households.* Portland, Ore.: Center for Urban Studies, Portland State University.

Davis, Judy S., Arthur C. Nelson, and Kenneth J. Dueker. 1994. The New 'Burbs. *Journal of the American Planning Association* 60, 1: 45–60.

Davis, Judy S., Arthur C. Nelson, and Kenneth J. Dueker. 1990. *The New 'Burbs*. Atlanta, Ga.: Center for Planning and Development, Georgia Institute of Technology.

DeGrove, John M. 1992. *Planning and Growth Management*. Cambridge, Mass.: Lincoln Institute of Land Policy.

DeGrove, John M. 1984. *Land Growth and Politics*. Chicago: Planners Press.

DeGrove, John M., and Nancy E. Stroud. 1980. *Oregon's State Urban Strategy*. Washington, D.C.: U.S. Department of Housing and Urban Development.

deHaven-Smith, Lance. 1985. Special Districts: A Structural Approach to Infrastructure Finance. In *The Changing Structure of Infrastructure Finance*, edited by James C. Nicholas. Lincoln Institute of Land Policy, Monograph #85-5. Cambridge, Mass.: Lincoln Institute of Land Policy, 59–77.

de la Barra, T., and P. A. Rickaby. 1982. Modeling Regional Energy Use. *Environment and Planning* B 11: 87–110.

Department of the Environment. 1974. *A Study of the Cambridge Sub-Region*. London: Her Majesty's Stationery Office.

Dideriksen, Ray, and R. Neil Sampson. 1976. Important Farmlands—A National Viewpoint. *Journal of Soil and Water Conservation* 31, 5: 195–97.

Dougherty, Laurence, Sandra Tapella, and Gerald Sumner. 1975. *Municipal Service Pricing: Impact on Fiscal Position*. Santa Monica, Calif.: Rand Corporation.

Dowall, David. 1986. Planners and Office Overbuilding. *Journal of the American Planning Association* 52, 2: 131–32.

Downing, Paul B. 1973. User Charges and the Development of Urban Land. *National Tax Journal* 26: 631–37.

Downing, Paul B., and Richard D. Gustely. 1977. The Public Service Costs of Alternative Development Patterns. In *Local Service Pricing Policies and Their Effect on Urban Spatial Structure*, edited by Paul B. Downing. Vancouver, B.C.: University of British Columbia Press.

Downs, Anthony. 1989. *The Need for a New Vision for the Development of Large U.S. Metropolitan Areas*. New York: Salomon Brothers.

Downs, Anthony. 1973. *Opening Up the Suburbs*. New Haven, Conn.: Yale University Press.

Duany, Andres, and Elizabeth Plater-Zyberk. 1991. *Towns and Town-Making Principles*. Cambridge, Mass.: Harvard University Graduate School of Design.

Duerksen, Christopher J. 1986. *Aesthetics and Land-Use Controls: Beyond Ecology and Economics*. Planning Advisory Service Report No. 399. Chicago: American Planning Association.

ECO-Northwest, Inc., Brown and Caldwell Consulting Engineers, and Government Finance Associates. 1989. *An Assessment of Funding for Sewerage and Drinking Water Facilities in the State of Oregon*. Portland, Ore.: Oregon State Department of Environmental Quality and Oregon State Department of Human Resources, Health Division.

Ely, R. T., and G. S. Wehrwein. 1940. *Land Economics*. New York: Macmillan.

Environmental Board of Vermont. 1981. *Act 250: A Performance Evaluation*. Montpelier, Vt.: Environmental Board of Vermont.

Ervin, David E. et al. 1977. Land Use Control: The Economic and Political Effects. New York: Praeger.

Esseks, J. D. 1978. The Politics of Farmland Preservation. *Policy Studies Journal* 6: 514–19.

Ewing, Reid. 1991. *Developing Successful New Communities*. Washington, D.C.: Urban Land Institute.

Feagin, Joe R. 1985. The State in the Free Enterprise City: The Case of Houston. *American Journal of Sociology* 90: 1209–30.

Fehr and Peers Associates. 1992. *Metropolitan Transportation Commission Bay Area Trip Rate Survey Analysis*. San Francisco: Association of Bay Area Governments.

Ferguson, Erik. 1990. Transportation Demand Management: Planning, Development, and Implementation. *Journal of the American Planning Association* 56, 4: 442–56.

Fischel, William. 1990. *Do Growth Controls Matter? A Review of Growth Management Literature*. Cambridge, Mass.: Lincoln Institute of Land Policy.

Fischel, W. A. 1985. *The Economics of Zoning Laws: A Property Rights Approach to American Land Use Controls*. Baltimore: Johns Hopkins University Press.

Fischel, William. 1982. The Urbanization of Agricultural Land. *Land Economics* 58, 2: 236–59.

Fischer, Michael L. 1985. California's Coastal Program: Larger-than-Local Interests Built into Local Plans. *Journal of the American Planning Association* 51, 3: 312–21.

Fisher, Ronald. 1988. *State and Local Public Finance.* Homewood, Ill.: Irwin.

Florida Advisory Council on Intergovernmental Relations. 1989. *Impact Fee Use in Florida: An Update.* Tallahassee, Fla.: Florida Advisory Council on Intergovernmental Relations.

Florida Atlantic University/Florida International University Joint Center for Environmental and Urban Problems. 1988. *Monograph #88-2.* Fort Lauderdale, Fla.: Florida Atlantic University/Florida International University Joint Center for Environmental and Urban Problems.

Florida Department of Community Affairs. February 1990. State Acts to Better Protect Coastal Islands. *Florida Planning* 10, 6: 1, 6.

Florida Department of Community Affairs. 1989. *Technical Memo* 4, 4. Tallahassee, Fla.: Florida Department of Community Affairs.

Florida Governor's Task Force on Urban Growth Patterns. 1989. *Final Report.* Tallahassee, Fla.: Office of the Governor.

Forkenbrock, David J., and Peter S. Fisher. 1983. Tax Incentives to Slow Farmland Conversion. *Policy Studies Journal* 11: 25–37.

Frank, James E. 1989a. *Pricing Strategies in the Promotion of Less Costly Development Patterns.* Tallahassee, Fla.: Florida Governor's Task Force on Urban Growth Patterns, Office of the Governor.

Frank, James E. 1989b. *The Costs of Alternative Development Patterns.* Washington, D.C.: Urban Land Institute.

Frank, James E., and Paul B. Downing. 1988. Patterns of Impact Fee Use. In *Development Impact Fees,* edited by Arthur C. Nelson. Chicago: Planners Press.

Freilich, Robert H. 1978. Saving the Land. *Urban Lawyer* 13: 27–40.

Freilich, Robert H. 1972. Golden v. Town of Ramapo: Establishing a New Dimension in American Planning Law. *Urban Lawyer* 4: ix–xv.

Fuller, Anthony M., and Julius A. Mage, eds. 1975. *Part-Time Farming: Proceedings of the First Rural Geography Symposium.* Guelph, Ont.: University of Guelph.

Fulton, William. 1990. Ventura, Calif.: personal communication, February.

Fulton, William. 1989. Two States Find a Way to Keep the Peace. *Planning* 55, 10: 16–17.

Furuseth, Owen J. 1981. Update on Oregon's Agricultural Protection Program: A Land Use Perspective. *Natural Resource Journal* 21: 57–70.

Furuseth, Owen J. 1980. The Oregon Agricultural Protection Program: A Review and Assessment. *Natural Resources Journal* 20: 603–14.

Furuseth, Owen J., and John T. Pierce. 1982. *Agricultural Land in Urban Society.* Chicago: Association of American Geographers.

Gaffney, Mason. 1964. Containment Policies for Urban Sprawl. In *Approaches to the Study of Urbanization,* edited by Richard L. Stauber. Lawrence: University of Kansas.

Gale, Dennis E. 1992. Eight State-Sponsored Growth Management Programs: A Comparative Analysis. *Journal of the American Planning Association* 58, 4: 425–39.

Geier, Karl E. 1980. Agricultural Districts and Zoning: A State-Local Approach to a National Problem. *Ecology Law Quarterly* 8: 655–96.

Gerbers, John. 1989. Take Me Home, Country Roads. Reprinted in *The Best of Planning.* Chicago: Planners Press.

Gleeson, Michael E. 1979. The Effects of an Urban Growth Management System on Land Values. *Land Economics* 55, 3: 350–65.

Glickfeld, Madelyn, and Ned Levine. 1992. *Regional Growth . . . Local Reaction.* Cambridge, Mass.: Lincoln Institute of Land Policy.

Gloudemans, Robert J. 1974. *Use-Value Farmland Assessments.* Chicago: International Association of Assessing Officers.

Godschalk, David R. March 1987. Balancing Growth with Critical Area Programs: The Florida and Chesapeake Bay Cases. *Urban Land:* 16–19.

Goldberg, Michael, and Peter Chinloy. 1984. *Urban Land Economics.* New York: Wiley.

Gordon, Dennis. 1990. Allen County, Ind.: personal communication, March 30.

Gottmann, Jean. 1961. *Megalopolis.* New York: Twentieth Century Fund.

Gurko, Stephen. 1972. Federal Income Taxes and Urban Sprawl. *Denver Law Journal:* 329–88.

Guskind, Robert. June 1988. New Jersey Says, "Enough." *Planning* 54, 6: 24–30.

Gustafson, Greg C., Thomas L. Daniels, and Rosalyn P. Shirack. 1982. The Oregon Land Use Act. *Journal of the American Planning Association* 48, 3: 365–73.

Hagman, Donald C., and Julian Conrad Juergensmeyer. 1987. *Urban Planning and Land Development Control Law.* St. Paul, Minn.: West.

Hales, Charles. 1992. Predictability + Certainty = Housing. *Urban Land.*

Hand, Jacqueline P. 1984. Right-to-Farm Laws: Breaking New Ground in the Preservation of Farmland. *University of Pittsburgh Law Review* 45: 297.

Hanson, David E., and S. I. Schwartz. 1975. Landowner Behavior at the Rural-Urban Fringe in Response to Preferential Property Taxation. *Land Economics* 51, 4: 341–54.

Hart, John Fraser. 1980. Land Use and Change in a Piedmont County. *Annals of the Association of American Geographers* 70, 4: 492–527.

Harvey, Robert O., and W. A. V. Clark. 1965. The Nature and Economics of Urban Sprawl. *Land Economics* 61, 1: 1–9.

Healy, Robert G., and James L. Short. 1981. *The Market for Rural Land: Trends, Issues, Policies.* Washington, D.C.: The Conservation Foundation.

Healy, Robert G., and Jeffrey A. Zinn. 1985. Environment and Development Conflicts in Coastal Zone Management. *Journal of the American Planning Association* 51, 3: 299–311.

Herbers, John. 1986. *The New Heartland.* New York: Times Books.

Hirsch, Werner Z. 1977. The Efficiency of Restrictive Land-Use Restrictions. *Land Economics* 53, 2: 145–56.

Howard, Charles. 1989. *Washington State 1990 Transportation Policy Plan—Subcommittee Report, Land Use.* Olympia, Wash.: Washington State Department of Transportation.

Howard, Ebenezer. 1898. *Tomorrow: A Peaceful Path to Reform.* Revised and republished in 1902 and 1970 as *Garden Cities of Tomorrow.* London: Faber and Faber.

Huddleston, Jack R. 1986. Distribution of Development Costs Under Tax Increment Financing. *Journal of the American Planning Association* 52, 2: 194–98.

Ingemoen, Mark. 1990. Communication with Joint Center for Urban and Environmental Problems, Florida Atlantic University/Florida International University, Ft. Lauderdale, Fla. August 1990.

Inman, Robert P. 1979. Subsidies, Regulations, and the Taxation of Property in Large U.S. Cities. *National Tax Journal* 32: 159–68.

Innes, Judith Eleanor. 1992. Group Processes and Social Construction of Growth Management: Florida, Vermont, and New Jersey. *Journal of the American Planning Association* 58, 4: 440–53.

Institute of Transportation Engineers Technical Input Committee. June 1988. Private Financing of Transportation Improvements. *ITE Journal* 58, 6: 43–52.

International Association of Assessing Officers. 1975. *Property Tax Incentives for Preservation: Use Value Assessment and the Preservation of Farmland, Open Space, and Historic Sites.* Chicago: International Association of Assessing Officers.

Isard, Walter, and Robert E. Coughlin. 1957. *Municipal Costs and Revenues Resulting from Growth.* Wellesley, Mass.: Chandler-Davis.

Jacobs, Jane. 1961. *The Death and Life of Great American Cities.* New York: Random House.

James Duncan and Associates. 1989. *The Search for Efficient Urban Growth Patterns.* Tallahassee, Fla.: Florida Department of Community Affairs.

Johnston, Robert A, Seymour I. Schwartz, and Steve Tracy. 1984. Growth Phasing and Resistance to Infill Development in Sacramento County. *Journal of the American Planning Association* 50, 4: 434–46.

Kain, John F. 1967. *Urban Form and the Costs of Urban Services.* Cambridge, Mass.: MIT–Harvard Joint Center for Urban Studies.

Kamara, Sheku G. 1987. Effect of Local Variations in Public Services on Housing Production at the Fringe of a Growth-Controlled Multicounty Metropolitan Area. *Urban Studies* 24: 109–17.

Kamara, Sheku G. 1984. *Fringe Area Growth in Metropolitan Portland.* Ph.D. dissertation. Portland, Ore.: School of Urban and Public Affairs, Portland State University.

Keating, Dennis W. 1986. Linking Downtown Development to Broader Community Goals: An Analysis of Linkage Policy in Three Cities. *Journal of the American Planning Association* 52, 2: 133–41.

Keene, John C. et al. 1975. *Untaxing Open Space.* Washington, D.C.: Council on Environmental Quality.

Kelbaugh, Doug, ed. 1989. *The Pedestrian Pocket Book.* Princeton, N.J.: Princeton Architectural Press.

Kelly, Eric Damian. 1993. *Managing Community Growth: Policies, Techniques, and Impacts.* Westport, Conn: Praeger.

Kelly, Eric Damian. 1988. Zoning. In *The Practice of Local Government Planning,* 2nd ed. Washington, D.C.: International City Management Association.

Keys, Dale L., and George R. Peterson. 1977. *Metropolitan Development and Energy Consumption.* Washington, D.C.: The Urban Institute.

Klein, William R. 1986. Nantucket Tithes for Open Space. *Planning* 52, 8: 10–13.

Knaap, Gerrit J. 1989. State Land Use Control and Inclusionary Housing: Evidence from Oregon. Paper presented at the 1989 meetings of the Association of Collegiate Schools of Planning, Portland, Oregon.

Knaap, Gerrit J. 1985. The Price Effects of an Urban Growth Boundary in Metropolitan Portland, Oregon. *Land Economics* 61, 1: 26–35.

Knaap, Gerrit J. 1982. *The Price Effects of an Urban Growth Boundary: A Test for the Effects of Timing.* Ph.D. dissertation. Eugene, Ore.: University of Oregon.

Knaap, Gerrit J. 1981. *The Price Effects of an Urban Growth Boundary.* Portland, Ore.: Metropolitan Service District of Portland, Oregon, and the Western Interstate Commission for Higher Education.

Knaap, Gerrit J., and Arthur C. Nelson. 1992. *The Regulated Landscape.* Cambridge, Mass.: Lincoln Institute of Land Policy.

Knaap, Gerrit J., and Arthur C. Nelson. 1988. The Effects of Regional Land Use Control in Oregon: A Theoretical and Empirical Review. *The Review of Regional Studies* 18, 2: 37–46.

Kolesar, John, and Jaye Scholl. 1972. *Misplaced Hopes, Misspent Millions.* Princeton, N.J.: The Center for Analysis of Public Issues.

Lafferty, Ronald N., and H. E. Frech, III. 1978. Community Environment and the Market Value of Single-Family Homes. *The Journal of Law and Economics* 21, 2: 381–94.

Land Conservation and Development Commission. 1989. *Report to the Oregon Legislature.* Salem, Ore.: Department of Land Conservation and Development.

Land Conservation and Development Commission. 1986. *Oregon Lands.* Salem, Ore.: Department of Land Conservation and Development.

Land Conservation and Development Commission. 1976. *Statewide Goals and Guidelines.* Salem, Ore.: Land Conservation and Development Commission.

Land Trust Exchange. 1989. Land Trusts: The Nation's Fastest-Growing Conservation Movement. *Exchange* (Spring): 188–219.

Landis, John D. 1986. Land Regulation and the Price of New Housing: Lessons from Three California Cities. *Journal of the American Planning Association* 52, 1: 9–21.

Lapping, Mark B. 1980. Agricultural Land Retention: Responses Foreign and American. In *The Farm and the City: Rivals or Allies?* edited by A. M. Woodruff. Englewood Cliffs, N.J.: Prentice-Hall.

Lapping, Mark B. 1979. Agricultural Land Retention Strategies: Some Underpinnings. *Journal of Soil and Water Conservation* 34: 124–26.

Lapping, Mark B., and J. F. FitzSimmons. 1982. Beyond the Land Issue: Farm Viability Strategies. *GeoJournal* 6: 519–24.

Lapping, Mark B., and Nels R. Leutwiler. 1987. Agriculture in Conflict: Right-to-Farm Laws and the Pari-Urban Milieu for Farming. In *Sustaining Agriculture in Cities*, edited by William Lockeretz. Ankeny, Iowa: Soil and Water Conservation Society of America.

Lapping, Mark B., John Keller, and Thomas L. Daniels. 1990. *Rural Planning in North America.* New York: Guilford Press.

Lapping, Mark B., George E. Penfold, and S. MacPherson. 1983. Right-to-Farm Laws. *Journal of Soil and Water Conservation* 38: 465–67.

Lawlor, James. 1992. State of the Statutes. *Planning* 58, 12: 10–14.

Lee, Douglass B . 1981. Market Failure. In *The Land Use Policy Debate in the United States,* edited by Judith Innes deNuefville. New York: Praeger.

Leinberger, Christopher B. 1994. Remarks made to the Atlanta regional meeting of the Urban Land Institute at Cobb Galleria Center, December 8, 1994.

Leonard, Jeffrey H. 1983. *Managing Oregon's Growth.* Washington, D.C.: Conservation Foundation.

Lessinger, Jack. 1962. The Case for Scatteration. *Journal of the American Planning Association* 28, 3: 159–69.

Leutwiler, Nels R. 1986. *Farmland Preservation Laws: What Do They Do? Can They Be Justified?* Masters thesis. Denver: Department of Urban Planning, University of Colorado at Denver.

Lewis, Sylvia. October 1989. Border Wars. *Planning* 55, 10: 8–13.

Lim, Gill C. 1983. *Regional Planning.* Totawa, N.J.: Rowman & Allanheld.

Lynch, Kevin. 1983. *Theory of Good Urban Form.* Cambridge, Mass.: MIT Press.

McKee, David L., and Gerald H. Smith. 1972. Environmental Diseconomies of Urban Sprawl. *The American Journal of Economics and Sociology* 31, 2: 181–88.

Marchand, J. M., and K. P. Russell. 1973. Externalities, Liability, Separability, and Resource Allocation. *American Economic Review* 63, 4: 611–20.

Mason, Robert J. 1992. *Contested Lands: Conflict and Compromise in New Jersey's Pine Barrens*. Philadelphia: Temple University Press.

Matuszeski, William. 1985. Managing the Federal Coastal Program. *Journal of the American Planning Association* 51, 3: 266–74.

Meier, Bruce W. 1989. *The Farmer's Response and the Surface of the Land Rent Cone of Green Bay*. Miami, Ohio: Department of Geography, Miami University.

Meier, Bruce W. 1988. An Urban Induced Ring of Disinvestment by Farm Operators. Paper presented to the 1988 Conference of the Association of American Geographers, Portland, Oregon.

Metropolitan Service District. 1979. *Urban Growth Boundary Findings*. Portland, Ore.: Metropolitan Service District.

Metropolitan Service District. Undated. *Comments on UGB Study*. Portland, Ore.: Metropolitan Service District.

Metropolitan Washington Council of Governments. 1991. *Transportation Demand Impacts of Alternative Land Use Scenarios*. Washington, D.C.: Metropolitan Washington Council of Governments.

Michael, Joel. 1987. Tax Increment Financing: Local Redevelopment Finance After Tax Reform. *Government Finance Review* 3: 17–21.

Middlesex–Somerset–Mercer Regional Council. 1991. *The Impact of Various Land Use Strategies on Suburban Mobility*. Princeton, N.J.: Middlesex–Somerset–Mercer Regional Council.

Miller, Thomas I. 1986. Must Growth Restrictions Eliminate Moderate-Priced Housing? *Journal of the American Planning Association* 52, 3: 319–25.

Mills, Edwin S. 1969. The Value of Urban Land. In *The Quality of the Urban Environment*, edited by Harvey Perloff. Baltimore: Resources for the Future, Johns Hopkins University.

Mills, Edwin S., and Bruce W. Hamilton. 1988. *Urban Economics*. 4th ed. Glenview, Ill.: Scott, Foresman.

Moore, Terry, and Arthur C. Nelson. 1992. *Assessing Urban Growth Boundaries*. Atlanta, Ga.: Center for Urban Planning and Development, City Planning Program, Georgia Institute of Technology.

Moudon, Anne Vernez, ed. 1990. *Master-Planned Communities: Shaping Exurbs in the 1990s*. Seattle: College of Architecture and Urban Planning, University of Washington.

Mumford, Lewis. 1961. *The City in History*. New York: Harcourt, Brace, and World.

Murdock, Pat. April 1989. Grow Now, Worry Later. *Planning* 55, 4: 20–27.

Muth, Richard F. 1961. Economic Change and Rural-Urban Land Conversions. *Econometrica* 29: 1–23.

National Agricultural Lands Study. 1981. *National Agricultural Lands Study*. Washington, D.C.: National Agricultural Lands Study, U.S. Department of Agriculture.

National Association of Home Builders. 1986. *Cost Effective Site Planning*. Washington, D.C.: National Association of Home Builders.

National Association of State Development Agencies. 1989. *Farmland Notes*. Washington, D.C.: National Association of State Development Agencies Research Foundation Farmland Project.

National Commission on Urban Problems. 1968. Federal Income Taxation and Urban Housing. In *Building the American City*, part IV, chap. 7. Washington, D.C.: U.S. Government Printing Office.

National Research Council. 1974. *Toward an Understanding of Metropolitan America*. San Francisco: Canfield.

Nelson, Arthur C. 1994. Toward Broadacre City. *Journal of Architecture and Planning Research* (Forthcoming).

Nelson, Arthur C. 1992a. Preserving Prime Farmland in the Face of Urbanization. *Journal of the American Planning Association* 58, 4: 467–88.

Nelson, Arthur C. 1992b. Improving Urban Growth Boundary Management. *Real Estate Finance* 58, 4: 11–22.

Nelson, Arthur C. 1992c. *New Communities and Florida Planning Policy*. Fort Lauderdale, Fla.: Joint Center for Environmental and Urban Problems, Florida Atlantic University.

Nelson, Arthur C. 1992d. Lessons of Urban Growth Boundary Design and Management in Oregon. *Real Estate Finance* 8, 4: 11–22.

Nelson, Arthur C. 1992e. Characterizing Exurbia. *Journal of Planning Literature* 6, 4: 350–68.

Nelson, Arthur C. 1991. The Analytic Basis for an Effective Prime Farmland Landscape Preservation Scheme in the U.S.A. *Journal of Rural Studies* 6, 3: 337–46.

Nelson, Arthur C. 1990a. Economic Critique of Prime Farmland Protection Programs in the United States. *Journal of Rural Studies* 6: 114–42.

Nelson, Arthur C. 1990b. Blazing New Planning Trails in Oregon. *Urban Land* 49, 8: 32–35.

Nelson, Arthur C. 1990c. Growth Strategies: The New Planning Game in Georgia. *Carolina Planning* 16, 1: 1–6.

Nelson, Arthur C. 1989. Benefits of Planning to Prevent Urban Sprawl. *Quality Cities* 63, 6: 16–20.

Nelson, Arthur C. 1988a. An Empirical Note on How Regional Urban Containment Policy Influences an Interaction Between Greenbelt and Exurban Land Markets. *Journal of the American Planning Association* 52, 2: 178–84.

Nelson, Arthur C. 1988b. Additional and Reduced Demand, Amenity and Disamenity Increment Recapture Considerations of Urban Containment Policies. *Real Estate Issues* 13, 1: 47–51.

Nelson, Arthur C. 1987a. The Effect of a Regional Sewer Service on Land Values, Growth Patterns, and Regional Fiscal Structure Within a Metropolitan Area. *Urban Resources* 4, 2: 15–18, 58–59.

Nelson, Arthur C. 1987b. How Regional Planning Influences Rural Land Values. In *Sustaining Agriculture Near Cities*, edited by William Lockeretz. Ankeny, Iowa: Soil and Water Conservation Society of America.

Nelson, Arthur C. 1986a. Using Land Markets to Evaluate Urban Containment Programs. *Journal of the American Planning Association* 52, 2: 156–71.

Nelson, Arthur C. 1986b. Towards a Theory of the American Rural Residential Land Market. *Journal of Rural Studies* 2, 4: 309–19.

Nelson, Arthur C. 1985a. Demand, Segmentation, and Timing Effects of an Urban Containment Program on Urban Fringe Land Values. *Urban Studies* 22: 439–43.

Nelson, Arthur C. 1985b. A Unifying View of Greenbelt Influences on Regional Land Values and Implications for Regional Policy. *Growth and Change* 16, 2: 43–48.

Nelson, Arthur C. 1984. *Evaluating Urban Containment Programs*. Portland, Ore.: Center for Urban Studies, Portland State University.

Nelson, Arthur C. 1983a. Comment on the Oregon Land Use Act. *Journal of the American Planning Association* 49, 1: 85–87.

Nelson, Arthur C. 1983b. Comment. *Natural Resources Journal* 23, 1: 1–5.

Nelson, Arthur C., and Kenneth J. Dueker. 1990. The Exurbanization of America With Planning Policy Implications. *Journal of Planning Education and Research* 10, 2: 91–100.

Nelson, Arthur C., and Kenneth J. Dueker. 1989. Exurban Living Through Improved Technology. *Journal of Urban Planning and Development* 115, 3: 101–13.

Nelson, Arthur C., and Gerrit J. Knaap. 1987. A Theoretical and Empirical Argument for Centralized Regional Sewer Planning. *Journal of the American Planning Association* 53, 4: 479–86.

Nelson, Arthur C., and Jeffrey H. Milgroom. 1994. Central City Revitalization Through Regional Growth Management. In *Central City Revitalization*, edited by Fritz Wagner. Beverly Hills, Calif.: Sage.

Nelson, Arthur C., and J. Richard Recht. 1988. Inducing the Rural Residential Land Market to Grow Timber in an Antiquated Rural Subdivision. *Journal of the American Planning Association* 54, 4: 529–36.

Nelson, Arthur C., William J. Drummond, and David S. Sawicki. 1992. *Exurban Industrialization*. Washington, D.C.: Economic Development Administration, U.S. Department of Commerce.

Nelson, Arthur C., James C. Nicholas, and Lindell Marsh. 1992. New-Fangled Fees. *Planning Magazine* 58, 11: 20–24.

Netter, Edith, and John Vranicar. 1981. *Linking Plans and Regulations: Local Responses to Consistency Laws in California and Florida*. Planning Advisory Report Number 363. Chicago: American Planning Association.

Newman, Peter, and Jeffrey Kenworthy. 1989. *Cities and Automobile Dependence*. Sydney, Australia: Gower.

North Central Texas Council of Governments. 1990. *Urban Form/Transportation System Options for the Future*. Arlington, Tex.: North Central Texas Council of Governments.

Northam, Ray M. 1971. Vacant Land in American Cities. *Land Economics* 47, 4: 345–55.

Office of Policy Development and Research. 1992. *Removing Regulatory Barriers to Affordable Housing: How States and Localities Are Moving Ahead*. Washington, D.C.: U.S. Department of Housing and Urban Development.

Ohls, James C., Richard C. Weisberg, and Michelle White. 1974. The Effect of Zoning on Land Value. *Journal of Urban Economics* 1, 1: 428–44.

Olson, Lyle. 1988. Fiscal Disparities Program—Not All It Is Purported to Be. *Public Investment*. Chicago: American Planning Association.

1,000 Friends of Oregon. 1981. *Administration of Exclusive Farm Lands in Twelve Oregon Counties: A Study of County Application of State Standards to Protect Oregon Farmland*. Portland: 1,000 Friends of Oregon.

Oregon Economic Development Department. 1989. *Oregon Shines*. Salem: Oregon Economic Development Department.

Oregon Health Division. 1991. *Safety on Tap: A Strategy for Providing Safe, Dependable Drinking Water in the 1990s*. Portland: Department of Human Resources, Oregon Health Division.

Pacific Meridian Resources. 1991. *Analysis of the Relationship of Resource Dwelling and Partition Approvals Between 1985–87 and Resource Management in 1990*. Salem: Oregon Department of Land Conservation and Development.

Pasour, E. C. 1972. The Capitalization of Real Property Taxes Levied on Farm Real Estate. *American Journal of Agricultural Economics* 52: 549–56.

Pease, James R. 1984a. *Profiles of Commercial Agriculture for the Southern Willamette Valley*. Oregon State University Extension Service Special Report 696. Corvallis: Oregon State University.

Pease, James R. 1984b. *Profiles of Commercial Agriculture for the Northern Willamette Valley*. Oregon State University Extension Service Special Report 696. Corvallis: Oregon State University.

Peiser, Richard B. 1989. Density and Urban Sprawl. *Land Economics* 65, 3: 194–204.

Peiser, Richard B. 1981. Land Development Regulation: A Case Study of Dallas and Houston, Texas. *Journal of the American Real Estate and Urban Economics Association* 9, 4: 397–417.

Peiser, Richard B. 1984. Does It Pay to Plan Suburban Development? *Journal of the American Planning Association* 50, 4: 419–33.

Penfold, George. 1988. Right-to-Farm as a Method of Conflict Resolution. Paper presented at the Conference on Resolving Rural Development Conflicts, Mount Allison University, New Brunswick.

Peterson, George E., and Harvey Yampolsky. 1975. *Urban Development of Metropolitan Farmland*. Washington, D.C.: The Urban Institute.

Pizor, Peter J. 1986. Making TDR Work: A Study of Program Implementation. *Journal of the American Planning Association* 52, 2: 203–211.

Platt, Rutherford H. 1985. The Farmland Conversion Debate. *Professional Geographer* 37, 4: 433–42.

Plaut, Thomas. 1977. *The Real Property Tax, Differential Assessment, and the Loss of Farmland on the Rural-Urban Fringe*. Regional Science Research Institute Discussion Paper Series No. 97. Amherst, Mass.: Regional Science Research Institute, University of Massachusetts.

Plaut, Thomas. 1976. *The Effects of Urbanization on the Loss of Farmland at the Rural-Urban Fringe: A National and Regional Perspective*. Regional Science Research Institute Discussion Paper Series No. 94. Amherst, Mass.: Regional Science Research Institute, University of Massachusetts.

Pope, C. Arden. 1985. Agricultural Productive and Consumptive Use Components of Rural Land Values in Texas. *American Journal of Agricultural Economics* 66, 1: 81–86.

Popenoe, David. 1979. Urban Sprawl: Some Neglected Sociological Considerations. *Sociology and Social Research* 63, 2: 255–68.

Popenoe, David. 1974. Urban Residential Differentiation. In *The Community*, edited by M. P. Elliott. New York: Free Press.

Porter, Douglas R., ed. 1992. *State and Regional Initiatives for Managing Growth: Policy Issues and Practical Concerns*. Washington, D.C.: Urban Land Institute.

Porter, Douglas R., and Lindel Marsh, eds. 1989. *Development Agreements: Practice, Policy, and Prospects*. Washington, D.C.: Urban Land Institute.

Porter, Douglas R., and Richard B. Peiser. 1984. *Financing Infrastructure to Support Community Growth*. Washington, D.C.: Urban Land Institute.

Porter, Douglas R., Patrick L. Phillips, and Terry J. Lassar. 1988. *Flexible Zoning*. Washington, D.C.: Urban Land Institute.

Prestbo, John. ed. 1975. *This Abundant Land*. Princeton, N.J.: Dow Jones Books.

Price Waterhouse. 1986. *Making the Right Turn: Protecting the Public Investment in Oregon's Roads and Bridges*. Portland: League of Oregon Cities, Association of Oregon Counties, and Oregon Department of Transportation.

Pucher, John. 1988. Urban Travel Behavior as the Outcome of Public Policy. *Journal of the American Planning Association* 54, 4: 509–20.

Puget Sound Council of Governments. 1990. *Summary and Comparison Between Alternatives—Vision 2020*. Seattle, Wash.: Puget Sound Council of Governments.

Pushkarev, Boris S., and Jeffrey M. Zupan. 1977. *Public Transportation and Land Use Policy*. Bloomington: Indiana University Press.

Ratcliff, Richard U. 1949. *Urban Economics*. New York: McGraw-Hill.

Real Estate Research Corporation. 1982. Infill *Development Strategies*. Washington, D.C.: Urban Land Institute and American Planning Association.

Real Estate Research Corporation. 1974. *The Costs of Sprawl*. Washington, D.C.: U.S. Department of Housing and Urban Development.

Reilly, William K., ed. 1975. The Use of Land: A Citizen's Policy Guide to Urban Growth. In *Management and Control of Growth*, vol. 1, edited by Randall W. Scott. Washington, D.C.: Urban Land Institute.

Resolution Trust Corporation. 1993. *Summary of Resolution Finance Data, by State, as of January 27, 1993*. Atlanta, Ga.: Resolution Trust Corporation.

Richardson, Harry W., and Peter Gordon. 1993. Market Planning: Oxymoron or Common Sense? *Journal of the American Planning Association* 59, 3: 347–52.

Rickaby, P. A. 1987. Six Regional Settlements Compared: Environment and Planning B. *Planning and Design* 14: 193–223.

Rickaby, P. A. 1981. Six Regional Settlement Patterns: Environment and Planning B. *Planning and Design* 8: 191–212.

Rickaby, P. A., and J. P. Steadman. 1981. Energy Conservation and Configuration of Settlements and Transport Networks. In *New Energy Conservation Technologies and their Commercialisation*, Volume 3, edited by J. P. Millhone and E. H. Willis. Berlin: International Energy Agency and Springer, 2853–61.

Rohse, Mitch. 1987. *Land-Use Planning in Oregon*. Corvallis: Oregon State University Press.

Rose, Jerome B. 1984. Farmland Preservation Policy and Programs. *Natural Resources Journal* 24, 3: 591–640.

Rosser, J. Barkley. 1978. The Theory and Policy Implications of Spatial Discontinuities in Land Values. *Land Economics* 54, 4: 430–41.

Sampson, Neal R. 1981. *Farmland or Wasteland*. Philadelphia: Rodale Press.

San Diego Association of Governments. 1991a. *On-Board Survey*. San Diego, Calif.: San Diego Association of Governments.

San Diego Association of Governments. 1991b. *Regional Growth Management Strategy*. San Diego, Calif.: San Diego Association of Governments.

Schaeffer, Peter V., and Lewis D. Hopkins. 1987. Behavior of Land Developers: Planning and the Economics of Information. *Environment and Planning A* 19: 1221–32.

Schallau, Con H. 1989. Oregon's Forest Resources. In *Oregon Policy Choices*, edited by Lluana McCann. Eugene: Bureau of Governmental Research and Service, University of Oregon, 155–90.

Schiffman, Irving. 1989. *Alternative Techniques for Managing Growth*. Berkeley: Institute of Governmental Studies, University of California.

Schmid, A. Allen. 1968. *Converting Rural Land to Urban Uses*. Baltimore: Johns Hopkins University Press.

Schneider, Devon M., David R. Godschalk, and Norman Axler. 1978. *The Carrying Capacity Concept as a Planning Tool*. Planning Advisory Service Report No. 338. Chicago: American Planning Association.

Schoennauer, Gary, and Tom MacRostie. 1988. Impact Fees in the Nation's Fastest Growing City. Paper presented to the Planners Training Service Symposium. Chicago: American Planning Association.

Schultz, Marilyn Spigel, and Vivian Loeb Kassen. 1984. *Encyclopedia of Community Planning and Environmental Management*. New York: Facts on File Publications.

Scott, R. A., ed. 1975. *Management and Control of Growth*. Washington, D.C.: Urban Land Institute.

Sharpe, Sumner, Cogan-Sharpe-Cogan. 1990. Portland, Ore.: personal communication, February 23.

Shoup, Donald C. 1970. The Optimal Timing of Urban Land Development. *Papers and Proceedings of the Regional Science Association* 25: 33–44.

Siemon, Charles L. 1989. Carrying Capacity Planning: Rx for the Future? In *Implementation of the 1985 Growth Management Act: From Planning to Land Development Regulations*, Monograph #89-1. Fort Lauderdale: Fla.: Florids Atlantic University/Florida International University Joint Center for Environmental and Urban Problems, 9–38.

Sinclair, Robert. 1967. Von Thunen and Urban Sprawl. *Annals of the Association of American Geographers* 57: 72–87.

Solomon, Barry. 1984. Farmland Protection: A Case of Quality Not Quantity. *Land Use Policy*: 357–66.

Southwest Center for Urban Research. 1974. *Environmental Analysis for Development Planning: Chambers County, Texas*. Houston, Tex.: Southwest Center for Urban Research.

Spectorsky, Auguste C. 1955. *The Exurbanites*. Philadelphia: Lippincott.

Spellman, John. 1984. King County's Purchase of Development Rights Program. In *Protecting Farmlands*, edited by Frederick R. Steiner and John E. Theilacker. Westport, Conn.: AVI Publishing.

Spreiregen, Paul D. 1981. *Urban Design: The Architecture of Towns and Cities*. Malabar, Fla.: Kreiger.

Starnes, Earl M. 1991. Concurrency: Linchpin or Nemesis? Paper presented at the 1991 meeting of the Association of American Collegiate Schools of Planning, Oxford, England.

Steadman, J. P. 1977. Energy Patterns and Land Use. *Journal of Architectural Education* 30, 3: 62–67.

Stein, Clarence. 1957. *Toward New Towns for America*. New York: Reinhold.

Stein, Jay M., ed. 1993. *Growth Management: The Planning Challenge of the 1990s*. Newbury Park, Calif.: Sage.

Stern, Robert A. M. 1981. *The Anglo-American Suburb*. London: Architectural Design Profile.

Stokes, Samuel N., A. Elizabeth Watson, Genevieve P. Keller, and J. Timothy Keller. 1989. *Saving America's Countryside: A Guide to Rural Conservation*. Baltimore: Johns Hopkins University Press.

Stoler, Frederick D. 1979. *Farm-Use Assessment Revisited*. Cambridge, Mass.: Lincoln Institute of Land Policy.

Stone, P. A. 1973. *The Structure, Size, and Costs of Urban Settlements*. Cambridge, England: Cambridge University Press.

Sullivan, Arthur M. 1985. The Pricing of Urban Services and the Spatial Distribution of Residence. *Land Economics* 61, 1: 17–25.

Tabors, Richard D., Michael H. Shapiro, and Peter P. Rogers. 1976. *Land Use and the Pipe*. Lexington, Mass.: D.C. Heath, Lexington Books.

Taub, Theodore, and Robert M. Rhodes. 1989. The Florida Local Government Development Agreement Act. In *Development Agreements: Practice, Policy, and Prospects*, edited by Douglas R. Porter and Lindel Marsh. Washington, D.C.: Urban Land Institute.

Thompson, Edward, Jr. 1982. Defining and Protecting the Right to Farm (Part 2). *Zoning and Planning Law Digest* 5: 67.

Thompson, Sharon. July 1986. Suburban Sprawl: How Counties Cope. *American City & County*: 58–64.

U.S. Department of Agriculture. 1990. *1987 Census of Agriculture*. Washington, D.C.: U.S. Department of Agriculture.

U.S. Department of Agriculture. 1985. *1982 Census of Agriculture*. Washington, D.C.: U.S. Department of Agriculture.

U.S. Department of Agriculture. 1975. *Perspectives on Prime Lands*. Washington, D.C.: U.S. Department of Agriculture.

U.S. Department of Commerce, Bureau of the Census. 1992. *Census of Government*. Washington, D.C.: U.S. Government Printing Office.

U.S. Department of Commerce, Bureau of the Census. 1987. *Census of Government*. Washington, D.C.: U.S. Government Printing Office.

U.S. Department of Commerce, Bureau of the Census. 1982. *Census of Government*. Washington, D.C.: U.S. Government Printing Office.

Urban Land Institute. 1992. *Market Profiles 1992*. Washington, D.C.: Urban Land Institute.

Urban Land Institute. 1982. ULI Policy Statement: The Agricultural Land Preservation Issue. *Urban Land* 41 (7): 18–26.

Urban Land Institute. 1968. *Community Builders' Handbook*. Washington, D.C.: Urban Land Institute.

Van der Ryn, Sim, and Peter Calthorpe. 1986. *Sustainable Communities*. San Francisco: Sierra Club Books.

Van Otten, George A. 1980. Changing Spatial Characteristics of Willamette Valley Farms. *Professional Geographer* 32, 1: 63–71.

Vining, Daniel R., Kenneth Bieri, and Ann Strauss. 1977. *Urbanization of Prime Agricultural Land in the United States: A Statistical Analysis*. Regional Science Research Institute Discussion Paper Series No. 99. Amherst, Mass.: Regional Science Research Institute, University of Massachusetts.

Vining, Daniel R., Thomas Plaut, and Kenneth Bieri. 1977. Urban Encroachment on Prime Agricultural Land in the United States. *International Regional Science Review* 2, 2: 143–56.

Volkman, Nancy J. 1987. Vanishing Lands in the USA. *Land Use Policy* 4, 1: 14–30.

Walker, David. 1985. Strategies. In *Proceedings of the Texas House and Senate Joint Special Committee on Urban Issues*. Arlington, Tex.: Institute of Urban Studies, University of Texas at Arlington.

Walmer, Tracy, and Kevin Johnson. 1990. Urban Development Plows Farmland Under. *USA Today*, March 7: 6A.

Wheaton, William L., and Morton J. Schussheim. 1955. *The Cost of Municipal Services in Residential Areas*. Washington, D.C.: U.S. Department of Commerce.

White, Michelle J. 1975. The Effect of Zoning on the Size of Metropolitan Areas. *Journal of Urban Economics* 2: 118–22.

White, S. Mark. 1993. *Affordable Housing: Proactive and Reactive Planning Strategies*. Planning Advisory Service Report No. 441. Chicago: American Planning Association.

Whitelaw, W. E. 1980. Measuring the Effects of Public Policies on the Price of Urban Land. In *Urban Land Markets: Price Indexes, Supply Measures, and Public Policy Effects*, Research Report No. 30, edited by J. Thomas Black and James E. Hoben. Washington, D.C.: Urban Land Institute.

Whiting, Charles C. 1989. Twin Cities Metro Council: Heading for a Fall? Reprinted in *The Best of Planning*. Chicago: Planners Press, 305–11.

Whorton, Joseph W., Jr. 1989. Innovative Strategic Planning: The Georgia Model. *Environmental and Urban Issues* 17, 1: 15–23.

Windsor, Duane. 1979. A Critique of the Costs of Sprawl. *Journal of the American Planning Association* 45, 3: 279–92.

Wyckoff. Mark A. 1989. Growth Management Techniques. *Planning & Zoning News* (August): 4–15.

Yaro, Robert D., Randall G. Arendt, Harry L. Dodson, and Elizabeth A. Brabec. 1990. *Dealing with Change in the Connecticut River Valley: A Design Manual for Con-servation and Development*. Cambridge, Mass.: Lincoln Institute of Land Policy.

York, Marie. 1991a. The Orlando Affordable Housing Demonstration Program. *Journal of the American Planning Association* 57, 4: 490–93.

York, Marie L. 1991b. *The Transportation Utility Fee*. Fort Lauderdale, Fla.: Florida Atlantic University/Florida International University Joint Center for Environmental and Urban Problems.

York, Marie L. et. al. 1989. *Encouraging Compact Development in Florida*. Fort Lauderdale, Fla.: Florida Atlantic University/Florida International University Joint Center for Environmental and Urban Problems.

Zehner, Robert B. 1977. *Access, Travel, and Transportation in New Communities*. Lexington, Mass.: Lexington Books.

Zeimetz, Kathryn A., Elizabeth Dillon, Ernest E. Hardy, and Robert C. Otte. 1976. *Dynamics of Land Use in Fast Growth Areas*. Agricultural Economics Report No. 325. Washington, D.C.: Economic Research Services, U.S. Department of Agriculture.

Zeman, Bobbie. February 1990. Growth Management—Colorado Style. *Florida Planning* 10, 6: 9.

Index